EUROPEAN STUDIES SERIES

General Editors	Colin Jones Richard Overy
Series Advisers	Joe Bergin John Breuilly

This series marks a major initiative in European history publishing aimed primarily, though not exclusively, at an undergraduate audience. It will encompass a wide variety of books on aspects of European history since 1500, with particular emphasis on France and Germany, although no country will be excluded and a special effort will be made to cover previously neglected areas, such as Scandinavia, Eastern Europe and Southern Europe.

The series will include political accounts and broad thematic treatments, both of a comparative kind and studies of a single country, and will lay particular emphasis on social and cultural history where this opens up fruitful new ways of examining the past. The aim of the series is to make available a wide range of titles in areas where there is now an obvious gap or where the existing historical literature is out of date or narrowly focused. The series will also include translations of important books published in Europe.

Interest in European affairs and history has never been greater; *European Studies* will help make that European heritage closer, richer and more comprehensible.

EUROPEAN STUDIES SERIES

General Editors: Colin Jones and Richard Overy
Advisory Editors: John Breuilly and Joe Bergin

Published

Robert Aldrich	Greater France: A Short History of French Overseas Expansion
Nigel Aston	Religion and Revolution in France, 1780–1804
Yves-Marie Bercé	The Birth of Absolutism: A History of France, 1598–1661
Janine Garrisson	A History of Sixteenth-Century France, 1438–1589
Gregory Hanlon	Early Modern Italy, 1550–1800
Michael Hughes	Early Modern Germany, 1477–1806
Dieter Langewiesche	Liberalism in Germany
Martyn Lyons	Napoleon Bonaparte and the Legacy of the French Revolution
Hugh McLeod	The Secularisation of Western Europe, 1848–1914
Robin Okey	The Habsburg Monarchy, c.1765–1918
Pamela M. Pilbeam	Republicanism in Nineteenth-Century France, 1814–1871
Helen Rawlings	Church, Religion and Society in Early Modern Spain
Tom Scott	Society and Economy in Germany, 1300–1600
Wolfram Siemann	The German Revolution of 1848–49
Richard Vinen	France, 1934–1970

Church, Religion and Society in Early Modern Spain

HELEN RAWLINGS

palgrave

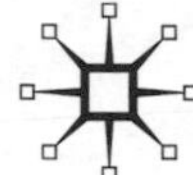

First published 2002 by
PALGRAVE
Houndmills, Basingstoke, Hampshire RG21 6XS and
175 Fifth Avenue, New York, N. Y. 10010
Companies and representatives throughout the world

PALGRAVE is the new global academic imprint of
St. Martin's Press LLC Scholarly and Reference Division and
Palgrave Publishers Ltd (formerly Macmillan Press Ltd).

ISBN 0–333–63694–5 hardcover
ISBN 0–333–63695–3 paperback

This book is printed on paper suitable for recycling and made from fully managed and sustained forest sources.

A catalogue record for this book is available from the British Library.

Library of Congress Cataloging-in-Publication Data

Rawlings, Helen
Church, religion and society in early modern Spain / Helen Rawlings.
p. cm.—(European studies series)
Includes bibliographical references and index.
ISBN 0–333–63694–5—ISBN 0–333–63695–3 (pbk.)
1. Spain—Church history. 2. Catholic Church—Spain—History. I. Title.
II. European studies series (Palgrave (Firm))

BX1584 .R38 2002
282'.46—dc21

2001057527

10 9 8 7 6 5 4 3 2 1
11 10 09 08 07 06 05 04 03 02

Printed in China

In memory of Glenn

Contents

Acknowledgements x
List of Tables and Maps xi
Introduction xiii

1 The Breakdown of Spain's Multi-Cultural Heritage **1**
Introduction 1
The Rise of Anti-Semitism in Spanish Society 2
The Establishment of the Spanish Inquisition 7
The End of Moorish Spain? 13
The Fate of the *Morisco* 18
The Decision to Expel 22
The Aftermath 24
Conclusion 26

2 Traditionalism and Innovation in the Spanish Church **27**
Introduction 27
Erasmian Humanism and Biblical Scholarship 28
The Attack on Erasmus and Erasmians 30
Catholic Reformers Condemned 32
The Protestant Threat of Mid-Century 37
Inquisitorial Censorship and the 1559 Index 42
The Archbishop of Toledo Accused of Heresy 44
Conclusion: Biblical Scholarship Under Scrutiny 47

3 The Reform of the Ecclesiastical Estate **50**
Introduction 50
The Condition of the Clerical Estate and Early Reform Initiatives 51
The Council of Trent and the Definition of Dogma and Discipline 54
The Application of Diocesan Reform 55
The Reform of the Episcopate 58
The Reform of the Priesthood 67
The Reform of the Religious Orders 73
Conclusion 76

4 The Church and the People **78**
Introduction 78
The Christianisation of the People 79
Sacramental Observance 84
Forms of Popular Religious Culture 89
The Universal Brotherhood of Believers 95
Conclusion 98

5 The Church in the New World **100**
Introduction 100
Colonisation and Evangelisation: the Jurisdictional Debate 101
Missionary Euphoria 107
A Clash of Cultures 110
Divisions of Authority 114
Conclusion 116

6 Crisis and Resilience in the Early Seventeenth-Century Spanish Church **119**
Introduction: Crisis in Castile 119
Arbitrismo and the Church 120
The Clericalisation of Spanish Society 124
The Growth of the Religious Orders 127
The Temporalities of the Spanish Church: Pressures and Survival 130
The Fiscal Burden 135
A Crisis of Religious Conscience in Society 139
Conclusion 142

Conclusion **144**

Profiles of Church Leaders and Reformers 148
Notes 161
Select Bibliography 171
Index 179

Acknowledgements

I am much obliged to Joseph Bergin for suggesting I write this book, for his careful reading of earlier versions of the manuscript and for the scholarly perceptions he brought to it. I am also grateful to John Edwards for his valuable comments and suggestions. Patrick Williams, who inspired my interest in the early modern Spanish Church many years ago, gave firm direction and encouragement throughout the project. While I warmly acknowledge their support, I in no way hold them responsible for the outcome. The Scouloudi Foundation provided a grant to support study in Spain at an early stage. The Inter-Library Loans staff of the University of Portsmouth Frewen Library helped enormously to expand the bibliography. Terka Acton and Gabriella Stiles at Palgrave patiently steered the book through to publication. Finally, I would like to thank my mother for her forbearance. The book is dedicated to my brother, whose memory we cherish.

List of Tables and Maps

Tables

1.1	Institutions adopting *limpieza de sangre* (purity of blood) statutes, 1482–1547	5
1.2	The expulsion of the *moriscos* by region, 1609–11	24
2.1	Protestant victims of the Valladolid and Sevillian *autos de fe* of 1559–60	41
3.1	The scale of Spanish bishoprics according to annual income, *c.*1570	62
3.2	Backgrounds of Castilian bishops appointed under Philip II	65
3.3	Householders per parish in Castilian bishoprics, 1587	70
3.4	Post-Tridentine Spanish seminaries	72
3.5	The growth in membership of male religious orders, 1591–1623	75
4.1	Percentage of defendants of the Inquisition of Toledo able to recite their prayers successfully, 1550–1650	81
4.2	Examples of cases of minor heresy brought before the Toledan tribunal of the Inquisition, 1551–1600	83
4.3	Increase in the number of devotional masses for the souls of the dead in Toledo, 1500–1700	89
4.4	The protective powers of local saints in New Castile, 1575–80	90
4.5	Number of votive festivals celebrated in New Castile, 1575–80	91
5.1	A chronology of the conquest and evangelisation of the New World, 1492–1575	117

6.1 The clerical population of Castile and Aragón in 1591 125
6.2 Secular and regular clergy in six major Castilian towns, 1591 128
6.3 Religious foundations in the city of Madrid, 1556–1665 129
6.4 Episcopal rents in early seventeenth-century Castile 132
6.5 The value of the Segovian tithe set against diocesan income, 1590–1659 134
6.6 Examples of direct deductions from episcopal incomes 136
6.7 Royal income, 1621 137

Maps

1 Diocesan divisions of Castile and Aragón at the end of the sixteenth century 60
2 Householders per parish in Castilian bishoprics, *c.*1587 68

Introduction

The Catholic Church has long been acknowledged as an institution of unparalleled importance in early modern Spain, central to the development of Spanish society during one of the most formative periods in its history, a period that many Spaniards still refer to as 'the Golden Age'. The firm direction given to religious policy by Ferdinand and Isabella (1474–1516) stimulated Spain's championship of the Catholic cause precisely as Europe was preparing to enter upon the era of the Reformation and Counter-Reformation that marked the sixteenth century. The new monarchs set up the Inquisition in 1478 to root out heresy and apostasy among converted Jews and, by extension, to enforce uniformity of belief throughout their newly unified kingdoms of Castile and Aragón. The fall of the ancient Moorish stronghold of Granada to Christian forces on 6 January 1492 was a major part of this initiative. Within a matter of months, practising Jews were forced to abandon the observance of their faith. Within a further decade, the same fate had befallen the Moors of Castile. The centuries-long cohabitation of Christians with their Jewish and Moorish neighbours – known as *convivencia* – began to disintegrate. By the end of the fifteenth century, the Spanish Church had become firmly associated with the authoritarian power of the monarchy and the repressive arm of the Holy Office. Spain's reputation as a major bastion of religious orthodoxy and racial intolerance was further reinforced in the early sixteenth century as it took on a leading role under Charles V (1516–56) in checking the spread of Protestant heresy through the lands of the Holy Roman Empire in northern and central Europe (which he inherited in 1519) and in combating the onslaught of Turkish power in central and n Europe. A further crusade began with dramatic suddenness across the Atlantic. In 1492 Christopher Columbus, in his quest to find a westerly route to 'the Indies', unknowingly embarked upon the discovery of the New World of the Americas. The conquest of the Aztec civilisation of New Spain by Hernán Cortés in 1519 was rapidly followed by that of the Incas of Peru by the Pizarro brothers in 1534. Spain now began the massive task of winning the souls of the conquered peoples of the New World for Christianity. These momentous events had a profound psychological impact upon Spain, confirming the identity that the *Reconquista* had forged between Spanish military expansion and divine purpose: clearly, as Spaniards witnessed it, the enlargement of their territories, in both Europe and the Americas, was a God-given opportunity to further the cause of Catholicism within them.

The Spanish Church was well placed to play its role in the expansion of Spanish power. When the Catholic Church began its own renewal at the Council of Trent (1545–63), the Spanish Church was already at the forefront of change. The decrees of Trent sought to raise educational and moral standards among Catholic clergy, as well as to extend an understanding of Christian doctrine among its peoples. Although the implementation of the Council's work brought many tensions to the surface, it also stimulated many positive developments in the Church, especially those sanctioned under Philip II (1556–98), whose own policy-making was underpinned by a powerful sense of Catholic zeal.

During the course of the sixteenth and seventeenth centuries, many theologians, canonists and members of religious orders played key roles at the centre of government. At local level the parish priest, as well as delivering the sacraments and leading the ceremonies of the Church, was also responsible for the collection of the tithe from his parishioners and, in addition, might perform the duties of public notary, sanctioning the issue of contracts, leases and wills. As a major land and property owner, the Church possessed vast material resources that enabled it to maintain its institutional power base in opulent style. As a provider of education and charity, it carried out an important social function. The Church's structures and traditions, its doctrinal and temporal authority, all exercised a powerful hold over the beliefs, the behavioural patterns, the values and outlooks of the people. The Spanish Church was thus deeply embedded in the whole fabric of everyday life. It was an ideological, political, economic and cultural force in society, all-embracing and all-powerful.

But for all its significance, no comprehensive history of the early modern Spanish Church has yet been written, comparable to those undertaken for the English, French or Italian Churches. Approaches to the religious history of early modern Spain have tended to be conservative in their interpretation, reflecting a view of the Church from within. The first ecclesiastical histories of Spain, published in the sixteenth and seventeenth centuries, were written by churchmen or laymen sympathetic with its Catholic mission. The works of Francisco Bermúdez de Pedraza, Gil González Dávila, Diego Ortiz de Zúñiga, Pedro Salazar de Mendoza, Prudencio de Sandoval, José de Sigüenza and Jerónimo de Zurita, to name but a few, serve as classic examples. They focused almost exclusively on histories of dioceses and religious orders, lives of saints, chronologies of popes, monarchs, bishops and church councils. Deeply apologetic in tone, extolling the virtues of churchmen and endorsing the supremacy of Spain's Catholic tradition, they established an historiographical tradition in keeping with the ideological climate of the age. Modern scholarship has tended to maintain an essentially orthodox approach to the history of the Church, as exemplified in the work of such distinguished Spanish historians as Quintín Aldea Vaquero, Tarsicio de Azcona, Antonio Domínguez Ortiz, José García Oro, Ricardo García Villoslada, José Luis González Novalín, Joaquín Pérez Villanueva and José Ignacio Tellechea Idígoras. Histories of the Spanish Inquisition have figured prominently within this historiographical tradition and in some respects have displaced histories of the Church *per se*. These contributions, substantial and scholarly as they are, only provide part of the framework for an understanding of the wider relationship between the Church, religion and society in early modern Spain. Nevertheless, significant advances have been made in the last 25 years to warrant a revision of the evidence. Current research initiatives by a younger generation of Spanish, French, British and American scholars are beginning to incorporate a broader, more critical approach to the history of the Spanish Church and religious life, forming part of a fundamental reappraisal of Spanish history that has been taking place since the end of the Franco era. The opening-up of Spanish archives, the improved cataloguing and accessibility of their holdings, along with the publication of important primary sources of evidence, have all helped in this process. Although gaps still exist in the overall picture (particularly in the history of the later seventeenth century), a new perspective on Spain's religious history is emerging from the work of early modern scholars that deserves close examination.

A reassessment of Spain's relationship with its religious minorities (examined in Chapter 1) suggests that the persecution of those of Jewish and Moorish blood was motivated by a number of tensions in society – economic, racial and cultural – rather than exclusively by the threat that they allegedly posed to the religious integrity of Catholic Spain. The *converso* and the *morisco* were valued members of society as well as being the victims of indiscriminate attack and marginalisation. Multi-culturalism partially survived official attempts to destroy it. Traditionally, the Spanish Church and Inquisition have been seen as instrumental in the creation of an exclusive, 'closed' society in early sixteenth-century Spain that suppressed humanist trends in intellectual circles and effectively sealed it off from the influence of the Reformation. This viewpoint has been challenged by an acknowledgement of the contribution of innovative alongside traditional expressions of spirituality and belief to the shaping of Spain's religious development (explored in Chapter 2). The issue of reform was one that dominated the Counter-Reformation period. Spain's leading role at the Council of Trent demanded that it take the initiative in implementing ecclesiastical reform within its own Church. But while the need for reform was universally accepted, an uneven picture emerges from a practical examination of the changes it brought to the various levels of leadership within the Spanish Church that have thus far been explored by modern historians. To add to this picture we now have the statistical data at our disposal to calculate with some degree of accuracy the size and distribution of the late sixteenth-century ecclesiastical estate, together with sections of its income, enabling us to apply quantitative as well as qualitative judgements to a study of the post-Tridentine Spanish Church (reviewed in Chapter 3). A number of modern historians have been assessing the practical implications arising from Spain's Counter-Reformation offensive at local church level. The degree of success achieved by the Church, in conjunction with the Inquisition, in imposing uniformity of belief on Spanish society in the post-Reformation era is currently open to debate. A study of local census records, topographical surveys and inquisitorial 'trials of faith' drawn from a wide regional spectrum have made it possible for historians to gain a unique insight into the behavioural patterns and religious beliefs of thousands of individuals scattered throughout the Iberian peninsula, adding to our understanding of popular culture in early modern Spain as well as providing a measure of the average Old Christian's response to Tridentine directives (the subject of Chapter 4). Recent research has also made for a more objective assessment of the success of the Church's programme of evangelisation in the New World, a study which has highlighted the tensions inherent in the process of cross-cultural exchange, as well as the fragile foundation of the missionary enterprise overseas (explored in Chapter 5). By the end of the early modern period, serious criticisms of the institutional Church were being voiced by contemporaries in respect of its excessive size, disproportionate wealth, the exclusivity of its doctrine and the rigidity of its values. These reflections (examined in Chapter 6), which reveal a partial questioning of the Church's authority over society, are adding a further dimension to the 'crisis' debate that has so dominated studies of seventeenth-century Europe in recent times. Insights such as these, although they cannot as yet provide a complete history of the interaction between the Church, religion and society in early modern Spain, are nevertheless forcing us to substantially revise previously held judgements. Traditional scholarship has vigorously promoted Spain's championship of Catholicism in the early modern period. Modern historians have identified inherent weaknesses in this image, in particular where the practice of the faith was concerned. There is increasing evidence to suggest that the forces of toleration coexisted alongside those of conservatism, ensuring the survival of a vibrant, diverse religious tradition. A more balanced, objective picture of Spain's religious history is emerging from recent research, which it is the purpose of this book to explore.

1 *The Breakdown of Spain's Multi-Cultural Heritage*

Introduction

On the eve of the early modern period, Spain occupied a unique position among other contemporary European nations: it was a land of diverse peoples, traditions and faiths, where for centuries Moslems and Jews had enjoyed freedom of worship alongside Christians. The War of Reconquest, fought sporadically between *c*.722 and 1492, had both a spiritual and a secular dimension. On the one hand it was a holy crusade against the ideological enemy Islam, and on the other it was an armed movement of human migration south in search of land and riches. Christian victory was won by the strength of the sword borne beneath the symbol of the crucifix. The Reconquest bred a warrior, crusader society that fed off the glories of war fought in the name of religion. It set a militant stamp on Spanish Catholicism that was to remain one of its distinguishing features throughout the early modern period. The Catholic Church emerged triumphant and secure in Spain at exactly the time when it was about to fragment under the stresses of the Reformation in much of the rest of western Europe. Christian victory also assisted the crown in its attempt to unify and consolidate control over its disparate kingdoms via a common faith. It was aided in this task by the repressive machinery of the Spanish Inquisition, established in 1478 to enforce orthodoxy and eliminate diversity of belief. By the beginning of the sixteenth century, Spain had forced its Jewish community into conversion or exile, while its Moorish inhabitants were about to be compelled to accept baptism or go into exile. Both converted Jews (known as *conversos*) and converted Moors (known as *moriscos*) were to suffer the stigma of being New Christians in a predominantly Old Christian society. But the breakdown of the centuries-long coexistence of three cultures, while heralded from within the Church as a great victory for Spanish Catholicism, is viewed by many modern scholars to have been neither as complete nor as widely accepted as was formerly thought. Nor was it exclusively prompted by ideological tensions. To a considerable degree multi-culturalism survived official attempts to suppress it and continued to shape Spain's religious identity until at least the beginning of the seventeenth century.

The Rise of Anti-Semitism in Spanish Society

On 30 March 1492, within three months of the fall of Granada, Ferdinand and Isabella signed an edict of expulsion, ordering all professed Jews who refused conversion to leave their kingdoms by the end of July. This marked the first official step towards the end of a pluralist Spain and the creation of a unified Catholic state. Ten years later, on 12 February 1502, all non-baptised Moors were ordered out of Castile. Similar action was taken against their co-religionists in Aragón a quarter of a century later. By pursuing a policy of religious unity with underlying political objectives, the monarchs capitalised on the spirit of the age, a militant, nationalist spirit born out of the *Reconquista*, that was intent on forging its own identity within Europe, freed from its two 'alien' civilisations, the Jewish and the Moslem.

The Jewish community, persecuted and then expelled from most other parts of western Europe between the late thirteenth and mid-fourteenth centuries, remained tolerated and highly valued in Spain. Although barred from holding public office and forced to live in segregated zones (known as *aljamas*), the Jews made a valuable professional and cultural contribution to society. Some established reputations as doctors, tax collectors and financiers, others worked as artisans and traders. Social and economic factors, rather than religious or racial ones, were initially responsible for a change in public attitude towards them. Protected by their separate existence, their wealth and their influence with Peter I of Castile (1350–69) and the aristocracy, the Jews escaped the widespread suffering and turmoil brought about by the Black Death in the mid-fourteenth century. But their fortunes were soon to decline under the turbulent three decades of Trastamaran rule that followed. Popular feelings of indignation at the Jews' superior social and economic status, inflamed via provocative sermons, found their expression in anti-semitic riots in major Castilian and Aragonese towns in 1391.[1]

Following these disturbances, more than half the original Jewish population of around 200 000 (three-quarters of whom were settled in Castile) chose to convert to Christianity rather than to suffer continuing persecutions and threats to their livelihoods. The *converso* was created. The dramatic reduction in the size of the Jewish communities in towns such as Seville, Toledo, Burgos, Segovia and Valladolid was matched by a corresponding increase in the number of *converso* inhabitants. During the first half of the fifteenth century, former Jews were easily absorbed into a tolerant Christian culture that accepted them as equals. Although conversion was not obligatory at this stage, it increasingly became advisable on grounds of self-interest. While the Jew continued to be subject to legal and social discrimination, major honours and offices remained open to the *converso*. Many converts rose rapidly under royal protection to occupy highly respectable positions within the Church and at court, in finance and administration, while also maintaining amicable relations with their Jewish relations. However, their critics regarded them as unscrupulous opportunists.

In the second half of the fifteenth century, as the sincerity of the *conversos'* religious conviction was placed under ever-closer scrutiny, Jewish converts to Christianity became increasingly marginalised. *Conversos* were widely believed to be public Christians but private Judaizers. Just how valid this perception was is difficult to judge. There appears to have been at best a mixture of loyalties and a complexity of religious attitudes within *converso* society: while some embraced Christianity fully others remained Jewish in all but name. The royal chronicler at the court of Ferdinand and Isabella, Fernando del Pulgar, who was himself of Jewish origin, related how a diversity of beliefs could be found within the same *converso* household, with genuine converts living alongside others who were secretly or openly reverting to the faith of their forefathers: 'And it happened that in some households the husband kept certain Jewish ceremonies and the wife was a good Christian, and that one son and daughter might be good Christians while another son was of the Jewish faith.'[2] Very little effort appears to have been made by the Church authorities to instruct the *converso* in the Christian religion. Jews and Jewish converts remained in contact with one another, thus maintaining the old spirit of *convivencia*. In the eyes of Christian society, a Jew revealed himself by his social and dietary habits, such as the keeping of the Sabbath, speaking and reading in Hebrew, the continued practice of Jewish ceremonies within the family, the eating of unleavened bread and a refusal to eat bacon or pork, rather than in his explicit rejection of Christian doctrine. It was evidence of this nature that was later to be used by the Spanish Inquisition as indicative of the 'heretical' inclinations of the accused.

In 1449, in the wake of further anti-semitic tensions in Toledo, all those of Jewish ancestry, however sincere and long-standing their conversion to Christianity, were barred from holding municipal office in the city by means of a civic law, known as the *Sentencia Estatuto*. The Toledan statute was instigated in response to a violent power struggle taking place between *converso* and non-*converso* families within a city once renowned for its climate of multi-cultural cooperation.[3] Jewish converts were resented for the monopoly they held over public office and for being too successful in their enterprises, thus threatening the careers and livelihoods of the Old Christian community. The Toledan statute established an important discriminatory code, soon to be adopted by other secular and religious institutions, one based on race rather than exclusively on religion. It confirmed the commonly held belief that the *converso* was a suspect, second-class citizen. To be of pure Old Christian ancestry was soon to become *the* essential prerequisite for social advancement and acceptability. However, at this early stage, discrimination against the *converso* was still not widely exercised or accepted, remaining largely confined to major towns. There was, indeed, considerable opposition to Toledo's anti-semitic legislation, notably within senior religious circles where it was deemed to be an act of supreme intolerance. Following papal condemnation of the *Sentencia* as unchristian, a number of prominent *conversos*, including the Dominican friar Juan de Torquemada (uncle of the first Inquisitor General of Spain) and the Bishop of Burgos, Alonso de Cartagena, declared themselves in writing to be opposed to the statute. In 1465 the General of the Jeronimites, Alonso de Oropesa, who actively encouraged Judaizers to become members of his order, also intervened in the debate. By the end of the fifteenth century, there was ample evidence of the successful professional, social and cultural assimilation of the *converso* into Old Christian society despite the growing impact of the statutes. Many converts to Christianity married into aristocratic circles where they formed powerful, expanding family alliances. Ferdinand the

Catholic himself was reputed to be of *converso* stock. A number of Castilian bishops who served in the second half of the fifteenth century were of known Jewish descent, including Juan Arias de Ávila, Bishop of Segovia (1461–97), and Alfonso de Burgos, Bishop of Córdoba (1477–82), Cuenca (1482–5) and Palencia (1485–99). But the forces of tolerance were never that far removed from those of intolerance. Despite the widespread level of criticism that the Toledan statute generated, the purity of blood movement soon gathered momentum. Statutes were first adopted by specific secular institutions (university colleges, guilds and town councils) in the second half of the fifteenth century, then by selective cathedral chapters and religious orders in the sixteenth, as illustrated by Table 1.1.

In 1547, following the precedent set by the civic authorities almost a century earlier, the cathedral chapter of Toledo adopted its own selective entry test requiring all those seeking capitular preferment to have their ancestry checked over four generations for any trace of Jewish lineage. Its instigator was, significantly, the first man of plebeian parentage to be appointed as Spanish Primate in the early modern period, Juan Martínez Siliceo (1546–57). His lowly origins provided him with a powerful weapon over his aristocratic enemies'

Table 1.1 Institutions adopting *limpieza de sangre* (purity of blood) statutes, 1482–1547

1482	The *Colegio Mayor* of San Bartolomé, University of Salamanca
1483	The Holy Inquisition (episcopal inquisitors)
1483	The Military Order of Alcántara
1483	The Military Order of Calatrava
1486	The Jeronimite Order
1488	The *Colegio Mayor* of Santa Cruz, University of Valladolid
1511	The Cathedral Chapter of Badajoz
1515	The Cathedral Chapter of Seville
1519	The *Colegio Mayor* of San Ildefonso, University of Alcalá
1525	The Franciscan Order
1527	The Military Order of Santiago
1530	The Cathedral Chapter of Córdoba
1531*	The Dominican Order (*onwards)
1537	The University of Seville
1547	The Cathedral Chapter of Toledo

Sources: Henry Kamen, *Inquisition and Society in Spain in the Sixteenth and Seventeenth Centuries* (Bloomington, 1985), pp. 116–17; Antonio Domínguez Ortiz, *Los Conversos de Origen Judío* (Madrid, 1957), pp. 57–68.

belief in their automatic birthright to capitular office. In his attack on the privileged elite, the Archbishop thus demonstrated that he was of pure, if humble, origins, whereas their 'superior' heritage, along with that of other leading members of the Castilian aristocracy, was highly suspect. This common assumption gained currency in 1560 when Francisco de Mendoza y Bobadilla published his *Tizón de la Nobleza de España* in which he provided evidence that the majority of the Spanish nobility were tainted with Jewish blood. In a highly competitive society, proof of *limpieza de sangre* thus became an important symbol of status and honour (attributes previously exclusive to the upper classes) for the ordinary man or woman, hence its popular appeal.

Religious and racial tensions continued to be motivated in part by prevailing social and economic conditions. The second half of the fifteenth century was characterised by a series of prolonged subsistence crises in Castile, the most serious taking place over the period 1465–73 and coinciding with the political anarchy that marked the end of the reign of Henry IV.[4] In these popular uprisings anti-semitic tensions ran high, reaching their climax in 1473 when a series of massacres of *conversos* took place in a number of Andalusian towns. The Jewish convert was victimised (as his forefathers had been at the end of the fourteenth century), not specifically for his race or his suspect religion, but on account of his social and professional advancement that enabled him to escape the worst effects of the crisis that so crippled the populace. Against this background of indiscriminate attack on the *converso* community, the Jews, although marginalised in major cities and subject to heavy taxation, continued to practise their faith and remained under the official protection of the crown. Jews held important roles at court as royal financiers, tax collectors, physicians and advisors. Among the most prominent were Abraham Senior, the chief rabbi of Castile and principal treasurer to the crown, and Luis de Santángel, secretary to the king. On the eve of Ferdinand and Isabella's reign, the Jews' contribution to society was clearly valued and their expulsion was certainly not high on the immediate political agenda. Nevertheless, there were clear anomalies between the position of Jews and of Jewish converts in Spanish society that had to be resolved.

Following the quelling of the Andalusian pogroms, a number of senior churchmen, including two powerful members of the Dominican Order, the royal preacher, Alonso de Hojeda, and the royal confessor, Tomás de Torquemada, began to press for the establishment of a Spanish Inquisition. The opportunity came when the monarchs made an official visit to the city of Seville (1477–8), which housed a prominent *converso* community. Here they were persuaded of the danger posed by this offensive religious minority whose dissident beliefs, so it was claimed, threatened to undermine the stability of the Catholic state. Hojeda and Torquemada drew upon the support of Cardinal Pedro González de Mendoza, Archbishop of Seville (1574–82). The queen, a deeply pious woman, totally committed to the Catholic cause, was shocked by their revelations of *converso* treachery and became convinced of the need to set up the appropriate secular machinery for the detection and punishment of heresy. In 1478 the monarchs made their official application to Rome to establish a Spanish Inquisition, to deal with the perceived threat to the Catholic identity of their kingdoms posed by backsliding Jews. The institution was to be modelled on that set up by the papacy in the thirteenth century in the neighbouring crown of Aragón to deal with the problem of Catharism. Unlike its Aragonese equivalent (now fallen into disuse), the Spanish Inquisition was to operate under the monarchs' direct control, thus extending their political authority over their Church (formerly responsible for heresy) and their spiritual authority over their people. Sixtus IV conceded, but later regretted, the relinquishing of papal authority over what was to become an awesome instrument of repression and intimidation. Two years later, in September 1480, the Spanish Inquisition began its operations in Seville under the supervision of two Dominican inquisitors.[5]

The Establishment of the Spanish Inquisition

The Spanish Inquisition was established to deal with a particular social group: it had sole authority over dubious Jewish converts to Christianity, suspected of reverting to their former faith, and had none over the Jewish community itself. The rigours of the institution soon made their mark. Crypto-Jews were rooted out and spared no mercy. At the first *auto de fe* of the Spanish Inquisition (the public ceremony at which those accused received their sentence), held in Seville on 6 February 1481, six prominent *conversos* were condemned to death at the stake. The contemporary chronicler and local Andalusian priest Andrés Bernáldez, representing the views of the ruling Old Christian elite, recorded that over 700 had been burnt and more than 5000 punished at the hands of the Sevillian Inquisition by 1488 and that 'the heretics of Córdoba, Toledo, Burgos, Valencia and Segovia, and the whole of Spain were discovered to be all Jews... Since the fire is lit it will burn until... not one of those who judaized is left'.[6] Fernando del Pulgar, not unnaturally, took a more sympathetic stance when describing the wave of persecution that followed throughout Spain: 'Up to two thousand men and women were burned on various occasions in different cities and towns; others were condemned to perpetual imprisonment; and to others was given as a penance that for all the days of their lives they should go marked with great red crosses placed on their clothing... And they as well as their children were declared unfit for all public office or responsibility.'[7] Although the exact numbers of those burnt at the stake varies according to sources, there is no doubt that the Inquisition was at its most brutal during the early years of its existence when its principal victims were *conversos*. It has recently been estimated that around 75 per cent of those who perished at the hands of the Inquisition did so during the period between 1480 and 1500. Some 250 *conversos* were condemned to death by the Toledan tribunal between 1485 and 1501, 124 by that of Zaragoza in the period up to 1502, while 754 were burnt alive by the Valencian Inquisition between 1484 and 1530.[8] Indeed, such was the severity of the Inquisition's activities that it generated a protest from Rome. In 1482, Sixtus IV threatened to bring the Aragonese tribunal under episcopal control on account of its unjust treatment of *conversos*.[9] It also prompted calls for clemency from certain prominent voices within elite circles, including that of Pulgar himself, who advocated a policy of preaching and persuasion. His expression of unofficial views led to him being relieved of his position as court historian. Fray Hernando de Talavera, confessor to Queen Isabella, was another influential dissenting voice, declaring that 'heresies need to be corrected not only with punishments and lashes, but even more with Catholic reasoning'.[10] In 1505, in his capacity as Archbishop of Granada, Talavera was to become a victim of the reign of terror unleashed by Inquisitor Diego Rodríguez Lucero in Córdoba, who, with the consent of the Inquisitor General, Deza (1504–7), sentenced 134 *conversos* to death over a six-month period between 1504 and 1505 and falsely accused the octogenarian friar of having Jewish blood, before himself being dismissed for his abuse of office in 1508. Against the background of these excesses, the machinery of the Inquisition expanded. A further 15 regional tribunals were established throughout Spain in the period up to 1495 to join in the task of extirpating heresy from their realms (some of which were later suppressed or merged). A General

Council of the Inquisition, known as the *Suprema*, was established in Madrid in 1483, presided over by the first Inquisitor General, Fray Tomás de Torquemada, to coordinate and control its operations in Castile and Aragón. By means of the Council, the two crowns became linked institutionally in pursuit of common religious objectives. The Aragonese, who jealously guarded their kingdom's laws and liberties, strongly objected to being subject to Castilian authority. The Catalan parliament (the Corts) complained to Ferdinand in 1484 that inquisitors, who had been appointed to investigate and punish heresy in Zaragoza, Huesca, Teruel, Lleida, Barcelona and Valencia, were acting 'against the liberties, constitutions and agreements solemnly sworn by Your Majesty'.[11] At the beginning of the reign of Charles V, the Aragonese parliament (the Cortes) petitioned the crown for a reduction in the powers of the Inquisition which were infringing upon areas of local jurisdiction (known as *fueros*). Complaints were also voiced in Castile. In 1518, the session of the Cortes held in Valladolid reported that as a result of the Holy Office's activities 'many innocent and guiltless have suffered death, harm, oppression, injury and infamy'.[12] But the protests were soon silenced. The Inquisition, despite evidence of abuses in its practices, was fast becoming a vital institution, protected by both the crown and the papacy, and tacitly supported by the vast majority of the Old Christian community whose values it reinforced. Its opponents, including members of the intellectual elite and the populace, were not sufficiently powerful to force a reform of its abuses.

We should also be aware that there were fundamental inconsistencies in the severity of punishment issued by regional tribunals. In the early years of the Inquisition's existence, harsher penalties were imposed in New Castile and Valencia, for example, than in Catalonia, where there were fewer *conversos* and the Holy Office's powers were restricted by local *fueros*. Inquisitors never set foot in certain areas of Galicia and the Basque country on account of their remoteness. The Toledan tribunal tended to issue New Christian artisans accused of adhering to Jewish religious practices with more severe punishments than those of higher social rank. Of the 1641 *conversos* who had dealings with the Toledan Inquisition in 1495, the majority held relatively modest occupations such as jewellers and silversmiths, shoemakers, tailors and tradesmen.[13] An analysis of trials of Judaizers brought before the Inquisition of Valencia between 1485 and 1530 has revealed similar findings: 90 per cent of those with identifiable professions were textile workers or merchants of moderate to poor means, suggesting that they were a target or vulnerable group.[14] John Edwards has demonstrated that when inquisitors visited the region of Soria in north-east Castile in 1486 and again in 1502 they typically found *conversos* guilty of 'crimes' of religious scepticism and irreverence. This scepticism did not necessarily imply either a rejection of Christianity or an affirmation of Judaism. Nor was it exclusive to the New Christian community, but rather symptomatic of the religious doubt that permeated much of Spanish, as well as European, society at the beginning of the early modern era.[15] When examined closely, the records of the Spanish Inquisition provide evidence of potential rather than actual incidence of Judaism among the *converso* community. Heresy was destined to remain a loose concept. In the period 1540–59, by which time crypto-Judaism had become a relatively minor preoccupation of the Holy Office, almost a third (31 per cent) of cases brought before its tribunals fell under the category of so-called 'propositions': casual verbal offences against the Catholic faith and its moral code, rather than intentional acts of heresy.[16]

The Inquisition's success was essentially based on the fear that it generated. When a local inquisitor arrived in a town, an 'edict of faith' was issued, listing all the activities that might be considered as 'heresies' against the Catholic Church. Old Christians were urged to come forward and confess their errors with the promise of 'reconciliation'. They were also under strict obligation to denounce members of their community whom they suspected of religious backsliding to their local tribunal, thus spreading an atmosphere of mistrust and prejudice within society. The Inquisition became notorious for its secret procedures, arrests without trial, occasional use of torture and indiscriminate use of the death penalty. Since the name of the informer was never revealed to the accused, the detection of heresy provided an opportunity for the settling of old quarrels or disputes between neighbours. Inquisitors were aided in their task of encouraging popular confessions by a network of local agents including laymen known as *familiares* and members of the priesthood known as *comisarios*, who enjoyed numerous privileges for the services they rendered. Set against a background of latent socio-economic grievances in society, the penalties to be incurred for the secret practice of Judaism were skilfully brandished by the crown in the closing decades of the fifteenth century to effectively control the religious persuasions of the Spanish people. According to the pioneering early twentieth-century liberal historian of the Inquisition, Henry Charles Lea, 'every individual [became] an agent of the Inquisition, bound by fearful penalties both spiritual and temporal, to aid it in maintaining the purity of the faith, and, at the same time, it made every man conscious that his lightest word or act might subject him to prosecution'.[17] Pulgar reported that many Jews were prepared to inform on *conversos* for their betrayal of the Jewish faith. Likewise, genuine converts sought to denounce false ones for bringing the whole of *converso* society into disrepute.

While *conversos* suspected of reverting to their former faith were being arrested, tried and tortured at the hands of the Inquisition, it was clear that tolerance of Jews in Spanish society could not long be sustained. Following a ruling issued by the Cortes of Toledo in 1480, they were forced to live a segregated existence, confined to urban ghettos where they were the victims of various forms of social and fiscal discrimination. In Segovia, Jews were not allowed to buy food during working hours or to eat fish on Fridays, while in Medina del Campo they were prohibited from participating in commercial activity in the local market. In Burgos, Jewish midwives were not permitted to attend to Christian women in childbirth. Any Jewish merchant who slept overnight in the port of Bilbao was subject to a fine of 2000 *maravedís*. Jews contributed disproportionately to the tax burden, bearing responsibility for as much as 25 per cent of the total sum collected in certain towns, notably Ávila.[18] As the first Inquisitor General, the infamous Tomás de Torquemada, took up office in 1483, a partial expulsion of Jews was authorised from the Andalusian dioceses of Seville, Córdoba and Cádiz. This was also the frontier zone for the advancement of Christian forces on Granada, amongst whom religious zeal ran increasingly high. Three years later, a similar expulsion of Jews was ordered from the Aragonese dioceses of Zaragoza, Albarracín and Teruel, but its effects were not felt immediately. Although the Inquisition lacked the authority to condemn them for their beliefs, it was indirectly forcing the Jewish community into an untenable position. The local expulsions were the prelude to a total expulsion.

On 31 March 1492 a royal decree was issued which gave those Jews who refused Christian baptism four months in which to leave Spain or face the death penalty. The timing of the announcement seemed propitious. Christian Spain was triumphant following the fall of Granada and eager to affirm itself. Columbus was about to depart on his first voyage of discovery. The expulsion order gave Spaniards a further sense of achievement by removing the 'pernicious presence' of Judaizers, suspected of encouraging New Christians to revert to their old faith. Now Ferdinand and Isabella could truly claim to be the champions of Christendom and worthy of their title 'the Catholic Kings', bestowed upon them in 1494 by Pope Alexander VI in recognition of their services to Catholicism. There was some last-minute hesitation on the part of the crown, which recognised the financial and professional losses likely to be incurred and perhaps foresaw the consequences of severing a cultural link that had its origins in Visigothic Spain. The Aragonese historian Jerónimo de Zurita warned his readers that 'many were of the opinion that the king was making a mistake to throw out of his realms people who were so industrious and hard-working, and so outstanding both in number and esteem as well as in dedication to making money. They also said that more hope could be entertained of their conversion by leaving them in the country than by throwing them out'.[19] But anti-semitic pressure from below and the drive for religious unity from above were the overriding considerations that led to the publication of the edict of expulsion. In a letter written to the Count of Aranda on the day of the decree's publication, Ferdinand expressed his obligation to serve the Spanish Inquisition before all else despite the possible economic repercussions:

> The Holy Office of the Inquisition, seeing how some Christians are endangered by contact and communications with the Jews, has provided that the Jews be expelled from all our realms and territories, and has persuaded us to give our support and agreement to this, which we now do, because of our debts and obligations to the said Holy Office; and we do so despite the great harm to ourselves, seeking and preferring the salvation of souls above our own profit and that of individuals.[20]

However, the decree of 'expulsion' also incorporated an open invitation to conversion. The Jews were to be given one last chance. As Andrés Bernáldez confirms in his chronicle, 'it was ordered that the holy Gospel and Catholic faith and Christian doctrine should be preached to all the Jews of Spain; and those who wished to convert and be baptized should remain in the realms as subjects, with all their goods'.[21] The findings of new research suggest a much smaller exodus and a much larger number of conversions than has previously been calculated. The social and economic consequences of expulsion were correspondingly less severe than anticipated and are now judged to have had minimal impact on Spain's seventeenth-century decline. Using the baseline figure of some 80 000 Jews in Spain on the eve of their expulsion, Henry Kamen now calculates that between the end of March and the end of July 1492 around 40 000–50 000 Jews left Spain (predominantly from Castile) for Portugal, Navarre and North Africa, while a similar number chose hasty baptism rather than enforced exile.[22] Perhaps as many as 80–90 per cent of those who left Spain returned between 1493 and 1499 ready to accept the Christian faith in principle, but in practice, as has been demonstrated for the region of Soria, uncertain of their real religious identity.[23] The edict of 'expulsion' thus served to increase the number of reluctant converts and to exacerbate the *converso* problem within society. Although Judaism had been officially banned from Spain, Jewish influences were still deeply ingrained in Spanish society and their eradication was to prove to be no simple exercise. Despite their increasing marginalisation, converted Jews continued to play an essential role in religious, intellectual and political life, trusted and resented in equal measure, long after the expulsion of their forefathers.

The End of Moorish Spain?

The establishment of the Inquisition to eradicate the contagion of Judaism from Spain and the enforced exile of those Jews who refused Christian baptism changed the whole nature of multicultural relations in Spain. As Catholicism became the identifying symbol of Spanish nationhood, so the Moorish community found itself in an increasingly vulnerable position. In the light of the Jewish persecutions, the royal decree of 12 February 1502 which ordered the obligatory conversion or expulsion of Moors from the kingdom of Castile seemed to represent a logical conclusion to the capture of Granada almost ten years to the day previously, and to set the seal on the religious policy of the Catholic monarchs.

The Moslem problem was more complex and deep-rooted than the Jewish one. From an ideological standpoint, the Spanish Moor was looked upon less as a heretic than as an infidel who could be persuaded into accepting the Christian faith. From a political standpoint, it was feared that he might give his allegiance to the Ottoman Turk, particularly if he landed troops on the soil of Spain. The capture of Constantinople in 1453 and the assembly of the Turkish fleet in the Black Sea and the Aegean in the 1470s augured a prolonged period of confrontation between Latin Christendom and

Ottoman Islam. Given the almost eight-centuries-long existence of the Moorish community within the peninsula and the potentially aggressive and expansive Ottoman empire, it was not surprising that Spain should have become more exigent over its Arab neighbours as the Reconquest came to an end. However, Spain still valued its Moorish past, hence the initial tolerance displayed towards Islam on its shores. The old enemy was also an old neighbour. There were two main geographical centres of Moorish habitation in the peninsula. In the eastern kingdom of Valencia, reconquered in the thirteenth century, there was a Moslem population of around 160 000, making up 30 per cent of the local rural community. In the Nasrid kingdom of Granada in the south, the final bastion of Islam in Spain, there was a concentration of some 500 000 Moors.[24] Although ultimately both communities suffered the same fate, their individual experiences of living under Christian rule were quite different.

Moslems living in eastern Spain worked as tenant farmers of the landed aristocracy. Their overlords valued them as hard-working labourers and respected their cultural identity. The Moors of Castile, including those of Granada, earned their living as small craftsmen: shoemakers, blacksmiths, carriers, muleteers, market gardeners, basket makers, tailors and joiners. As with their co-religionists in the east, they formed a vital labour force, prepared to live and work in conditions that were not acceptable to Old Christians. In both regions they lived in segregated communities, known as *morerías*, enjoying civil liberties but resented by Christians for their thriftiness, their sobriety and their separateness. It was the Granadine Moors who aroused most suspicion, given the proximity of Granada to the North African coast and the potential for Turkish attack, hence the priority that Ferdinand and Isabella attached at the beginning of their reign to seizing the kingdom of Granada and to bringing the War of Reconquest to an end. It seems that, at least initially, the monarchs were more concerned with establishing national unity and securing political stability along the vulnerable southern frontier than they were with imposing Catholicism on their Moorish subjects. We should not forget that they were simultaneously engaged in seeking a solution to the serious problem posed by Jewish converts in their kingdoms, and it seems unlikely that they would have wished to add to these. Indeed, very generous terms of surrender were negotiated with the Moors of Granada in 1491, prior to the Christian capture of the city in January 1492. The terms of the settlement, known as the *capitulaciones*, allowed for those Moors who chose to remain in Castile (some 200 000) to keep their language, customs, laws and property, as well as permitting them to practise their Islamic faith without interference, just as the *mudéjars* had done for centuries in the rest of Spain. The conciliatory terms of settlement granted to the vanquished Moors of Granada, which allowed for 'all the common people, great or small, to live in their own religion',[25] suggests that religious uniformity was not an official priority at this stage.

In the decade that followed, the traditional spirit of *convivencia* was revived largely through the activity of Hernando de Talavera, Archbishop of Granada (1493–1507). His strategy was one of conciliation: he made Christianity accessible to his new flock, not by using forceful or coercive tactics, but by adapting the faith to their needs. Known as 'the great *alfaquí* of the Christians', he set about learning Arabic and encouraged his clergy to do likewise. Moslem music replaced Christian music in many religious ceremonies. A converted Moor became a member of the Archbishop's household and his personal confessor. A fellow Jeronimite noted that Talavera 'detested the evil custom prevalent in Spain of treating members of the sects worse after their conversion than before'.[26] But the Archbishop's conciliatory approach was at once the measure of his success and the instrument of his downfall. His sympathy for and easy acceptance of the Moorish people and their culture raised doubts, later unsubstantiated, as to the purity of his own origins. By the end of the decade, Talavera's universal, tolerant approach to the delivery of Christianity was out of step with the increasingly intransigent religious policy of the crown.

The year 1499 marked a major turning point in the Granada mission as Francisco Jiménez de Cisneros, the Archbishop of Toledo (1495–1517), took charge of its direction. Increasing pressure and inducement, via sermons, bribes and threats, were placed on the Granadine Moors to abandon their cultural traditions and accept Christian baptism. This policy, which clearly violated the terms of surrender, prompted a series of uprisings against Cisneros's repressive measures. The atmosphere of trust between the majority and minority faiths now turned to one of mistrust, threatening the delicate balance of power within the kingdom. A revolt in the Albaicín district of Granada in December 1499 was followed in January by an armed struggle of three months' duration in the Alpujarras mountains outside the city. A programme of forced conversions, mass baptisms and the violent persecution of offenders of the faith followed. By the end of February 1500, there were a reported 50 000 new converts to Christianity in

Granada, but in the majority of cases theirs was nothing more than an outward show of conformity. The indiscriminate attack on Moorish culture culminated in October 1501 with the ritual burning of thousands of precious Arabic manuscripts and books. A royal pragmatic was published on 12 February 1502 which bore all the hallmarks of that issued against the Jewish community ten years earlier. According to Isabella, the Moors posed the same threat to the religious stability of Spain as had the Jews a decade before, 'since there is much danger in the communication of the said Moors of our kingdom with the newly converted [who] may be drawn and induced to leave our faith and to return to their original errors ... as already by experience has been seen in some of this kingdom and outside of it'.[27] The pragmatic required all non-baptised Moors to leave Castile and León within 12 months, thus bringing to an end almost 800 years of coexistence between the faiths in the kingdom. The majority chose to stay. It was rumoured that Ferdinand was about to take similar action against the *mudéjars* of Valencia, but he remained true to the promise he made to his Aragonese subjects in 1500 when he declared that 'Our holy Catholic faith in the conversion of the infidels admits neither violence nor force but [only] full freedom and devotion'.[28] The local Inquisition tried to take action against the practice of calling a Moslem to prayer five times a day via the sounding of a horn, but the custom continued. It was another quarter of a century before Christianity was imposed on the Moorish populations of Valencia (1525) and Aragón (1526). Here mass conversion came about not as a result of royal decree, but following the revolt of the *Germanías* led by rebels seeking a reduction in the powers of the landed aristocracy. By hounding Moorish labourers into reluctant conversion, the rebels indirectly attacked the privileged elite whom they served. The *mudéjar* community of Spain thus became one of *moriscos*. But in the eastern kingdoms, as in Granada, it was a nominal arrangement. In practice they were now baptised but uninstructed Christians, who continued to live as a separate and potentially dangerous Islamic community, suspected of collusion with French Huguenots and of maintaining close contact with their Turkish allies.

The operation of the Moslem doctrine of *taqiyya* (meaning precaution) allowed the *morisco* to adopt all the appropriate external features of Christianity as long as he remained privately faithful to Islam. The falsity of his Christian belief, from a Catholic point of view, was revealed in his performance of daily prayer and his observance of periods of fast, most notably that of Ramadan, as well as his Sunday labours, his non-attendance at mass, his feigning of confessional sins, his washing off of the chrism after baptism and his refusal to acknowledge the consecration of the eucharistic bread and wine, acts which a non-Christian observer might regard as indicative of his passive resistance to rather than his open defiance of the Catholic faith. A continued adherence to Islam was identifiable not just in a *morisco*'s deceptive religious behaviour, but also in his whole way of life: in his dietary habits (such as his abstention from eating pork and drinking wine and his cooking with oil instead of lard), his attention to personal hygiene (engaging in ritual bathing on a Friday), his maintenance of group solidarity, his use of the Arabic tongue and his style of dress. There thus evolved an assault by the Christian authorities, not merely on the alleged religious deviance of the *morisco*, but on his whole cultural identity, a culture which had flourished in Spain for centuries and was intimately interwoven with his religious beliefs.[29] The doctrinal conformity of a newly baptised Christian effectively could not be separated from his pattern of social behaviour. As Archbishop Talavera had reminded the Moors of the Albaicín at the beginning of the century, it was necessary to conform 'in your dress and your shoes and your adornment, in eating and at your tables and in cooking meat as they cook it; in your manner of walking, in giving and receiving, and, more than anything, in your speech, forgetting in so far as you can the Arabic tongue'.[30] Although the Inquisition (established in Granada in 1526) acted leniently towards the newly converted Moorish population during the first half of the sixteenth century, it nevertheless regarded an adherence to Islamic customs (as well as religion) as an obstacle to the acceptance of Christianity and therefore a punishable offence. The dancing of the *zambra* (a typical Moorish dance) and the eating of couscous resulted in a *morisco* from Toledo being accused of 'heresy' in 1538. Inquisitor General Manrique de Lara (1523–38), in his list of acts that a Christian must denounce to the Inquisition, included the giving of Moorish names to children 'or showing pleasure at others doing so'.[31] This was a particularly sensitive issue as the Arab name identified the clan to which each *morisco* belonged. Identification of family clans underpinned the Islamic legal system, based on arbitration, kinship and blood feuds. The ban on the use of Arabic surnames thus threatened the stability of Moslem society and increased resentment and fear of the Christian oppressor.

On a visit to Granada in 1526, Charles V was informed that 'the *Moriscos* are truly Moors: it is twenty-seven years since their conversion and there are not twenty-seven or even seven of them who are Christians'.[32] In December of the same year, following recommendations put forward by an ecclesiastical congregation, attempts were made to eradicate all existing traces of a still flourishing Moorish civilisation in Granada (including the use of Arabic, the wearing of traditional Moorish dress and the performance of the *zambra*). The congregation also urged the local clergy to take greater responsibility for the integration of the *morisco* into the Christian Church via training programmes for priests and educative initiatives for parishioners. Neither proposal was fully implemented. A financial compromise was reached by which Charles suspended the legislation and received payment of a large subsidy of 90 000 ducats over six years from the Granadine *moriscos*, principally derived from the profits of the silk industry, in return for which the local tribunal of the Inquisition exercised minimal vigilance over them. At the same time they remained protected by the Captaincy General of Granada, an hereditary office held in succession by three Counts of Tendilla, members of the powerful aristocratic house of Mendoza, to whom the *moriscos* paid military taxes (known as the *fardas*) to support the cost of security in the region. Upon their submission to Christian baptism in 1526, the *moriscos* of Valencia were granted a 40-year period of grace from inquisitorial prosecutions in return for a payment of 40 000 ducats to the crown. Both Castilian and Aragonese Moorish converts were thus able to maintain virtually intact all the essential features of their cultural inheritance without fear of reprisal. The fact that the *moriscos*' nominal Christianity was quietly tolerated suggests that they were still valued for the contribution they made to society as skilled labourers, artisans and craftsmen – and, most importantly for the crown, as taxpayers – which more than made up for the doubtful status of their conversion. The *modus vivendi* of Moorish society in Spain was effectively to remain intact throughout most of the first half of the sixteenth century.

The Fate of the Morisco

During the early 1560s, the Granadine *moriscos* became more restive as the terms of their immunity expired and the local tribunal of the Inquisition stepped up its activity against them. Ninety-two per cent of the prosecutions it mounted in 1566 concerned *moriscos*, as compared with 50 per cent in 1550.[33] It was now no longer possible to superficially satisfy the rules of conformity where the adherence to Christian doctrine was concerned, as many had previously managed to do. Turkish advances in the western Mediterranean, combined with corsair raids along the southern coast, compounded fears of the possible recapture of Granada. Pedro Guerrero, the Archbishop of Granada (1546–76), recently returned from the Council of Trent, instructed his clergy, assembled in provincial council between 1565 and 1566, to engage in a rigorous Christianisation programme throughout the archdiocese in accordance with Tridentine requirements. But the initiative was not seized and a further opportunity for instruction and integration was lost at a vital moment. The failure of Granadine clergy to accommodate the *morisco* and his reluctance to abandon his native culture increased tensions between the local church and its parishioners. A royal edict (known as a *pragmática*) was published on 1 January 1567, prohibiting the practice of Moorish traditions within the kingdom of Granada. Measures included a ban on the use of Arabic and the wearing of silk garments, as well as the destruction of private and public baths, including those of the Alhambra. It amounted to a cultural annihilation. The *pragmática* was deliberately announced on the anniversary of the surrender of Granada, thereby giving pointed offence. The age of cooperation between the two cultures had all but passed away. The conciliatory approach was about to be replaced by one of hardline coercion.

The enforcement of the edict sparked off the outbreak of a violent uprising of Granadine *moriscos* in the Alpujarras mountains on Christmas Eve 1568 which lasted for two years and resulted in many atrocities on both sides.[34] The king and senior ministers totally underestimated the local response to the imposition of the *pragmática*. It was naively assumed that forcing the *morisco* to abandon his ancient traditions would make him into a loyal Christian subject, that one civilisation could simply impose itself on another after centuries of cohabitation. The second revolt of the Alpujarras was also part of a wider jurisdictional struggle between the fourth Count of Tendilla, Captain General of Granada from 1543, who was regarded as being the protector of *morisco* peasants, and members of central government (represented via the legal tribunal known as the *Audiencia*), determined to impose their own administrative authority on the kingdom via the edict. Following the quelling of the revolt, a policy of resettlement was put into immediate effect. Over 80 000 of the rebels were rounded up in November 1570 and the majority despatched in convoy to major cities in southern Castile. Toledo, Córdoba and Albacete took at least half of the exiled community. The dispersal of the seditious Granadine *morisco* community, so it was envisaged, would solve the problem. In practice it merely served to exacerbate it. The contagion spread throughout Castile rather than being confined to its southernmost kingdom.

In 1588 the Archbishop of Toledo, Gaspar de Quiroga, reported to the Council of State on the failure of *morisco* integration within his own archdiocese. He took as his evidence a statement produced by a commissioner of the Toledan tribunal. He spoke of the lax orthodoxy of the *morisco* community in scathing terms:

> Diabolical unbelievers, they never go to mass, never accompany the Holy Sacrament through the streets, only go to confession for fear of sanctions against them. They marry amongst themselves, hide their children to avoid having them baptized, and when they do baptize them take the first passers-by on the church steps as godparents. Extreme unction is never requested except for those who are practically dead and unable to receive it. And since the people responsible for supervising and educating these unbelievers do very little supervision or education, the latter do as they please.[35]

This last remark reflects the real root of the problem: almost a hundred years after the Moors had been forced into Christian baptism, the Primate of Spain was obliged to acknowledge that evangelisation had never made any significant progress. His Church had failed in its mission. The *morisco* was still the Moor of old. But instead of condemning his clergy, he proposed condemning the alien race itself. At a meeting of the Council of State held on 5 May 1590, several councillors first raised the possibility of expulsion as a practical solution to the *morisco* problem.

Following the crushing of the second Alpujarras revolt, the focus of concern shifted to Spain's eastern provinces. Two-thirds of all Aragonese *moriscos* (some 200 000) inhabited the area between Zaragoza and Alicante where they formed a large percentage of the rural population. The vast majority of them (135 000) were concentrated in the kingdom of Valencia where there was one *morisco* for every two Christians. In the neighbouring kingdom of Aragón there were 61 000, making up a fifth of the local population. In both areas the New Christian community was multiplying fast. A 70 per cent growth rate was recorded in the kingdom of Valencia between 1565 and 1609, compared with a 45 per cent increase in the size of the Old Christian population.[36] The fear was that the New might soon outnumber the Old Christian population. The *moriscos* of the eastern kingdoms did not suffer the same level of cultural repression as their co-religionists in the south. They lived in separate, mainly rural, settlements where they retained most of their traditions, including their practice of worship. They were protected by their noble overlords who hampered the conversion process by preventing the Inquisition taking action against their highly valued labour force. Here the old Castilian proverb 'the more Moors, the more profit' certainly rang true. The Valencian tribunal stepped up its prosecution of *moriscos* following the second Alpujarras uprising. It brought 2500 to trial between 1560 and 1614, as compared with 82 between 1540 and 1559.[37] These persecutions, which also affected neighbouring Zaragoza, heightened political tensions between Old and New Christians. By the end of the sixteenth century, the *moriscos* in the east were regarded as a serious potential security risk. It was feared that the Aragonese were in collusion with the French and that those of Valencia were seeking aid from their Ottoman allies.

Against this background, a meeting of Valencian bishops took place in 1573, under the chairmanship of Archbishop Juan de Ribera (1568–1611), to discuss ways of better instructing and integrating their *morisco* flock into the full body of the local church. A scheme was discussed to establish 22 new parishes in areas of high *morisco* settlement. Ribera, who had gained a reputation for his generous support of pastoral work in the archdiocese, promised to contribute 3000 ducats per year to the project. The *plan parroquial* received papal approval in 1576 but a lack of funds and enthusiasm amongst the local clergy meant that the proposals made little headway in the decade that followed.[38] A *Junta* of senior clergy met in Valencia in 1587 at the insistence of the crown to discuss new initiatives. An increasingly inflexible line of approach emerged. Martín de Salvatierra, the Bishop of Segorbe (1583–91), came out firmly in favour of expulsion. Ribera himself was likely to have been of the same opinion but continued to support the official programme of evangelisation and the extension of the parochial infrastructure. In 1597, an edict of grace was published by Pope Clement VIII by which Valencian *moriscos* were encouraged to abjure their errors and enter fully into the Catholic Church. As he ended his visit to Valencia in May 1599, Philip III instructed Ribera to press ahead with the publication of a catechism for the newly converted and to intensify the preaching mission. But by the end of 1601 the Archbishop could not contain his frustrations any longer. In a letter to the king he insisted on the obstinacy of the *moriscos* and the danger they represented. In January 1602 he wrote again to Philip III vigorously insisting on the need for expulsion or risk losing Spain to 'heretics and traitors'.[39] The matter was now referred to the Council of State.

The Decision to Expel

There was no unanimous call to expel the *moriscos* at this stage, from within either government, the Cortes or the Church. The Inquisition was not formally consulted. Divisions of opinion and of conscience continued to obstruct the decision-making process, just as they had done the attempted programme of assimilation. The Council of State came close to agreement in 1602 but the Duke of Lerma and the royal confessor, Fray Gaspar de Córdoba, were not yet convinced. Those who favoured expulsion – men motivated by the political threat rather than the religious one – were still in the minority. Ecclesiastical opinion in general did not support the harsh stand made by Ribera. Cardinal Fernando Niño de Guevara, as Inquisitor General (1599–1602), refused to allow a global condemnation of the *moriscos*. In 1606 Pedro de Valencia, chronicler to Philip III, wrote a treatise in which he put forward a series of rational solutions to the *morisco* problem. He strongly advised against the use of force, proposing instead that measures should be taken to integrate the *morisco* into Christian society on equal terms and to provide for their proper conversion. Valencia's paper bore witness to the endurance of a tolerant, dispassionate current of thought in Spanish society, humanist in spirit, free from religious prejudice and fanaticism.[40] A *Junta* of three senior ministers (including the newly appointed royal confessor Fray Jerónimo de Javierre, General of the Dominican Order), which met in January and October 1607, recommended a renewal of Christian teaching and missionary work under the direction of committed priests and members of religious orders. But within a matter of months, a majority decision was taken at a session of the Council of State (convened on 30 January 1608) to support a policy of expulsion. This dramatic reversal of intent may have been prompted by the Duke of Lerma, persuaded by Archbishop Ribera, who seized an opportune moment to reap maximum personal and political advantage. The shock discovery of a planned *morisco* uprising in Valencia, scheduled for Maundy Thursday 1605, involving French and Algerian participation, may also have forced events. However, the decision taken by the council was not publicly disclosed at this juncture. Indeed, there was still considerable division of opinion on the issue. In November 1608 a group of leading Valencian theologians met to consider the *morisco* problem at the insistence of Pope Paul V, who continued to advocate a conciliatory solution. The Bishops of Orihuela, Tortosa and Segorbe declared themselves in favour of the continuation of the Christianisation programme (providing evidence of success within their own dioceses), a recommendation quite at odds with that which had already been taken in Madrid. The formal decision to expel the *moriscos* was made by the Council of State on 4 April 1609 and approved by Philip III five days later, the same day on which Spain signed a 12-year truce with the Dutch rebels. Public attention was thus diverted from the humiliating withdrawal of troops from the Netherlands while Spanish garrisons reassembled to aid in the deportation process.[41] The first expulsion order was published in Valencia on 22 September 1609. Five days later, Archbishop Ribera delivered a sermon in which he justified the banishment of the *morisco* on religious grounds. He referred to the dishonour suffered by true Christians through their forced coexistence with infidels and the need to placate God for having tolerated non-believers for so long. The old crusading militancy of the Spanish Church was thus dramatically rekindled in order to win over public opinion. Lerma skilfully avoided confrontation with his fellow Valencian overlords by allowing them to retain the personal property and real estate (*bienes muebles y raíces*) of their *morisco* tenants. Between September 1609 and January 1610, an estimated total of 135 000 *moriscos* were deported from the kingdom of Valencia – potentially the most dangerous area of *morisco* habitation. They were followed by their co-religionists from Castile, Extremadura, La Mancha, Andalusia, Murcia, Catalonia and Aragón. By the end of March 1611, the main part of the operation was complete, with pockets of resistance having been successfully crushed. A total of 300 000 *moriscos* had been forced to leave Spain for France and North Africa. To these must be added the 10 000–12 000 identified by Domínguez Ortiz and Vincent as having lost their lives in rebellions en route to their places of departure. The expulsion marked the ultimate failure of Spanish society to accept the cultural diversity of the *mudéjar* community and to properly assimilate the *morisco* into the Christian faith. By presenting the event as a great moral victory for Catholicism, the political calculations

Table 1.2 The expulsion of the *moriscos* by region, 1609–11

	No. of expulsions	*% loss*
Kingdom of Castile		
Old and New Castile, La Mancha, Extremadura	45 000	0.9
Murcia, Andalusia, Granada, Canaries	50 000	2.7
Crown of Aragón		
Aragón	61 000	15.2
Catalonia	5 000	1.0
Valencia	135 000	23.0
Total losses	296 000	3.7

Source: Henri Lapeyre, *Geografía de la España Morisca* (Valencia, 1986), p. 252.

inherent in the dispersal were disguised, as was the conflict of attitudes within both lay and ecclesiastical circles that lay behind it.

The Aftermath

The catastrophic 23 per cent demographic depletion of the kingdom of Valencia prompted a severe agricultural and economic recession in the region, compounding the national crisis. As early as May 1610, the *Audiencia* of Valencia was lamenting the scarcity of hard-working labourers caused by the expulsion of the *moriscos*. Landowners, dependent on *morisco* rents, failed to make their mortgage payments to their creditors, who included ecclesiastical communities. In February 1612 the court historian, Cabrera de Córdoba, reported that the rental income of the Archbishop of Valencia had declined from 70 000 to 50 000 ducats per annum following the depopulation of the area.[42] The economic stability of the Inquisition in the eastern kingdoms was also severely affected by the expulsion. The Valencian tribunal suffered a 42.7 per cent loss of income from annuities and subsidies payable by the *morisco* population. Its counterpart in Zaragoza had its income reduced by 48 per cent.[43] Both tribunals sought financial compensation from the government for their loss of victims. The crown made considerable ready profit from the expulsion, via seizures of goods and property, but the monies were soon dissipated. Ecclesiastical opinion remained divided. In January 1610, the Archbishop of Seville made a plea for clemency on behalf of those *moriscos* remaining in the city of Granada who were respected members of the local church.[44] In October 1611, all the 2500 inhabitants of the community of the Valle del Ricote in Murcia were expelled, although acknowledged as being faithful Christians. Cervantes, via the character of Ricote in Part II of *Don Quijote*, expressed his own underlying sympathy (and possibly that of a wider public) for the banished *morisco* by making him the mouthpiece of the sadness and bitterness of a condemned race. 'To us', claimed Ricote, 'it [exile] was the most terrible [punishment] that could be inflicted. Wherever we are we weep for Spain; for, after all, we were born here and this is our native country. Nowhere do we find the reception our misery requires', he lamented.[45] By 1614 the 'poisoned fruit', representing approximately 3–4 per cent of the overall population, had been removed from the flesh of Spain. The Moorish enemy, the false convert, who had refused to abandon the traditions of his mother culture, who was reported to be in collusion with Spain's foreign enemies and who had reaped profit at the expense of the Spaniard by his hard work and thriftiness, had been excluded. The religious motivation for the expulsion, compounded by the political threat, concealed a long-standing animosity on the part of the Christian towards the Moorish convert, partly rooted in the successful survival of the alien culture. As Fernand Braudel has acknowledged, 'The *Morisco* after one, two or even three centuries, remained still the Moor of old, with his Moorish dress, tongue, cloistered house and Moorish baths. He had retained them all. He had refused to accept western civilization and this was his fundamental crime'.[46] The expulsion of the *moriscos* both symbolised the bitterness felt by a defeated nation and was at the same time symptomatic of the internal dilemma of a society ill-at-ease with its past and uncertain about its future. The doubts lingered. Antonio de Sotomayor, the royal confessor, remarked in 1633: 'It is a very short time since the Moriscos were expelled, an action that did much harm to these kingdoms, that it would be a good idea to have them back, if they could be persuaded to accept our Holy Faith.'[47] The *morisco* may have been forced out of Spain but his influence lived on, most notably in its artistic and architectural heritage, its gastronomic habits and in the very physical features of the Andalusians themselves. As a French traveller noted towards the middle of the nineteenth century, 'there is some Arab blood in all these people'.[48]

Conclusion

The breakdown of Spain's multi-cultural heritage and the imposition of Catholicism as the only acceptable faith have been interpreted by the traditional school of Spanish historians as policies that definitively shaped the development of Spain's religious identity in the early modern period. According to this viewpoint, it gave rise to a Church characterised by its militancy and exclusivity. Its power was strengthened by the support of the crown on the one hand, which controlled ecclesiastical patronage and determined religious policy, and on the other by the Holy Inquisition, which rigorously enforced the practice of orthodox principles of belief and behaviour. But there is now sufficient evidence from the work of modern historians to suggest that Spain's Catholic mission was never as complete or as successful as has previously been suggested. According to this new research, the extent of the Church's control over the religious persuasions of the Spanish people was fragmented, making way for the survival of elements of Jewish and Moorish practice in Spain long after the edicts of expulsion against its religious minorities were published. By forcing Jews and Moors to accept Christian baptism rather than integrating them via a full programme of instruction, the crown ensured that they would long remain reluctant converts. The Inquisition, while brutally efficient in certain areas of the peninsula (most notably in central-southern towns), was ineffectual in others (such as the remote rural areas of north-west Spain). Not every Spaniard who came under its scrutiny was willing to either confess or inform. The propaganda initiatives of the crown were not sufficient in themselves to ensure the undivided spiritual allegiance of its subjects. Furthermore, had the campaign to impose orthodoxy been successful, the Inquisition would never have continued with its work as long as it did. As we shall see, it widened its role in the sixteenth century beyond the pursuit of backsliding Jews, targeting diverse groups of alleged heretics, be they intellectuals, spiritualists or uninstructed peasants. Spanish Catholicism, by virtue of Spain's unique religious heritage as well as its cultural and regional diversity, would always be a faith that derived from multiple roots. This was the real precondition of its development in the early modern period.

2 *Traditionalism and Innovation in the Spanish Church*

Introduction

During the opening decades of the sixteenth century, the religious foundation of early modern Europe underwent a dramatic transformation. The rise of Lutheranism in Germany in the 1520s prompted a movement of radical reform within the western Church, referred to by modern historians as the Reformation. It resulted in the formation of a Reformed Church, which promoted a broader, more inclusive approach to Christian belief and worship set to rival the Church of Rome, which in turn responded by reinforcing the orthodox principles of its foundation. Spain, despite its firm commitment to Catholicism, was not unaffected by these events. It possessed a large New Christian population whose faith, as we have seen, was regarded at best as ambivalent and thus in need of constant vigilance. The emergence of the Reformed Church led to a hardening of traditional, conservative attitudes within the Catholic Church hierarchy and their representatives on the Inquisition, intent on purging Spain of any potentially subversive infiltrations of belief. The Inquisition deliberately set about associating innovative trends in religious and intellectual life with the 'heresy' perpetrated by Martin Luther, however far removed they were from such a definition in actual fact. Furthermore, by actively seeking new sources of contagion, it substantially expanded its own power base, which had been considerably diminished since the end of the period of intense anti-*converso* persecutions. The tactic of the Holy Office can be illustrated in its approach to the activity of a small, elite group of spiritual devotees, based in New Castile, known as the Illuminists or the *Alumbrados*. Inspired by their reading of devotional literature, they advocated the virtues of private, meditative prayer over formal ceremony as a means of attaining perfect union with God. In the mid-1520s, prominent members of the Illuminist movement, which attracted many New Christian followers and was supported by many leading Franciscans, were hounded by the Inquisition as heretics for disseminating an obscure, and therefore in its judgement deviant, form of spirituality. In practice, many of those accused had their cases dropped due to lack of evidence. Despite the unremitting nature of the campaign to exclude any such innovative tendencies of belief, which extended over much of the first half of the sixteenth century, Spanish religious and intellectual life continued to be invigorated by complementary creative trends and outlooks of a reformist nature.

Erasmian Humanism and Biblical Scholarship

During the 1520s, the writings of the distinguished Dutch humanist scholar Desiderius Erasmus (*c*.1466–1536) began to influence Spanish religious and intellectual life as a result of his following at the imperial court of Charles V, King of Spain (1516–56) and Holy Roman Emperor (1519–58). Erasmus supported the dissemination of a new form of religious culture, known as Christian Humanism. The humanist tradition, in which piety and learning were intimately linked, evolved from ideas promoted in northern Europe during the Renaissance. It encouraged the wider interpretation of biblical scholarship via its classical routes, leading to a revitalised expression of belief. Erasmus outlined these notions in his *Enchiridion Militis Christiani* (*Handbook of a Christian Soldier*), first published in 1503. In it he criticised paganism, superstition and immorality in the Church (notably within the monastic orders). He called for a reformed, less ritualistic, more tolerant faith, that accommodated intellectual freedom, private prayer and meditation. Erasmus hoped that peace and spiritual reconciliation might be achieved between traditionalists and reformists within the Christian Church, a notion that accorded with Charles V's vision of himself as a universal Emperor ruling over a universal Church. Erasmianism was a cosmopolitan movement with political, social and religious overtones that responded to the climate of the early modern age. It soon acquired an enthusiastic following in Spain, especially among those who had travelled with the imperial court through northern Europe, stimulating a vibrant atmosphere of religious enthusiasm among intellectuals, courtiers and certain members of the Church hierarchy. The two most senior ecclesiastics in Spain, Alonso Manrique de Lara, the Inquisitor General (1523–38), and Alonso de Fonseca, the Archbishop of Toledo (1523–34), were both ardent supporters of Erasmus's views. Outside immediate court circles, many Erasmian sympathisers were characterised by their New Christian ancestry, their Illuminist (*alumbrado*) background and their association with the Complutensian University of Alcalá.

In 1498 Cardinal Fray Francisco Jiménez de Cisneros, Archbishop of Toledo (1495–1517), announced his intention to establish the University of Alcalá de Henares outside Madrid as a centre for theological training and biblical study. Ten years later it accepted its first students. Its centrepiece was the *colegio mayor* of San Ildefonso, set to rival the elite educational establishments of Salamanca and Valladolid. Alcalá was soon transformed into a lively centre for theological debate and inquiry into the Scriptures. In 1522 (the same year in which Luther's New Testament appeared in print), the famous Polyglot Bible was published at Alcalá – a six-volume critical edition of the Scriptures produced in parallel text format in Latin, Hebrew and Greek. Many distinguished Spanish and foreign scholars (including Erasmus) were invited to take part in the project, whose objective was 'to improve the dissemination of the word of God'. It was a work conceived in an atmosphere of tolerance and cooperation that paid tribute to the diverse origins and interpretations of the word of God. The publication of the Complutensian Bible represented a major cultural and scholastic achievement. It set the seal on the reputation of the university as one of the most advanced seats of learning in Europe. It soon became a thriving centre for the development of humanist culture in Spain, producing some of the most eminent spiritual leaders and religious reformers of the period.

From 1525, the writings of Erasmus began to roll off the Alcalá printing press. In 1526 a Castilian version of the *Enchiridion*, translated by the canon of Palencia, Alonso Fernández de Madrid, appeared in print for the first time. Such was its appeal that it immediately sold out. Eight editions were printed in Spain over the next four years. The book was reported to be so popular that it was read 'in the cities, in the churches, in the convents, even in the inns and highways . . . by people of every sort'.[1] The propagation of Erasmian humanism through the printed word injected new life into the Illuminist movement, with which it shared much common ground. But the success of Erasmianism in Spain was to be short-lived. Within a year of the publication of the *Enchiridion* in Castilian, attempts were underway to undermine Erasmus, his supporters and the whole spirit of religious regeneration with which he was associated.

The Attack on Erasmus and Erasmians

In June 1527, an ecclesiastical Congregation met at Valladolid. The official reason for the gathering of theologians, religious and inquisitors was to approve a subsidy to help the Emperor fund the defence of Christendom against the Turk in the Mediterranean. Some of those assembled took advantage of the opportunity to discuss their views on Erasmus. The anti-Erasmus faction was led by Franciscans and Dominicans, profoundly suspicious of his anti-monastic views, as summed up in his famous dictum on the false piety of monks – *monochatus non es pietas*. They were supported by leading theologians from Salamanca, who disapproved of his attack on scholastic theology. They exposed the 'twenty-two errors of Erasmus' before those gathered in Congregation.[2] The pro-Erasmus faction was led by humanist scholars from Alcalá and his partisans within the ecclesiastical hierarchy. Two fundamental interpretations of Christian belief, which were at the heart of the emerging divisions within the western Church, appeared to be brought under public scrutiny: the traditional and the reformist. However, new research suggests that this may be an over-simplistic interpretation, that Spanish intellectuals were capable of crossing the boundaries between scholasticism and humanism and that those theologians who assembled at Valladolid were inconsistent in their approach to Erasmus.[3] When Archbishop Manrique brought the proceedings of the conference to a sudden end two months after its opening, nothing had really been resolved. Charles wrote to Erasmus in December 1527, assuring him of his continued support.

Three events in 1529 prompted a dramatic downturn in the fortunes of Erasmus and his followers in Spain. In July Charles left Spain for Italy, taking with him the leading Erasmians from his household. Shortly afterwards, Inquisitor General Manrique fell from favour and was forced to retire to his archdiocese of Seville. In the same year Francisca Hernández, the leader of the Valladolid

Illuminist circle, was arrested and proceeded to maliciously denounce fellow devotees to the Inquisition as Erasmian humanists of Lutheran orientation. The position of Erasmians was reduced to that of a vulnerable minority of intellectuals, deprived of support and suspected of unorthodox leanings. The strengthened campaign against Erasmus, launched in the early 1530s, represented a tactical display of force by the conservatives who dominated the Inquisition, now enjoying a much freer hand in Spain in the absence of the Emperor and his foreign advisers. The Inquisition's moves to eradicate Erasmianism also have to be set against the background of emerging religious turmoil within Europe. In 1529, a number of German princes signed a 'Protestation', pledging their support for what henceforth became known as the Protestant Church. Two years later, they banded together against imperial religious policies by forming the League of Schmalkalden. The Holy Roman Empire was set to become a divided land of two Churches, one Protestant and the other Catholic, and susceptible to the growth of extreme sects within. The Inquisition responded by attempting to discredit any potentially damaging currents of belief that it suspected might be associated with the heresy spreading through northern Europe, and therefore capable of destabilising the authority of the Catholic state. It chose as its first victim one of the most highly acclaimed humanist scholars in Spain.

In June 1533, Juan de Vergara was arrested by the Holy Office. A charge of triple heresy ('Lutheran, Illuminist and Erasmian') was levelled against him. Vergara, who had collaborated in the Polyglot Bible project at Alcalá, first met Erasmus in 1520 while visiting the Flemish court as private secretary to the Spanish Primate, Guillermo de Croy (1518–21), and established a firm friendship with him. Throughout the decade that followed, Vergara distinguished himself as one of the leading exponents of Erasmian reform in Spain, while at the same time occupying a position of considerable rank within the established Church, that of canon of Toledo. He vigorously defended himself at his trial, refusing to accept that his friendship with Erasmus constituted a crime or that he had any sympathy with Lutheran doctrine. The Inquisitors' verdict was announced, significantly, following the death in February 1534 of Vergara's patron, the Spanish Primate, Alfonso de Fonseca. Vergara was forced to abjure his errors in an *auto de fe*, held in the Plaza de Zocodover in Toledo on 21 December 1535. The trial represented a show of force by the Inquisition, but the punishment – a year of monastic seclusion and a 1500 ducat fine – was an extremely moderate one. Vergara still had influential friends within the Spanish Church who helped secure his release in February 1537, whereupon he resumed his position within the Toledan cathedral chapter.[4] Vergara was a member of the intellectual and ecclesiastical elite, stimulated by his contact with new ideas emanating from northern Europe. He embraced a flexible religious culture, one that was perhaps more widespread among Spanish scholars than has hitherto been acknowledged. He was far removed from being a subversive figure within the Catholic Church as the Holy Office sought to label him. Other prominent Erasmians, such as the *converso* theologian and commentator on the Holy Scriptures Juan de Valdés and the Chancellor of the University of Alcalá, Pedro de Lerma, chose to leave Spain rather than fall victim to the campaign to discredit their tolerant tradition. By the mid-1530s, the Inquisition – under heavy Dominican influence – had effectively enforced silence on humanist scholarship as part of its campaign to turn Spain into a fortress against heresy. It now turned its attention to hounding some of the great Catholic reformers who forged Spain's religious revival in the first half of the sixteenth century – Juan de Ávila, Ignatius Loyola and Teresa de Jesús – all of whom, significantly, were later recognised as saints.

Catholic Reformers Condemned

Juan de Ávila made a major contribution to the revitalisation of religious life in early sixteenth-century Spain in his role as a popular preacher, writer and clerical reformer. During his formative years as a student at the University of Alcalá, he had become familiar with the writings of Erasmus. In 1526, with the support of Archbishop Manrique de Lara of Seville, Ávila began his career as a priest in southern Spain, where he appealed directly to the spiritual needs of the people. Such was the extent of his influence that he became known as 'the Apostle of Andalusia'. He travelled through the region preaching, hearing confessions, organising aid for the poor and promoting religious education. He called for a renewed sense of vocation amongst the priesthood and criticised the system of patrimonial appointments to chaplaincies that enabled young men to become priests simply on account of their family lineage. In 1531, at the height of his success, Juan de Ávila was arrested for publicly suggesting that 'it was better to give alms than to found chaplaincies' and that '[in Andalusia] there is [an] insufficient number of masses and extreme misery amongst the poor'.[5] His theology, with its emphasis on works of charity and acts of simple faith, attracted many who, like their 'Apostle', had descended from New Christian families. In the prevailing climate of spiritual unease, Ávila's reformist ideals and his methods of devotion, which had much in common with those advocated by the *alumbrados* and humanist thinkers, set a dangerous challenge to orthodoxy in the eyes of the ecclesiastical authorities. Above all, it was the power and success of Ávila's apostolate that prompted the mistrust (and jealousy) of academics and theologians within the Church and their representatives on the Inquisition who refused to accept any other than the traditional route to God, with its emphasis on doctrine, ceremony and public prayer.

Such was the flimsiness of the inquisitorial case against Ávila that within two years he was cleared of all charges and released from imprisonment. He returned to take up his preaching role in Andalusia, developing around him a sacerdotal school, dominated by New Christians, which engaged in apostolic missions and was later to provide a model for the Tridentine seminary. While in prison, Juan de Ávila had begun to write his most celebrated work – a commentary on Psalm 44, the *Audi, filia* – in which he warned his readers of the dangers of *alumbradismo* – the very 'crime' of which he had been accused. The text, which first appeared in manuscript form in 1556, was seized upon by the heavy hand of Inquisitor General Valdés in 1559 for its heretical content and withdrawn from circulation. A man of highly suspect spirituality in the eyes of the Inquisition, Ávila nevertheless continued to influence the course of Spanish Catholicism into the Counter-Reformation period. He wrote a number of catechisms that transformed the religious education of the laity. He prepared a written outline of his proposals for clerical reform which the Archbishop of Granada, Don Pedro Guerrero, incorporated into his address to the second session of the Council of Trent.[6] Five years after Juan de Ávila's death in 1574, under the more accommodating regime of Inquisitor General Gaspar de Quiroga (1573–95), the *Audi, filia* was published in Toledo. The influence of Juan de Ávila, which combined recognition of the need for change with a respect for tradition, would live on.

Juan de Ávila's methods of prayer and meditation, as well as his reforming zeal, won him a number of keen disciples, among them Ignatius Loyola, the founder of the Jesuits. Born into an aristocratic Old Christian family from Guipúzcoa in 1491, Loyola entered into military service for the crown. While recovering from war wounds received in the siege of Pamplona (1521), he became profoundly influenced by his reading of devotional literature, and in 1522 chose to withdraw from secular life and adopt a semi-monastic existence of extreme austerity. In pursuit of spiritual guidance, the former soldier set out on a pilgrimage to Jerusalem and the Holy Land. He had begun the first draft of his *Spiritual Exercises* – a practical guide for the direction of souls – which set out a month-long programme of intensive self-examination, meditation and prayer, leading to a strengthening of the novice's will and his total submission to the cause of Catholicism. The *Exercises* were a unique statement of spiritual commitment. Not only did they become the fundamental manual of Jesuit instruction but furthermore, while predating the Council of Trent, they embodied the essential elements of its doctrine. On his return to Spain, Loyola took up the study of theology at Alcalá (1526) and soon became deeply involved in Erasmian circles. The intense activities of his prayer groups aroused the suspicions of the Inquisition. He was arrested in April 1526 as an alleged *alumbrado*. No sooner had he been absolved (and banned from preaching for three years) than he found himself in a similar confrontation, this time with Church authorities in Salamanca. To avoid further persecution he left Spain for France in 1527, never to return to his homeland. While studying at the Sorbonne he assembled around him nine 'brothers', the founder members of the Society of Jesus, who included four Spaniards. In August 1534 at Montmartre they committed themselves to their apostolic ideal: the propagation of the faith through contemplative prayer, popular preaching and missionary work, supported via voluntary contributions of alms. The Society, born out of the desire for spiritual renewal within the Catholic Church as it adapted itself to the challenges of the early modern era, was formally established by a papal bull of September 1540. It was set to become the international cornerstone of the Counter-Reformation's worldwide teaching mission. In 1556, it had a Spanish membership of 300. By the beginning of the seventeenth century, this figure had risen to over 2000.[7]

But controversy continued to surround the Society in Spain. In the early 1550s, Melchor Cano, a Dominican professor of theology at Salamanca and a fierce opponent of innovative forces within the Church, attacked Jesuit philosophy for harbouring Illuminist leanings. The *Spiritual Exercises*, so he claimed, promoted an interior form of religious experience rather than one that adhered to the formalities of orthodox tradition. The new Society, Cano feared, would 'corrupt the simplicity and Christianity of Spain'.[8] There was also a racial element to the attack: although Loyola himself was of Old Christian origin, his successor as General, Diego de Laínez, was not. Many *conversos* – some original disciples of Juan de Ávila – joined the Society, which operated a policy of 'open membership' until 1592, thereby raising further suspicions of Jewish infiltration within its ranks. Loyola continued to be hounded by his enemies beyond his death in 1556. Along with so many works of mystical inspiration, the *Spiritual Exercises* fell victim to inquisitorial censorship in the 1559 Index. Traditionalists within the Spanish Church regarded the Jesuits as rivals who owed allegiance to the papacy before the crown and whose commitment went far beyond Spain. Despite these setbacks, the Jesuits remained among the most vociferous opponents of the stifling of innovative forms of spiritual expression in sixteenth-century Spain and key individuals in the application of religious reform in neglected rural areas, demonstrating that the agents for change were active rather than passive forces within the early modern Spanish Church.

Similar suspicions surrounded the mystical experiences and writings of the founder of the Discalced Carmelite movement, Teresa de Ahumada y Cespeda, canonised in 1622 as Saint Teresa de Jesús, known to us as Teresa de Ávila. Teresa was a product of the vibrant expression of spirituality that characterised Spanish religious life during the opening decades of the sixteenth century. Her spiritual calling had begun in the 1530s, when Juan de Ávila and Ignatius Loyola were establishing their movements. As a young Carmelite nun, she too was deeply influenced by the reading of devotional literature (especially Francisco de Osuna's *Spiritual ABC*) which described the inner spiritual life, oriented towards the quiet reception of God through mental prayer. She now embarked upon a long, often tortuous, spiritual journey, as she recalled in her autobiography: 'On one side God called me, and on the other I followed the world. All divine things gave me pleasure; yet those of the world held me prisoner'.[9] In the 1540s, she was drawn through a series of divine revelations to renounce the things of this world and seek instead a humble life of prayer and devotion. During the following decade her spiritual callings became more intense, incorporating powerful visions and raptures, culminating in her most celebrated mystical experience (1559/60) – the piercing of her heart by an angel with a burning arrow – referred to as the transverberation and immortalised in Bernini's sculpture *The Ecstacy of Saint Teresa* (1646). One of Teresa's closest spiritual mentors was Juan de Ávila, whom she described as 'a man deeply versed in everything relating to prayer'.[10] Inspired by his example, as well as by that of other religious reformers (especially the austere spirituality of the founder of the Discalced Franciscans, Pedro de Alcántara), Teresa dedicated herself to religious reform. In 1561, she embarked upon her missionary role – to reform the lax rule of the Carmelites. Her aim was to replace the elitism that had governed entry to the order for generations by the preconditions of poverty, humility, piety and obedience – characteristics of the primitive rule that had inspired the Carmelite movement's original foundation in the mid-thirteenth century. Furthermore, the emphasis placed on doctrine and discipline within the order's constitution accorded with the proposals for monastic reform outlined at the Council of Trent. Following the inauguration of the first Discalced Carmelite convent of Saint Joseph in Ávila on 24 August 1562, Teresa embarked upon a 20-year period of radical reforming activity. A total of 17 female and 15 male Carmelite communities were founded in Spain and Portugal between 1562 and 1582.[11]

Teresa's mystical experiences, intimately described in her writings, coincided with a period of intense reaction on the part of an influential sector of the Church hierarchy against any form of innovative spiritual expression that was not subject to its direct control and therefore threatened to undermine its authority. In 1562, Teresa finished writing her autobiography, *Libro de la Vida*, in which she recorded in simple, direct prose her own personal experiences of divine revelation, and gave instructions as to how others could follow the mystical way. Its publication, however, was deferred on account of the suspicions surrounding her meditative practices. As her writings fell under scrutiny, she was denounced to the Inquisition, accused in 1575 of spreading superstition and of influencing the *alumbrado* community of Seville. Teresa's Jewish blood (inherited from her paternal grandfather, a wealthy New Christian merchant and tax farmer in Toledo) cast a further layer of suspicion on her person and her movement that permitted the participation of *conversos*. With the support of Philip II and Inquisitor General Quiroga, the campaign against Teresa was temporarily dropped. A remarkable reappraisal of Spanish mysticism took place during the later sixteenth century as the Inquisition entered a less repressive phase of its history and Trent stimulated a revival of intense forms of pious devotion that had earlier been stifled in Spain. The deep spirituality that Teresa espoused and transmitted to her movement was now recognised as a fundamental aid to Catholic reform, rather than as a threat to it. In her commitment to radical reform through prayer and her conscious desire to counteract heresy, Teresa personified the intense devotional and contemplative spirit of Spanish Catholicism in the Counter-Reformation era. Her writings, collected and edited by Fray Luis de León, were finally approved for publication in 1588, six years after her death. The acknowledgement of Teresa's contribution to Spain's religious regeneration provides further evidence of how the different forces within the Spanish Church were capable of harmonisation. Described by a Carmelite friar as 'a human angel, a divine woman, a spirit wholly divinised',[12] her elevation to sainthood in 1622 formally confirmed her exalted status within the Catholic Church. Teresa is still acknowledged as one of the most remarkable women in Spanish history.

The Protestant Threat of Mid-Century

The precautionary investigations made into those of suspect religious persuasion by the Holy Inquisition during the first half of the sixteenth century were followed in the 1550s by the launching of a vigorous attack on what was perceived to be an infiltration of Protestant influences into Spain. Before the Council of Trent met in its first session (1545–8) to redefine Catholic doctrine, there was still genuine ignorance and misunderstanding among Spaniards as to what actually constituted Protestantism. Until mid-century, Luther's teachings had been read by only a small minority of intellectuals – erudite clergy and liberal-minded professors – who had access to trends in European thought but whose influence over religious persuasion in Spain was marginal. Inquisitors' principal definition of a Lutheran was somebody who made a careless religious statement or a passing reference to a Reformer as opposed to deliberately attacking the Catholic Church. Of the alleged 105 'Lutherans' brought before the Spanish Inquisition prior to 1558, 66 were of foreign origin. Cases of Protestant heresy were dealt with predominantly by frontier tribunals – Logroño, Zaragoza and Barcelona in the north and Seville in the south – situated in peripheral areas 'open' to the passage of trade and ideas. In practice, the Reformation stood little real chance of establishing itself in Spain, the only country in western

Europe which possessed a powerful institution whose designated purpose was to preserve its orthodoxy. Nevertheless, as we have seen, the Spanish kingdoms did not remain totally impervious to the dramatic effects of the spread of the Reformed Church through northern Europe. When it was announced in the late 1550s that Lutheran heresy had apparently penetrated Spain's religious defences and established a native root, it threatened to destabilise the country's image at home and abroad as the guardian of the faith.

The discovery of alleged Protestant cells in Seville and Valladolid (1558), swiftly followed by the imposition of rigorous laws of censorship (1559), has to be understood within the context of the prevailing political climate in Spain and be set against a background of mounting religious turmoil in England, France, Germany and the Spanish Netherlands. The anti-Lutheran campaign, which fanned the fears of the Catholic hierarchy, was deliberately mounted in response to the internal and external tensions that Spain faced at a major turning point in its history – the transitional period following the abdication of Charles V from the throne of Spain in 1556, in favour of his son Philip II, to the return of the new monarch from the Netherlands in 1559 to assume his Spanish kingship. During the intervening years of regency government, Spanish court politics were dominated by the ruthless and ambitious Inquisitor General, Fernando de Valdés (1547–65).

In May 1558 the Inquisition announced the discovery of a group of Protestant believers, of high secular and ecclesiastical standing, centred on Valladolid, where the royal court was in residence. Within a matter of months, the existence of a parallel group of Protestant sympathisers in Seville was revealed. The detection of heresy within senior religious and courtly circles sent a wave of panic through the political establishment. Alarmed at the discovery of Lutheranism within the most Catholic of his kingdoms, Charles wrote immediately to his daughter Juana, the princess regent, from his monastic retreat at San Yuste. He demanded that 'heretics be punished with all the force and vigour that their errors merit... admitting no pleas, having respect for no one'.[13] A copy of the letter was sent to his son Philip in Brussels who supported his father's insistence on the need for resolute action. The Inquisition quickly took charge of the crisis.

The scandal unleashed by the Protestant discoveries threatened the position of the Inquisitor General, but he skilfully seized the opportunity to strengthen rather than undermine his power base at the Holy Office.[14] Valdés had risen spectacularly through the ranks of both secular and ecclesiastical office during the absence of the Emperor. His career lay in the balance, however, as Spain awaited the return of its new king. The Eboli faction, led by the Portuguese favourite, Ruy Gómez de Silva, was now working its way into a position of power at court and seeking to oust the former servants of the Emperor.[15] In March 1558, the Inquisitor General found himself out of favour with the crown over his refusal to grant a royal subsidy for military campaigns in Europe, and he feared that he might be about to be removed from court to his archdiocese of Seville (from which he had been absent for most of his ten years of tenure). The Council of Trent's recent decree on episcopal residence (1547) provided his adversaries (who included the future Archbishop of Toledo, Bartolomé de Carranza) with further reason to isolate him from the capital. The discovery of heretical dissent in Valladolid arose at precisely the moment when Valdés most needed it. He quickly took charge of the situation, exaggerating its gravity to achieve maximum political effect. The first arrests were made in April. By the end of May 1558, following the intervention of Charles V, the Inquisitor General had returned to royal favour by rendering himself, and the Holy Office, indispensable to the absentee king in the campaign to combat heresy. The Valladolid discoveries made it even more imperative for the Inquisitor General to remain at court to deal with the crisis and for Philip to return to Spain. It was not until August that he publicly exposed the full extent of Protestant activity within his own archdiocese. The Sevillian religious crisis was astutely dealt with as a local rather than a national issue, its significance initially underplayed to avoid embarrassment to its absentee archbishop. In September, Valdés secured the approval of Paul IV to extend the investigative powers of the Inquisition beyond the secular reaches of society to include members of the Church hierarchy. This was a crucial papal concession and a turning point in the history of the Inquisition.[16] Armed with its increased authority, the Holy Office embarked on a new, aggressive and highly politicised phase in its history.

The origins of the Sevillian Protestant movement were discovered within the very heart of the cathedral chapter itself in the early 1550s. Many humanist scholars from Alcalá had been appointed as canons of Seville under the Erasmian Archbishop Alonso Manrique. They included the magistral canon, Dr Juan Egidio, and his successor, the *converso* preacher and royal chaplain Dr Constantino Ponce de la Fuente. In August 1552 Egidio, whose nomination for the Aragonese bishopric of Tortosa had been suspended in 1549 due to suspicions as to his religious orthodoxy, was found guilty of unorthodox teachings and sentenced to a year of reclusion. Following Egidio's death in 1556, the Holy Office began to hound Dr Constantino. He was an ideal victim for the 'sombre men' of the Inquisition who sought to remove all traces of what they considered to be religious deviance from Spain: he was of New Christian origin, schooled in the humanist tradition, and had come in contact with Protestant propaganda during his travels with the Emperor through Germany (1548–53). He was tainted by his blood and his 'foreign' connections and therefore was inevitably branded a heretic. In November 1557, an 'active' cell of approximately 120 Protestant reformers of Calvinist orientation was exposed from within the Jeronimite communities of San Isidro del Campo and Santa Paula. Some of their leading friars, including Cassiodoro de la Reina (the first translator of the Bible into Castilian), took flight before their discovery. In the wake of this scandal, Constantino was seized in August 1558 and died in the cells of the Inquisition two years later. Both he and Egidio were burnt in effigy in the second Sevillian anti-Protestant *auto de fe* of 22 December 1560.

Another distinguished Alcalá scholar (and former student of Archbishop Carranza's) was a key member of the Valladolid Protestant cell – Dr Agustín Cazalla, son of Pedro de Cazalla and the *conversa* Leonor de Vivar. The family's house in Valladolid had operated as a centre of *alumbrado* activity in the early 1520s under the direction of Francisca Hernández, who later defected from the group and informed on it. Dr Cazalla was a highly respected figure in both ecclesiastical and courtly circles. As imperial chaplain and preacher he was part of the same cosmopolitan entourage of the Emperor to which Constantino belonged. He, too, had travelled widely in northern Europe where he came in contact with reformist views. In 1552, he was appointed a canon of Salamanca. By 1557, he had fallen under the influence of the leader of the Valladolid group, the Italian Carlos de Sesso. Within two years, the whole Cazalla family had turned towards Protestantism. Agustín, together with his brother Francisco, a local priest, and his sister Beatriz, a spiritual devotee (*beata*), were all burnt at the stake in the first anti-Protestant *auto de fe* held in Valladolid, on Trinity Sunday 1559. An effigy of their mother was also burnt at the same ceremony. Another brother, Pedro (also a local priest), was condemned to death in the second such *auto* staged in the city five months later. Dr Cazalla, whose background was touched by Illuminist, Erasmian and Lutheran sympathies, was both a product of the rich and varied spiritual climate of the first half of the sixteenth century and, at the same time, a victim of the campaign of suspicion and mistrust mounted against exponents of what were deemed to be 'alien' strands of belief at the beginning of the second half of the century. He stood at the crossroads of the tolerant 'Catholic' and the highly disciplined 'Counter' Reformations.

Philip's first official act as king on his return to Spain from Flanders in 1559 was to preside over the *auto de fe*, held on 8 October in the Plaza Mayor of Valladolid, at which 12 suspected Lutherans were condemned to death at the stake, including the leader of the group, Carlos de Sesso, whose last-minute appeal to the king for mercy was refused. In the fires that raged on the outskirts of Valladolid on 21 May and 8 October 1559, the outward traces of liberal spiritual persuasion that permeated the early sixteenth-century Spanish Church were dramatically extinguished. By giving his support to the Inquisition's spectacular propaganda exercise waged against Protestantism right at the beginning of the new reign, Philip associated himself directly with the ruthless extirpation of heresy from his realms. The rejection of 'contaminated' northern European thought and the imposition of a strictly regulated ideology from the centre served to reinforce social cohesion and a sense of national identity at a time when Spain felt particularly under threat from outside influences. By taking on the task of 'keeping at bay the enemies of God', the Holy Office imposed a model of conformity that met all the objectives of the Counter-Reformation Church and at the same time bolstered

Table 2.1 Protestant victims of the Valladolid and Sevillian *autos de fe* of 1559–60

Date of auto de fe	*Total no. accused*	*Total no. of Protestants accused*	*Total no. of Protestants burnt*
Valladolid			
21 May 1559	31	30	14
8 Oct 1559	30	25	12
28 Oct 1559	37	14	3
Seville			
24 Sept 1559	80	22	20
22 Dec 1560	44	40	17

Sources: Matías Sangrador Vitores, *Historia de Valladolid*, vol. 1 (Valladolid, 1851), pp. 386–94; José Luis González Novalín, *El Inquisidor General Fernando de Valdés (1483–1568)*, vol. 2 (Oviedo, 1971), pp. 233–5, 260–6.

the authority of the Catholic monarchy. The Inquisition used the spectre of Lutheran heresy, rather than the real existence of it, to instil fear into the Spanish people and to reinforce its ideological control over them. The calculated campaign directed by the Holy Office over the ten-year period 1555–65, which reached its climax in the Valladolid and Seville *autos* of 1559–60, successfully prevented Protestantism from establishing a native root in Spain. As a result, it never posed a major threat to the religious stability of the Spanish kingdoms.

Inquisitorial Censorship and the 1559 Index

Inquisitor General Valdés had yet another powerful weapon at his disposal – that of censorship. During the course of the 1550s a degree of selective, but harshly administered, censorship was imposed by the crown in conjunction with the Holy Office to prevent the penetration of contaminating foreign culture into Spain through the printed word. On 7 September 1558 the princess regent, Juana, issued a royal pragmatic prohibiting the import of any foreign texts into the kingdom and ordered the retention of those circulating within Spain that were condemned by the Inquisition. The pragmatic invested responsibility in the Council of Castile for the licensing of all new texts for publication, while the Inquisition set the rules of censorship and imposed the sanctions. The ultimate penalty for disobedience was death, hence the pragmatic's notorious reputation as 'the law of blood' (*la ley de sangre*). In August 1559, Valdés published the first Spanish Index of prohibited texts, modelled on that produced by the University of Louvain in 1550. As well as banning the works of Protestant reformers and vernacular translations of the Bible, Valdés's Index delivered a heavy blow to some of the most popular works of Spanish devotional literature. The new laws were applied with rigour. Bookshops and libraries were regularly searched and local tribunals made responsible for the collection and public burning of all works by heretics. In November 1559, Philip II removed the key source of contact with foreign intellectual ideas by recalling to Spain all those students studying abroad. It appeared that, within the space of just over a year, an iron curtain had descended on Spanish learning and scholarship. However, in practice, the effects of the cultural 's new Index was not exclusively prohibitory as unterpart (published in the same year). A more nent existed in Spain, by which certain less contro- were expurgated (their offensive passages deleted), being banned altogether. There were many anomalies in ication of the rules of censorship. Francisco de Osuna's classic anual of prayer and meditation, *The Third Spiritual ABC* (1527), an essential guide for all *alumbrados*, escaped inquisitorial scrutiny until 1612. Fernando de Rojas's *La Celestina* (1499) – one of the most widely read works of Spanish literature of the period which overturned the traditional values of orthodox society – was not expurgated until 1632, and only then on account of the author's *converso* background. One of those who helped compile the 1583 Index, the eminent Jesuit historian Juan de Mariana, had his own writings expurgated by inquisitorial censors in 1640. Spanish culture certainly suffered a setback as a result of the measures of 1558–9, but it was not permanently destroyed. Of the 670 texts on Valdés's Index, less than 15 per cent were Castilian. European (as opposed to Spanish) literature continued to be the main target of Gaspar de Quiroga's Index, published in two parts in 1583 (prohibited texts) and 1584 (expurgated texts). The majority of the 3500 prohibitions it contained were unknown or inaccessible to the ordinary Spanish reading public. Notwithstanding the restrictions imposed on the publication of devotional and creative literature by the laws of censorship, the second half of the sixteenth century witnessed a great flowering of Spanish culture as it entered its much acclaimed 'Golden Age'.

The Archbishop of Toledo Accused of Heresy

In the wake of the hysteria generated by the first Protestant discoveries, the Inquisition seized its most illustrious victim – the Spanish Primate. On 22 August 1559 (exactly a week before the arrival of Philip II in Spain from the Netherlands), the Archbishop of Toledo, the Dominican friar Bartolomé de Carranza y Miranda, was arrested at Torrelaguna on the outskirts of Madrid on a charge of heresy. The news of the Archbishop's arrest sent shock waves throughout Spain and scandalised Catholic Europe. The whole Dominican order felt the weight of his disgrace. The controversy surrounding Archbishop Carranza was symptomatic of the many conflicts and tensions that existed in mid-sixteenth-century Spain – professional, political and ideological – that found their expression in his persecution at the hands of the Inquisition.

The Dominican friar, of humble *hidalgo* parentage, was a former student and professor of theology at San Gregorio in Valladolid. He made a name for himself as a distinguished theologian at the first and second sessions of the Council of Trent, where he took a determined stand against Protestantism and strongly supported the obligatory nature of episcopal residence – the subject of a treatise he published in 1547. In 1550, he was elected Provincial of the Castilian branch of his order and his talents soon brought him to the attention of the heir to the throne. He spent three years with Philip in England (1554–7) as his religious adviser and then accompanied him to Flanders to take up his Burgundian inheritance. The new king was so impressed by Carranza that he nominated him to be Archbishop of Toledo in September 1557, in succession to Martínez Siliceo. The bull of appointment was issued by Rome on 10 December – the same day the nomination was received in Consistory – without any of the regular profile checks being undertaken, such was the strength of the royal recommendation. Carranza's rapid rise to the primacy, despite his humble pedigree, incurred the animosity of leading figures at court and within the Church hierarchy – aristocratic rivals, disappointed at being overlooked for promotion themselves – who soon began to plot against him.

Fernando de Valdés greatly resented Carranza's rapid rise to the most senior office in the Spanish Church, especially in view of the hard line he took on absentee prelates. Fearing that he might be ousted from his post at the Holy Office to comply with Trent's dictate on residence, he turned the tables and took the leading role in instigating the Archbishop's arrest on a charge of heresy. He had prepared the legal ground well in advance. As we have seen, immediately following the discovery of Protestant influences within religious circles, he judiciously sought and obtained papal permission to extend the Inquisition's powers of investigation to bishops, previously exempt from its purview. From this juncture not even the most senior ecclesiastic in Spain would be excluded from its net of inquiry. Valdés, with or without the king's full approval, was determined to exercise his newly acquired authority at the first opportunity. He found an able accomplice in Melchor Cano, a fellow Dominican friar and a former academic rival of Carranza's at San Gregorio, who now held the influential position of religious adviser to Philip II, with specific responsibility for literary censorship. This role provided him with the perfect springboard for attack. While investigating heretical literature in Flanders in 1558, Carranza had published his *Commentaries on the Christian Catechism*. Zealous inquisitors, including Cano and Domingo de Soto (both companion theologians of Carranza at Trent, now turned enemies), soon found ample evidence in it of Lutheran (as well as *alumbrado*) doctrine, prompting a fundamental questioning of his orthodoxy. The intervention of another of the Archbishop's adversaries, the Franciscan friar and a rival royal confidant Bernardo de Fresneda, was also crucial to the outcome of events. He first denounced the Dominican to the Inquisition over a year before his arrest on account of his association with Cardinal Pole, the papal legate at the court of Mary Tudor.[18] He was also accused of being a former Erasmian and of having influenced the beliefs of the Valladolid heretics Carlos de Sesso and Pedro de Cazalla. In a sermon preached shortly after entering his new archdiocese in December 1558, Carranza spoke of the spiritual malaise that existed within society. 'People call prayer, church-going, communion and confession *alumbrado*. They will soon call them Lutheran', he remarked.[19] He could not have made a more prophetic statement about his own future.

The Archbishop's protracted trial, which began in 1561 in Valladolid and ended in 1576 in Rome, also opened up the jurisdictional dispute between the crown and the papacy over who controlled the Spanish Church. Philip claimed supreme authority over the right to try bishops. Rome contested and reserved its right in episcopal cases. In 1565, a delegation of cardinals arrived in Madrid to negotiate. Their mission failed but the report of one of their members spoke for many in Spain who were forced to keep silent. Rome was informed that 'Nobody dares to speak in favour of Carranza for fear of the Inquisition. ... The most ardent defenders of justice here consider that it is better for an innocent man to be condemned than for the Inquisition to suffer disgrace'.[20] To criticise the Inquisition was to jeopardise the whole reputation of the Catholic monarchy. While the efforts of Pope Pius IV to expedite the trial proved fruitless, the hardline tactics employed by his more combative successor, Pius V (including a threat to excommunicate the Spanish sovereign), forced Philip to yield. Finance eventually became the ultimate arbiter. The king, who managed to appropriate the substantial revenues of the Toledan archbishopric during Carranza's imprisonment (amounting to between 150 000 and 200 000 ducats per year), desperately needed papal approval for a renewal of the *cruzada* tax.[21] In order to obtain it he had to concede the prisoner's removal from Valladolid to Rome. By the time Carranza left Spain in December 1566, Valdés, who had gradually fallen from favour at court since the Protestant discoveries, had been forced under pressure from Rome to resign from the Holy Office.

In 1567 the trial began again, all the evidence being re-examined by papal judges. Pius V was known to favour acquitting Carranza of the charges brought against him but died on 1 May 1572, shortly after denouncing 'the theologians of Spain [who] want to make him a heretic although he is not one!'[22] A final 'compromise' judgment on the case was issued by Gregory XIII on 14 April 1576. Carranza was accused of being 'gravely suspect of heresy' (*vehementemente sospechoso de herejía*) and was ordered to abjure 16 suspect propositions from his writings. He was forbidden from returning to his post as Archbishop for five years. However, Carranza's freedom was to be short-lived: he died in Rome on 2 May, less than one month after his release. None of the protagonists in this drama could claim outright victory or defeat. The verdict, which avoided a direct charge of heresy, may have saved the Spanish crown from considerable embarrassment, but its jurisdiction over the Church had been compromised by being forced to concede to papal supremacy. The Inquisition had effectively exceeded its powers and emerged severely discredited from the episode. Although it was still capable of striking with vengeance in the name of orthodoxy, the case marks something of a watershed in its history. There would be no more Carranzas.

Conclusion: Biblical Scholarship Under Scrutiny

It was no coincidence that the conciliatory ending of the Archbishop's trial also saw the case against the biblical scholar Fray Luis de León brought to a similar conclusion. The Augustinian friar, elected at the age of 34 to the Thomas Aquinas chair in theology at Salamanca, was frequently involved in scholastic debates with fellow professors over the authority of the Scriptures. The liberal thinking of this youthful professor made him an obvious target for attack. His opponents, who included rival Dominican colleagues, were exponents of the traditional school of biblical scholarship (based on the philosophy of Aristotle and Thomas Aquinas), which had recently been endorsed by the Council of Trent. The campaign against Fray Luis was mounted late in 1571 by two of his fiercest enemies at Salamanca, a fellow professor, León de Castro, and the Dominican Bartolomé de Medina. He was denounced to the Inquisition the following year for preferring the original Hebrew version of the Bible to the Latin Vulgate one, translated by Saint Jerome in the fifth century. 'To emend the Vulgate by the Hebrew and Greek is exactly what the heretics seek to do', so it was claimed during the friar's ensuing trial.[23] Fray Luis's *converso* background – a trait which, as we have seen, was common to many of the great religious reformers of the period – made him all the more vulnerable to accusations of harbouring Jewish sympathies. Furthermore, his unconventional translation into the vernacular of the Song of Solomon (1561) was seen to confirm suspicions about his orthodoxy. Aware of the attacks being made on him (as well as other fellow scholars), but confidant of his own innocence, Fray Luis submitted his works to the Inquisition for examination and in his subsequent trial defended himself on all charges. However, the vigour of the friar's defence encouraged further accusations to be made against him. Hopes of a speedy release soon faded. Although it soon became clear that there were no grounds for prosecution, endless discussions between censors (*calificadores*) over the subtleties of theological interpretation caused the trial to drag on for over four and a half years. A judgment needed to be made against the friar, however flimsy, to vindicate his enemies. The Jesuit Juan de Mariana expressed his disquiet at events. 'What a miserable state is that of the virtuous man! As a reward for his achievements he has to endure the hatred and accusations of the very people who should be his defenders', he lamented.[24] Fray Luis's downfall came about as a direct result of his intellectual prowess which was too powerful for the contemporary climate. On his release in December 1576, eight months after Carranza's conditional acquittal, he was reprimanded and required to retract several offensive propositions made in a lecture on the Vulgate. Fray Luis was warmly received on his return to the university in January 1577 and quickly resumed his academic career. Within two years he had risen to the post of regular professor of Scripture. When a further attempt was made to condemn him for his interpretation of the Scriptures in 1582, the Inquisitor General himself, Gaspar de Quiroga, intervened to overturn the prosecution.

As Fray Luis awaited the verdict of his trial, León de Castro turned his attention to defaming another Hebraist scholar, Benito Arias Montano.[25] Montano, a participant at the third session of Trent, had been sent by Philip II to Antwerp in 1568 to collaborate with French and Dutch scholars in the production of a new edition of the Polyglot Bible at the Plantin press. Three years later, half a century after the *Biblia Complutense* had revolutionised the reading of the Scriptures, the new Polyglot Bible was in print in the Netherlands and soon received papal approval. Meanwhile in Spain, León de Castro, who had prompted the arrest of Fray Luis, was preparing to denounce Montano to the Inquisition for producing a work of doubtful orthodoxy on account of its loose interpretation of the Vulgate alongside the Hebrew text. Fearing his own arrest, Montano travelled to Rome in 1575 to plead for support from a Congregation of cardinals. While approving of the new Polyglot, they refused to concede any challenge to the authority of the Latin Vulgate Bible. Montano was 'retired' to the post of curator of the royal library at the Escorial, where, ironically, his duties included the classification and expurgation of suspect texts! But the case was not yet over. In 1577, on behalf of the Inquisition, Mariana issued a favourable verdict on the new Polyglot and it was allowed to circulate freely in Spain. Shortly after Fray Luis was let off with a reprimand, the charge against Montano was also dropped.

These cases reveal much about the change of climate at the Holy Office under Inquisitor General Quiroga (1573–94), as well as the relationship between the innovative and the traditional branches of Spanish spiritual and intellectual life. Although those who shaped the renewal of Catholicism in early sixteenth-century Spain had effectively been silenced by the end of the 1570s under the repressive arm of the Inquisition and in response to the rigid intellectual climate of the Counter-Reformation, the conservative, authoritarian tendency within the Spanish Church was not able to perpetually justify its censorship of the tolerant, progressive forces that remained prominent within it. Spanish Catholicism in the early modern period, far from being a monolithic force, was capable of embracing a variety of perspectives that drew upon its diverse roots and the range of dialectic that lay within it.

3 The Reform of the Ecclesiastical Estate

Introduction

The Spanish Church, along with other western churches, came in for considerable criticism in the course of its transition from late medieval to early modern times – a period of heightened religious tensions in society. According to the official reports of church councils and synods, as well as popular anti-clerical literature of the time, it was a Church riddled with secularism, absenteeism, ignorance, and low levels of morality and discipline.[1] In response to these criticisms – both real and exaggerated in nature – an ambitious programme of ecclesiastical reform was laid down in Spain towards the end of the fifteenth century, a quarter of a century before the rise of Lutheranism in Germany and half a century before the Catholic Church launched its official response to the Protestant and Radical Reformations. It was a crucial moment for such initiatives: the Church had taken on a leading role in the recovery of southern Spain for Christianity, and Catholicism was being heralded as the defining feature of national identity, adding a particular intensity of fervour to the religious enterprises of the crown. By endorsing such a programme, Ferdinand and Isabella were at the same time able to skilfully extend their authority over the Spanish Church, whose enormous wealth and power lay beyond their direct control. However, the drive for reform was not always matched by the will or the commitment to implement it, either in the short or the long term. As the Catholic monarchs and their successors were to discover, outward enthusiasm for change was often inhibited by an underlying resistance to eradicating centuries-old traditions, structures and interests. This chapter will look specifically at pre- and post-Tridentine attempts to reform the Spanish ecclesiastical estate and will assess their outcome.

The Condition of the Clerical Estate and Early Reform Initiatives

Two important assemblies of clergy were convened in Castile as Ferdinand and Isabella prepared to officially assume royal authority throughout the kingdom: a Toledan Provincial Council was held at Aranda in 1473 (the first since 1429) and a Congregation of Castilian clergy gathered at Seville in 1478.[2] These assemblies put forward a number of reforming measures designed to raise standards of recruitment to clerical office and eradicate the ill-discipline that lay within the ecclesiastical estate. Latin became an obligatory requirement for those seeking a benefice at parochial or capitular level. At least ten clergy per cathedral or collegiate church were to have undergone a minimum of three years' training in theology, canon law or the liberal arts. Residence was required in all church offices, with or without care of souls, except for the minor office of prebendary. Ordained priests were to celebrate mass at least four times per year and bishops a minimum of three times. Concubinage was fiercely condemned and penalties were imposed on licentious clergy. Members of the clerical estate were barred from entering the service of their temporal overlords and from carrying arms. They were ordered to abstain from gambling and acts of usury and to dissociate themselves from the extravagance of secular church celebrations. Regular episcopal visitations would ensure that these targets were adhered to. These proposals, radical for their day, were endorsed by the Castilian Cortes, which met at Toledo in 1480.

In practice, however, Ferdinand and Isabella did little more than establish the foundations for long-term ecclesiastical reform. A number of major obstacles prevented them from fully achieving their objectives. Firstly, their programme was directed primarily at the lesser ranks of the clerical estate (priests, curates, chaplains, friars, and so on), whose appointment was largely controlled by lay patrons, and secondly, it was essentially a Castilian rather than an Aragonese initiative. Thirdly, the disparate geography of the Spanish kingdoms severely inhibited progress. Some clergy based in remote parts of the peninsula were literally beyond the physical reach of reform. Finally, the monarchs had no real authority over senior clergy through whom they could enforce their proposals. While bishops, heads of religious houses and cathedral clergy each followed different directives, a thorough reform of the Spanish Church would be long delayed.

The key to raising standards of leadership within the Spanish Church lay in securing control over appointments to major ecclesiastical benefices, including highly prized bishoprics, dependent on the see of Rome. During the opening years of their reign, Ferdinand and Isabella worked determinedly to this end. Papal intervention in nominations to Spanish benefices had increased during the dynastic disputes of the fourteenth and early fifteenth centuries, leading to foreign incumbents in office, widespread absenteeism and the misappropriation of ecclesiastical income by Rome. Nepotism and pluralism went unchecked. The Borja family, including Rodrigo Borja, the future Pope Alexander VI (1492–1503), held a monopoly over the see of Valencia between 1429 and 1511. Rafael Galeote Riario, nephew of Pope Sixtus IV, acted as administrator *in absentia* over a 40-year period for the dioceses of Osma (1483–93) and Cuenca (1479–82 and 1493–1518). The bishopric of Cádiz was held by a succession of absentee Italian cardinals between 1495 and 1525. Pamplona was similarly a seat of papal nepotism. Ferdinand and Isabella, with the approval of powerful cathedral chapters and the loyal delegation of Castilian clergy who attended the Sevillian Congregation of 1478, intervened successfully in the presentation of candidates to the sees of Cuenca (1482 and 1485) and Seville (1485), rejecting papal nominations. They called upon the 'ancient right of supplication' of Spanish kings in matters of ecclesiastical jurisdiction and presentation to benefices, held from the sixth to the twelfth centuries and endorsed in the *Siete Partidas* of Alfonso X, in order to further their claims. As the War of Reconquest came to an end and their own power base was consolidated, the opportunity arose for the Spanish monarchs to press formally for rights of patronage over their Church.

In December 1486, Pope Innocent VIII granted Ferdinand and Isabella the right to establish churches, control ecclesiastical appointments and levy taxes in the newly conquered kingdom of Granada and the Canary Islands. It was an historic agreement, extended to the New World in 1508, and gave the crown the opportunity to raise a new category of bishop to office, not just in Granada, but increasingly beyond its confines. The old warrior, aristocratic prelates such as Alfonso Carrillo of Toledo (1446–82) and Pedro González de

Mendoza of Seville (1474–82) were replaced by churchmen such as Hernando de Talavera of Granada (1493–1507), Pascual de Ampudia of Burgos (1496–1512) and Francisco Jiménez de Cisneros of Toledo (1495–1517). Drawn from the middle to lower nobility, these men further distinguished themselves by their contribution to government and learning, as well as church reform. Although it was to be almost a quarter of a century before the Spanish crown officially achieved its objective of being able to nominate to all Spanish bishoprics (conceded by Pope Adrian VI in 1523 in the bull *Eximiae devotionis affectus*), Ferdinand and Isabella had won a degree of control over preferment to and management of their Church that was unique in western Europe. The *Patronato* agreements, as they were known, constituted a major source of authority at the crown's disposal and its bishops were to become the key reforming agents of the Spanish Church as it launched its counter-attack on the Protestant Reformation.

The first half of the sixteenth century saw little progress being made in the field of ecclesiastical reform. Early sixteenth-century synods, may of which survive in print, reiterate the same concerns over low levels of clerical training and conduct as did late fifteenth-century ones, suggesting that the realisation of Isabelline initiatives often remained in practice a dead letter. There were a number of reasons for this. Charles V, absent from Spain for almost 24 of the 40 years of his kingship (1516–56), to a large extent allowed the Spanish Church to run its own course. The Emperor's concerns lay elsewhere: with his conflict with the Protestant princes in Germany, with the advance of the Turk in the Mediterranean and with the Habsburg–Valois wars in Italy. In Spain, the religious implications of the Reformation were handled by the Inquisition, which, as we have seen, took on the role of cleansing the Church of all alien ideological influences, while the raising of standards of discipline and the wider dissemination of Catholic doctrine were largely neglected. The rise of Protestantism therefore can be seen as diverting the Spanish Church from the urgent task of putting its own house in order. As negligible as the impact of the Reformation was on Spain, during the reign of Charles V *counter* reform was prioritised over *Catholic* reform. Furthermore, the prolonged political disputes between the Emperor and the papacy over their respective interests in Italy, together with their disagreement over the objectives of a General Church Council, hindered progress towards universal Church reform.

The Council of Trent and the Definition of Dogma and Discipline

A General Council of Catholic bishops and theologians met in December 1545 at Trent in northern Italy to address the religious crisis affecting Christendom. This was to be the first of three separate sessions of debate, lasting a total of seven years, spread over the period 1545–63. Over 200 Spanish bishops and theologians attended the Council where they made a vigorous contribution to debate and the drawing up of its decrees. Heralded as a counter-attack on Protestant heresies, the Council of Trent was unable to effect any reconciliation between Protestants and Catholics. Its overriding concern was to reinvigorate the Church of Rome by reaffirming its doctrinal beliefs, in contrast to those set out by the leaders of the Reformation, and by setting out a programme for institutional reform that would eradicate the corruption and lax discipline to be found within its professional body. By the time its second session met (1551–2), the unity of Christendom was all but lost. In 1555, the principle of freedom of worship (*cius regio eius religio*) was established in the Empire by the Peace of Augsburg. The influence of the Reformed Church was spreading rapidly throughout northern Europe. As delegates assembled for the crucial final session (1562–3), the rise of international Calvinism (a rival, militant current of the Lutheran Church) threatened to penetrate the heart of Catholic Europe. The redefinition of the theory and practice of Catholicism that emerged from the Council of Trent was designed to strengthen the Church from within and preserve it from further disintegration.[3]

Trent reinforced the traditional foundations of Catholic doctrine. The Latin Vulgate edition of the Bible was confirmed as the official version of Scripture. Bible study was acknowledged as a fundamental source of the word of God, but not the sole one, as asserted by the leaders of the Reformation. God's message was also transmitted via the preaching authority of the Catholic Church and through the observance of its apostolic traditions, including the sacraments. Faith alone was not sufficient for salvation, as claimed by Martin Luther. For a Catholic believer to avail himself of God's grace and favour, his demonstration of faith had to be accompanied by good works and the repentance of sin. Trent exalted the sacrifice of the mass and its powers of deliverance. It was to become the focal point of Catholic worship. While Protestants supported the notion of the priesthood of all believers, Trent confirmed the hierarchical structure of the

Catholic Church, with the authority of those entrusted to the ministry enhanced over the laity.

As well as addressing doctrinal matters, Trent also put forward a radical programme for ecclesiastical reform at all levels. The calibre of the episcopate and the authority invested in it were to be strengthened. Bishops were to reside in their benefices (except where official leave of absence had been granted). They were to effect reform via diocesan synods, following the lead set at provincial councils. They were to visit their dioceses regularly, preaching and guiding their flock. Furthermore, they were required to regulate admissions to holy orders and watch over religious communities. Attempts were also made to raise the standard of leadership within the middle ranks of the Church, where much hereditary and venal interest prevailed. Four professional canonries were to be created in each cathedral and collegiate church: a canon lector, a canon magister, a canon penitentiary and a canon theologian. All senior capitular officeholders and at least half of all canonries were to be conferred on those of graduate status. Priests were to be better instructed and disciplined. Seminaries were to be set up for their training. Absenteeism, pluralism and abuses of clerical conduct were to be checked. Priests were to preach every Sunday, provide for the Christian education of the laity and keep records of baptisms, marriages and deaths. Regular clergy were to train as novices before entering the profession. They were to adhere rigorously to the rule of their order, maintaining vows of obedience, poverty and chastity. Strict observant rule was to replace lax conventual rule.

The Council of Trent represented an historic moment in the evolution of the western Church. Where the Spanish Church was concerned, its proposals largely *reaffirmed* previously established objectives. The fundamental question was whether Philip II, with the support and enthusiasm of those who had taken part in the Council, would be able to succeed in taking forward the Tridentine recommendations where previous attempts at reform had barely made discernible progress.

The Application of Diocesan Reform

On 13 June 1564, Pius IV officially approved the work of the Council of Trent in the bull *Benedictus Deus*. One month later, on 12 July 1564, Philip II issued a royal patent (*cédula*) confirming his acceptance of the Tridentine decrees, but in practice, as we shall see, this acceptance was conditioned by terms he dictated as the *de facto* leader of the Spanish Church. In April 1565, instructions were issued by the Royal Council for the convening of provincial assemblies by archbishops throughout Spain to set the agenda for the adoption of reform at local church level via diocesan synods. Five months later, the Provincial Council of Toledo met in its first session. This was the first such council to be held in Spain (excepting Catalonia) for over 50 years and its proceedings were to set the pattern for those held in the metropolitan sees of Granada, Santiago de Compostela, Valencia, Zaragoza and Tarragona, all convened in the same year. The Toledan Council proved to be an important testing ground. Dissent was rife even before the council met. A large group of Castilian cathedral clergy from Burgos, León, Zamora, Oviedo, Osma, Segovia and Calahorra had met in secret at Valladolid in June to discuss their grievances, following which they made a direct appeal to the Pope to revoke certain Tridentine decrees that threatened to undermine their traditional independence from episcopal jurisdiction. 'If Spanish bishops are allowed to carry forward the Council's recommendations', they observed, 'there will be no honourable men left in Spain prepared to enter the clerical profession.'[4] Philip quickly intervened, ordering his senior clergy to abide by Trent and not to enter into private correspondence with His Holiness, with whom the king had recently broken off diplomatic relations following Carranza's enforced transfer to Roman custody. Don Francisco de Toledo, the future Viceroy of Peru, was appointed to monitor proceedings on the crown's behalf at this and subsequent assembles, and to submit all recommendations for royal approval before publication, thereby furthering the mistrust of Rome, already suspicious of the nature and purpose of Spanish reform. By the time the Toledan Council completed its agenda in March 1566, Philip had confirmed in law royal rights of patronage over the Spanish Church, granted by apostolic concession.[5] It was a clear statement of intent. Although he was genuinely committed to implementing Trent's edicts where they stood to elevate the institutional status of the Church, Philip wanted reform to develop under the aegis of his *patronazgo* rather than in response to papal decree. This gave rise to conflicts between his religious and political agendas, which ultimately inhibited the whole process of reform.

The constitutions of the six provincial councils convened in 1565 set out a comprehensive programme for reform at diocesan level to be carried forward by Spanish bishops. Trent had decreed that every bishop was to hold an annual diocesan synod. In practice this proved to be an over-ambitious proposal, particularly it seems for Castilian bishops who between them held an average 2.5 synods per year in the period 1545–1600, while in Aragón the comparable figure was 3.7, with the Catalan Church taking much of the initiative. Synods generally proved to be more often a forum for conflict rather than for cooperation over reform. On his return from the second session of Trent in 1554, Don Martín Pérez de Ayala, Bishop of Guadix (1548–60), immediately called a synod to restructure the whole pattern of ecclesiastical life in his diocese, heavily embedded with *morisco* influences.[6] But his ambitions went beyond the aspirations of both his clergy and his flock and he soon found himself in conflict with members of the chapter and the local church over his proposals for reform. The raising of standards of pastoral leadership and the assimilation of the *morisco* population into Christian culture were sacrificed to the preservation of vested interests. This was to be the first and last synod to be held in Guadix during the whole of its diocesan history. Ayala's reforming initiatives were likewise greeted with little enthusiasm by the privileged capitular clergy of his new diocese of Segovia, to which he transferred in 1560. His recall to the final session of Trent saved him from further immediate conflict. While the erudite theologian swayed the opinion of the council with his solid performances in debate, the application of Tridentine decrees at grass-roots level proved a much more difficult task. In June 1562, from the closing session of the assembly, he wrote in disillusion to Philip II informing him that 'loud voices are raised on the issue of reform but it is obvious that little will be achieved of lasting value'.[7] Both the high ideals of Trent and the harsh realities of delivering reform were embodied in the initiatives of Ayala. His experience was similar to that of Don Cristóbal de Rojas y Sandoval, also a delegate at the second session of Trent. As the most senior prelate in the archdiocese of Toledo, he presided over the Toledan Council of 1565–6 in the absence of Archbishop Carranza and energetically supervised its implementation in his own diocese of Córdoba, where he convened six diocesan synods during his nine-year term as bishop (1562–71). However, his initial enthusiasm soon waned in the face of increasing clerical hostility to his reforming endeavours. In correspondence with the king from Córdoba in September 1568, he wrote of 'seeing how divine matters so necessary for the preservation of the Catholic Church have fallen into relaxation and neglect'.[8] When the diocesan clergy of Cuenca met in synod in July 1566 they firmly demonstrated their unwillingness to cooperate with conciliar decisions. The parish clergy presented a list of grievances including an objection to the cost of annual synods, the rigours of the residence requirement, the obligation to pay for the upkeep of the poor and unfair competition in appointments to benefices. The cathedral clergy, who had already made a direct appeal to Rome, were ill-disposed towards measures designed to ensure the performance of their official canonical duties, as well as the erosion of their financial and jurisdictional independence from the ordinary.[9] Bishop Fresneda (1562–71) took a firm stand and managed to force his clergy to accept the constitutions in principle. In practice, however, the tensions persisted. The intervention of the crown, the mistrust of cathedral chapters, who still formed semi-autonomous power bases within many diocesan churches, and the generally poor commitment of clergy to reform all hindered Spanish bishops in the implementation of Tridentine objectives. The Toledan Provincial Council of 1582–3, convened by Archbishop Quiroga (1577–94), to a large extent reinforced the recommendations of the previous council of 1556–66. The Spanish Church had, in practical terms, moved on very little in the intervening period. The papacy continued to object to the presence of a royal legate at church councils and was sympathetic to appeals by cathedral chapters for the modification or revocation of synodal decrees. The friction with Rome, together with competing jurisdictions within the national Church, remained severe stumbling blocks in taking forward the recommendations of the Council of Trent in Spain. This was the last provincial council to be held in Toledo for over 350 years!

The Reform of the Episcopate

The raising of the professional and pastoral profile of the episcopate and the strengthening of its authority and jurisdiction at the apex of Church hierarchy was undoubtedly the cornerstone of Tridentine reform. In order to carry out its mission of renewing the faith of its members, the institutional Church had first to reform itself. There was common accord over the need to eradicate pluralism, nepotism and aristocratic privilege from preferment practice. Bishops were to be worthy, conscientious, morally sound and intellectually able men who would lead the whole ecclesiastical estate by their example. The fundamental requirement of all bishops was residence. Trent condemned those prelates whose 'sole occupation in life is wandering idly from court to court, or abandoning their flock and neglecting the care of their sheep in the flurry of worldly affairs'.[10] Nevertheless, leave of absence for short periods and certain exemptions from service – notably for those engaged in affairs of state – were permitted. Bishops were to preach regularly, carry out annual visitations of their dioceses, promoting works of charity, learning and discipline within them; they were to hold yearly diocesan synods and attend provincial councils every three years; they were to found seminaries for the training of priests and supervise ordinations to holy orders. In December 1563, as the final session of the Council came to a close, the Venetian bishop, Jerome Ragazzoni, summarised the expectations of Trent in the area of episcopal reform: 'Great ecclesiastical offices will in future be filled by those in whom virtue prevails over ambition . . . and bishops will remain in the midst of their flocks', he proclaimed.[11] The test lay in how far his optimistic words would translate into effective actions.

Before examining the principles and procedures that governed appointment to episcopal office in the post-Tridentine period, it is important to look first at its structure. The Castilian branch of the late sixteenth-century Spanish Church was divided into 5 archdioceses (Toledo, Seville, Santiago, Granada and Burgos) and 30 dioceses. The Aragonese branch was smaller: it held 3 archdioceses (Tarragona, Zaragoza and Valencia) and 17 dioceses (see Map 1). As a whole the Spanish Church, with its 55 territorial divisions, was relatively modest in size when compared with the 113 dioceses of neighbouring France or the 315 of the Italian states.[12] The diocesan structure of early modern Spain was distinctly irregular. Dioceses were concentrated in northern Castile and Aragón, where the roots of Christianity ran deepest, and were more widespread further south, where Moorish civilisation had survived the longest. Toledo, recaptured by Christian forces in 1085, was the largest archdiocese in Europe and the richest after Rome. Its archbishop, Primate of Spain, ruled over eight suffragan dioceses set within a vast geographical expanse, rich in agricultural production, which extended as far north as Valladolid in Old Castile, south to Córdoba in Andalusia and east to Cartagena on the Mediterranean coast. These were the territories, including major regional capitals and commercial ports, that had been granted to former Toledan archbishops for assisting the crown in pushing forward the Christian frontier in the eleventh and twelfth centuries.

Map 1 *Diocesan divisions of Castile and Aragón at the end of the sixteenth century*

Source: Map based on 'Geografía Eclesiástica' in *Diccionario de Historia Eclesiásica de España*, vol. 2 (Madrid, 1972), p. 1009.

By contrast, dioceses set within the remote, under-developed northern areas of the peninsula, untouched by the Moorish invaders, such as the newly erected sees of Elna (1573), Jaca (1571), Barbastro (1571) and Solsona (1593) in upper Aragón and those of Tuy, Mondoñedo and Orense in outer Asturias, bore more of a resemblance to large parishes. These imbalances in the diocesan map of Spain were to become more marked in the changing demographic and economic landscape of the seventeenth century. Apart from the readjustments made to diocesan boundaries by Philip II, so that they corresponded with national frontiers, resulting in a total of six new bishoprics being created in the crown of Aragón and 14 in the Spanish Netherlands, the territorial divisions of the Spanish Church remained unchanged, rooted in the historical foundation of Christianity in the peninsula more than ten centuries earlier and compounded by its fragmented geography.

By following the career patterns of Spanish bishops appointed by Philip II, it is possible to subdivide these dioceses into three groups according to promotional trends linked to financial return, as illustrated in Table 3.1.[13] There were 27 dioceses with annual incomes of up to 15 000 ducats, predominantly located in the peripheral, isolated regions of the peninsula, serving small, impoverished communities either close to mountains, on coasts or near frontiers, in much need of pastoral guidance. The majority of these low-income dioceses were granted as first appointments, often to men with regional links in the area, and tenure lasted some seven years. Dioceses with annual rents of between 15 000 and 30 000 ducats constituted the middle ranks of the episcopal hierarchy. Fifteen dioceses fell into this category, divided broadly into two types – those centred on major regional capitals (such as Granada, Tarragona, Salamanca, Ávila, Zamora and Segovia) and those serving peripheral areas (such as Pamplona, Cartagena, Badajoz, Calahorra and Tortosa). These middle-status bishoprics were often reserved as promotional positions, either for bishops from lower-status sees or as rewards for experienced royal administrators. Finally, there were 13 dioceses with annual incomes of between 30 000 and 200 000 ducats, which stood at the apex of the episcopal career ladder. Appointment to one of these dioceses represented the culmination of a long ecclesiastical career, frequently combined with service for the crown.

In the case of Spain, the reform of the episcopate took its initiative first and foremost from its patron, the crown. The crown's right of nomination to Spanish bishoprics, conferred by the papacy in 1523,

Table 3.1 The scale of Spanish bishoprics according to annual income (in ducats), *c.*1570 (archbishoprics indicated in bold, post-1570 dates of erection in parentheses)

High-status dioceses (13) – income of over 30 000 ducats	
Toledo	**220 000**
Seville	**88 000**
Zaragoza	**55 000**
Cuenca	50 600
Valencia	**49 500**
Córdoba	47 700
Santiago	**44 000**
Sigüenza	44 000
Plasencia	43 800
Burgos	**40 500** (1574)
Jaén	35 500
Málaga	33 000
Palencia	31 000
Middle-status dioceses (15) – income between 15 000 and 30 000 ducats	
(a) *Central* (serving major regional centres)	
Coria	26 400
Salamanca	26 400
Granada	**26 400** (1483)
Zamora	22 000
Tarragona	**17 600**
Ávila	17 500
(b) *Peripheral* (serving outlying areas)	
Segovia	26 400
Osma	24 200
Cartagena	17 600
Badajoz	17 600
Calahorra	17 600
Tarazona	17 600
Tortosa	16 500
Pamplona	16 000
León	15 400
Low-status dioceses (27) – income below 15 000 ducats	
(a) *Mountainous areas*	
Astorga	12 500
Mondoñedo	12 000
Oviedo	9 500
Orense	8 800
Lugo	8 800
Guadix	7 700

Teruel	13 200 (1577)
Huesca	13 200
Lérida	11 000
Segorbe	11 000
Urgel	7 700
Albarracín	5 500
Barbastro	4 400 (1571)
Solsona	4 400 (1593)
Jaca	3 300 (1571)
Elna	2 200 (1573)
(b) *Coastal and frontier*	
Canaries	13 200
Cádiz	13 200
Ciudad Rodrigo	11 000
Tuy	9 300
Almería	3 200
Gerona	13 200
Mallorca	13 200
Orihuela	11 000 (1564)
Vich	5 500
Barcelona	5 500
Additional low-status see	
Valladolid	12 200 (1595)

Source: See note 13 on page 165.

ensured that there remained a close professional alliance between the Church and the state. Not only were Spanish bishops to be dependent on their monarch for patronage and promotion, moreover, they were to be subservient to the different fiscal and political pressures imposed upon them by the crown. The preferment policy that Philip II had laid down at the very commencement of his reign, in response to the heightened religious tensions in Europe, preempted the resolutions of the fathers at Trent. His episcopate would stand as a supreme example of the revived force of Catholicism in the west. A new generation of career professionals began to accede to office during the 1550s and 1560s. By studying the backgrounds and career patterns of those 115 men who rose to bishoprics in the kingdom of Castile in the second half of the sixteenth century, coinciding with the reign of Philip II (1556–98), it is possible to construct a profile of a majority section of the episcopate in post-Tridentine Spain and measure this against some of the aspirations of Trent.

The period in question saw a significant change in the social circle from which Spanish bishops were drawn. Notwithstanding the appearance of illustrious family names among lists of appointees to major bishoprics in sixteenth-century Spain (such as members of the royal house of Austria and the aristocratic houses of Fonseca, Mendoza, Zúñiga, Guzmán, Valdés, Guevara, Moscoso, Sandoval and Borja), they were increasingly to become exceptions to the rule, thereby counteracting criticisms that bishops were born rather than made. Overturning the preference of his father to appoint members of the titled aristocracy, and reviving the trend established under Ferdinand and Isabella, Philip chose to elevate second or third sons of lower to middle noble family origins as bishops. Some 70 per cent of his appointments went to such men, who regarded senior ecclesiastical office as a profession as opposed to a sinecure, a factor that made for greater loyalty and dedication to service, hence the appeal of middle men to the crown. Social background apart, the other essential prerequisite for successful career progression within the upper echelons of the Spanish Church, beyond that of being an ordained priest of legitimate Old Christian birth, was to have an appropriate academic record. Those men educated to degree level in theology, philosophy or canon law at one of the elite university colleges (*colegios mayores*) of Salamanca, Alcalá or Valladolid – the academies of the professional classes in early modern Spain – stood the best chance of promotion. Almost half of Philip II's Castilian episcopate obtained their degrees from these privileged institutions, which served the educational needs of the secular and ecclesiastical elite alike. Bishops were now men of letters, enhancing their role as teachers and guardians of their flock (see Table 3.2). The king made efforts to match bishops' training with regional and diocesan requirements. Theology graduates tended to be preferred over those with a legal training in the competition for office under Philip II on account of their doctrinal knowledge, so necessary for the furtherance of the Church's teaching mission, especially in remote areas of the kingdom such as Galicia, Cantabria and the Canaries.[14] Bishops with a legal background were destined for border areas – Extremadura and Andalusia – where litigious disputes often arose. In the practice of preferment former church servants (including delegates at the Council of Trent and members of cathedral chapters) tended to be favoured over those who had previously served in secular office, although there were exceptions to this rule. For example, long-serving inquisitors were key potential candidates, taking 27 per cent of posts, whereas

Table 3.2 Backgrounds of Castilian bishops appointed under Philip II

		% of total no. appointed
Family origins		
Titled nobility	22	19.1
Middle nobility	81	70.4
Educational background		
University graduates	77	66.9
Colegio mayor graduates	54	47
Degree discipline		
Theology	67	58
Law	30	26
Background of service*		
Church	84	73
State	34	30
Total bishops appointed	115	

* Some bishops had joint careers.
Source: See note 16 on page 165.

members of religious orders only gained 13 per cent of appointments. Furthermore, as we shall see, a considerable number of bishops combined church and state service. The balance between law and theology graduates in Castilian bishoprics narrowed in the following century, as a legal training became a more universal route to a career in the royal service, whether secular or ecclesiastical in nature. Philip sought to avoid generating excessive promotional opportunities that merely satisfied careerist ambitions, supporting the principle that dioceses were to be rewarded with bishops and not bishops with dioceses. Although less than 30 per cent of his Castilian episcopate earned promotion to a second or third see, this still made for a relatively high level of mobility and potential lack of stability in office. In contemporary France (1589–1661), by comparison, it was rare for a bishop to be promoted beyond his first see.[15] By the middle years of the reign, the distinct qualities sought in a prospective bishop had been formally laid down. In 1578, it was established by royal decree that would-be prelates 'should be graduates of theology or canon law from approved universities, of sound judgement, exemplary lifestyle, modest disposition, charitable conduct, worthy reputation, pure-blooded and legitimate birth ... for upon them rests the correction ... of the Christian world'.[16] The *Cámara de Castilla* (a branch of the Royal Council with specific responsibility for patronage) set up a systematic procedure for selecting future bishops and promoting serving ones that closely followed these criteria and was rigorously supervised by the crown. A new professionalised episcopate emerged in Castile to meet the challenges of Trent and the exigencies of royal policy, exigencies that were ultimately to lead to an undermining of its profile.

The Tridentine decree on residence was strongly supported by Spanish delegates who considered it to be a fundamental obligation of all priests and bishops. This view was expounded in a number of early sixteenth-century treatises on episcopal office, including those of Juan Bernal Díaz de Luco (1530), Bartolomé Carranza (1547), Domingo de Soto (1554) and Luis de Granada (1565).[17] However, there is ample evidence to suggest that the principle was not adhered to in practice. For example, when the see of Sigüenza fell vacant in 1579, Philip was reminded that for close on a century there had been no long-term resident prelate in the diocese! Burgos found itself in a similar position. Much absenteeism was in fact prompted by the crown itself. It frequently suited the monarch to appoint senior prelates to key posts in the secular administration, which inevitably led to the neglect of their pastoral obligations. Out of a total of seven presidents of the Council of Castile who served between 1556 and 1598, three concurrently held episcopal office, while five of the six Inquisitors General appointed by Philip II were non-resident bishops. The more conscientious prelates felt that their professional loyalties were being stretched in such circumstances. Cristóbal Fernández de Valtodano refused to accept the presidency of the legal tribunal (*Chancillería*) of Valladolid in 1564 precisely because he considered it incompatible with his office as Bishop of Palencia (1561–70).[18] Diego de Covarrubias, as Bishop of Segovia (1564–77), hesitated to accept the presidency of the Council of Castile when it was offered to him in 1572. He applied for papal dispensation from residence to allow him to undertake state service at senior level and it was granted.[19] The archbishopric of Toledo – the highest ecclesiastical office in the Spanish Church – was almost exclusively held by an absentee servant of the crown in the early modern period. The career of Gaspar de Quiroga as Archbishop of Toledo (1577–94) and Inquisitor General (1573–94) provides a fitting example.[20] When Quiroga was appointed to Toledo in 1577 – the same year in which he refused the presidency of Castile on the grounds of being overburdened – the Spanish Church was much in need of strong leadership following the Carranza affair. For close on 20 years there had effectively been no primate. During that period, much of the early initiative of Trent had been lost. While Quiroga made considerable efforts to further the cause of reform in his archdiocese (including his convening of a provincial council in 1582, his support of the work of the Jesuits, his patronage of the artist El Greco, as well as his endorsement of a new Manual of Sacraments in 1581), his residence at court meant that his day-to-day duties as archbishop were principally carried out by a suffragan bishop or vicar general. Although considerable advances were made in raising the calibre of those appointed to episcopal office in the post-Tridentine period, the diversion by the crown of the professional expertise of bishops to service the needs of the state led to the neglect of their primary role and to the reduction of their authority within their dioceses at a crucial juncture, overturning some of the key objectives of Trent. Diego de Colmenares, the early seventeenth-century chronicler of Segovia, was all too familiar with the outcomes: 'The greatest calamities which have befallen our community', he wrote, 'have occurred when its bishops were not around or had died.'[21]

The Reform of the Priesthood

Priests with care of souls made up just under half of the secular division of the Castilian clerical estate. The parish priest (known as the *cura* or *beneficio curado*) held the leading pastoral role in the rural community. He governed the parish, supervised the lesser clergy, was responsible for the religious instruction of his flock, as well as providing for their basic spiritual needs via the celebration of mass and the administration of the sacraments. He had the power to fine those who did not attend mass and excommunicate those who did not pay their ecclesiastical dues. The parish priest was thus, in theory, a figure of some authority in the immediate community. He was often, but not exclusively, of local origin.

Priests were recognised as key agents in directing the work of the Counter-Reformation at parochial level. The Council of Trent sought to raise the professional profile of parish clergy by insisting on the selection of appropriately trained and disciplined priests who would reside in their benefices and bring God to the laity via prayer,

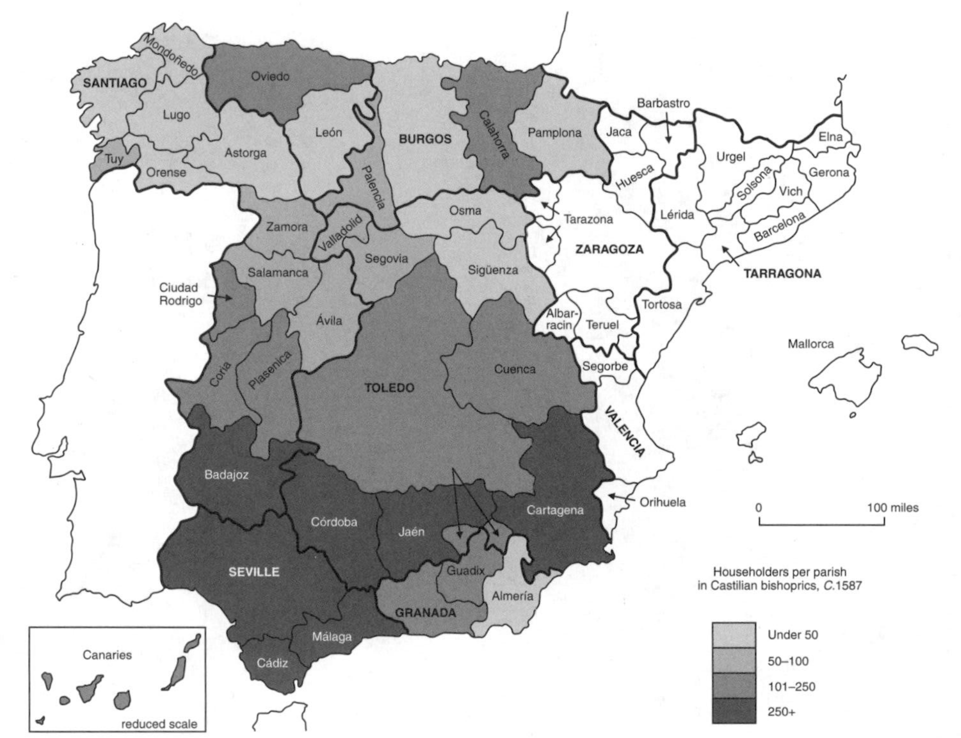

Map 2 *Householders per parish in Castilian bishoprics,* c.*1587*
Source: Tomás González, *Censo de la población* (Madrid, 1829).

preaching and the delivery of the sacraments. Following Trent, only a cleric ordained in major orders who had undertaken a minimum of two years of undergraduate study and had an independent income of between 40 and 50 ducats could become the holder of a parish living. The application of Tridentine recommendations in respect of the reform of the priesthood was in practice subject to numerous restraints.

The parish was the local unit of church organisation, the central place of worship in each village or community. There were some 20 000 parishes in late sixteenth-century Spain, 15 344 of which were concentrated in Castile. In common with the kingdom's diocesan divisions, Castilian parishes were of uneven size, wealth and distribution.[22] The average parish served 83 families or 415 inhabitants (see Table 3.3). Nearly three-quarters of all Castilian parishes were located in the northern expanse of the kingdom, the bedrock of Spain's centuries-old Christian tradition. The dioceses of Santiago, Astorga, Oviedo, León, Lugo, Calahorra and Burgos, where just over a quarter of the Castilian population lived at the end of the sixteenth century, held half the kingdom's parishes. The high density of parishes in northern Castile was clearly inconsistent with prevailing demographic trends. Many of the tiny rural parishes in the north (measuring between 7 and 35 sq km in size) were becoming semi-populated in the second half of the sixteenth century as their inhabitants moved southwards in search of better livelihoods. Such was their poverty that they did not attract resident priests, let alone well-educated ones. By contrast, in the southern half of the kingdom, where the closing stages of the Reconquest had been fought out and substantial divisions of land conceded to the Church and aristocracy, parochial units were much larger and therefore the pastoral responsibilities attached to them far greater. There were 234 parishes within the archbishopric of Seville serving a population of just over 123 000 households (an average of 1 per 525 families) – a ratio over ten times greater than that to be found in the majority of northern sees such as Burgos and Santiago. The most heavily worked priests were those based in the southernmost diocese of Cádiz. Here there were 14 parishes for a population of nearly 12 000 households (an average of 1 per 864). The large size of parishes in the south (covering over 75 sq km) was such that priests had little real contact with their parishioners. The unevenness of the Castilian parochial infrastructure, which by the end of the sixteenth century was seriously at odds with changing patterns of lay habitation, meant that for the

Table 3.3 Householders per parish in Castilian bishoprics, 1587

Bishopric	*(a) Households*	*(b) Parishes*	*Average (a per b)*
Santiago	33 535	1 008	33.2
Astorga	40 622	913	44.4
Ávila	41 425	460	90
Badajoz	24 014	53	453
Ciudad Rodrigo	12 805	55	232.8
Coria	26 523	117	226.6
Lugo	20 400	1 020	20
Mondoñedo	15 971	371	43
Orense	28 412	663	42.8
Plasencia	28 376	142	199.8
Salamanca	33 201	606	54.7
Tuy	13 834	240	57.6
Zamora	23 284	273	85.2
Burgos	66 722	1 708	39
Calahorra	70 000	1 000	70
Pamplona	41 901	852	49.1
Palencia	43 316	439	98.6
Toledo	167 051	817	204.4
Cartagena	20 117	47	428
Córdoba	49 171	93	528.7
Cuenca	58 190	341	170.6
Jaén	34 281	98	349.8
Osma	21 518	455	47.2
Segovia	24 598	443	55.5
Sigüenza	24 351	516	47.1
Valladolid	7 691	23	334.3
Seville	123 014	234	525.7
Cádiz	11 850	14	846.4
Canaries	7 741	45	172
Málaga	19 090	70	272.7
Granada	20 077	187	107.3
Almería	3 476	47	73.9
Guadix	5 747	37	155.3
Exempt sees			
León	33 544	981	34.1
Oviedo	80 000	976	81.9
Totals	1 275 848	15 344	83.1

Source: Adapted from Tomás González, *Censo de la Población* (Madrid, 1829), pp. 391, 394–5.

majority of the kingdom's population the Church, at least in its pastoral capacity, exercised minimal influence over their daily lives. During the last quarter of the sixteenth century, poor returns from the land and the depopulation of the countryside forced many parish priests to abandon their flocks in the rural environment and seek a more lucrative living in a neighbouring town. The uneven geographical distribution of neighbourhood pastors was to provide a serious handicap to raising the standard of religious instruction in early modern Spain. Complaints about lay superstition and ignorance were most common in those areas where resident priests were lacking – the hostile mountains of Galicia, the rugged Basque lands, the remote Canary Islands and the Alpujarras region outside Granada.

Although the nomination of priests was the official responsibility of the local bishop, considerable powers of ecclesiastical patronage were held by cathedral chapters and the military orders, as well as lay bodies (including town councils) and senior members of the aristocracy. In the northern outreaches of the peninsula (Galicia, Asturias and the Basque lands), the Benedictine monasteries together with the local nobility effectively controlled the appointment of parish clergy, as well as the collection of the tithe (frequently misappropriated for secular ends). They nominated their own monks, noble sons or poorly paid vicars to parishes, some of whom had little or no vocation and a very poor grasp of Catholic doctrine. Such pockets of independence clearly inhibited official attempts to improve standards of priestly conduct.

The raising of standards of clerical education lay at the heart of reforming measures. Philip supported the recommendation that seminaries be set up for the training of priests and sought to validate the initiative via the Cortes of Castile. Although the need for seminaries was readily accepted in principle to make good the serious deficiency in training programmes for the priesthood, it proved much more difficult to put into practical effect. Cathedral chapters were reluctant to provide the necessary funding for their establishment, while the traditional universities – the majority concentrated in the Crown of Castile – feared a loss of their status and potential to attract students. The realisation of the proposal was therefore ultimately left to rest on the charity and goodwill of bishops. Some 20 seminaries were established in the period 1564–1600 (14 in Castilian and 6 in Aragonese dioceses). One of the most successful was that set up in Tarragona in 1568 by Cardinal Gaspar Cervantes de Gaeta, which later achieved university status. Among those prelates failing to carry

Table 3.4 Post-Tridentine Spanish seminaries

Established 1564–1600	*Established 1601–1700*
Granada (1564–5)	Coria (1603)
Burgos (1565)	León (1606)
Mondoñedo (1565–73)	Almería (1610)
Tarragona (1568–73)	Vich (1635)
Huesca (1580)	Jaén (1660)
Córdoba (1583)	Badajoz (1664)
Cuenca (1584)	Plasencia (1670)
Palencia (1584)	Sigüenza (1670)
Valladolid (1588–98)	
Cádiz (1589)	
Gerona (1589)	
Ávila (1591–4)	
Murcia (1592)	
Urgel (1592)	
Barcelona (1593)	
Tarazona (1593)	
Lugo (1593–9)	
Osma (1594–1601)	
Guadix (1595)	
Málaga (1597)	

Source: *DHEE*, vol. 4, pp. 2422–9.

out their obligation on an appeal of penury was the Spanish Primate himself, Gaspar de Quiroga. Enthusiasm and financial support waned dramatically in the following century, which saw only eight new seminaries being erected, while some of those previously opened were forced to close down due to lack of support. Table 3.4 illustrates these anomalies. In post-Tridentine Spain the clerical elite continued to be drawn from those university colleges that specialised in law and theology, leading to the demise of the seminary, which tended to be regarded as a second-rate educational institution.

As a result of these circumstances, there remained profound regional variations in the standard of pastoral leadership to be found in post-Tridentine Spain. According to the findings of a recent study, reform never touched the priesthood of Cantabria, the majority of whom regarded their office as a means of material gain.[23] In 1580, half the clergy of Oviedo were still not versed in Latin or able to administer the sacraments, earning Asturias its reputation as the 'veritable Indies' of Spain.[24] Illiterate priests could still be found in rural Catalonia at the end of the seventeenth century. Friars were employed as preachers and confessors in certain areas to make up for the deficiencies of priests. It was in central Castile, in dioceses close to major centres of learning, that standards of recruitment to the priesthood improved dramatically in the years following Trent, even exceeding official requirements. In Cuenca, 87 per cent of priests who served in the post-Tridentine period (after 1565) were educated to degree level, as compared with 53 per cent who served in the pre-Tridentine period (before 1565). The graduate status of assistant priests rose from 16 to 31 per cent over this same period. Residence improved as livings were offered to local men.[25] A survey of the educational backgrounds of a sample of 90 priests serving in the Toledan archdiocese between 1590 and 1660 reveals a similar upward trend in the calibre of appointees to office: while 15 per cent had doctoral degrees, 53 per cent had graduated at licentiate level (equivalent to an honours degree) in either canon law or theology.[26] These snapshots of educational improvement do not conceal the fact that the calibre of the post-Tridentine priesthood was uneven. The full application of reform at parochial level was hindered by the irregular distribution of parishes within the geographical map of Spain, the restraints of the patronage system and the deficient provision of clerical training.

The Reform of the Religious Orders

Although some advances had been made in reforming the male mendicant orders under Ferdinand and Isabella, giving rise to the establishment of Observant Franciscan, Augustinian and Dominican congregations, progress was patchy, especially outside Castile, and made little or no headway under Charles V. Philip II had already devised his own ambitious proposals for the reform of the religious orders before the Council of Trent delivered its general programme for their reform in 1563. The king's initiatives, which fell in line with his perception of reform as a means to extend his powers of patronage over the Church, aimed broadly at rooting out abuse and ill-discipline within the Spanish orders and reducing their dependency on foreign superiors. His proposals included the transfer of all relaxed conventual foundations to strict observant control under the supervision of episcopal commissaries, appointed by the crown.

A *Junta de Reforma* was set up in Madrid to supervise the whole exercise – a small committee of men, drawn from the king's advisory circle, including the royal confessor and the Inquisitor General. After some initial vacillation, Rome eventually ceded to Philip's plans to assume personal control over monastic reform in a series of briefs issued by Pius V between 1566 and 1567. But the task proved much more complex than the crown had envisaged: the proposed restructuring of certain religious communities via the absorption of smaller into larger congregations (affecting the Third Order of Franciscans and the Premonstratensians) provoked appeals to Rome; female religious orders refused to accept strict enclosure; the original rule of some foundations, to which there was a general requirement to conform, was found to be far removed from the spirit of Trent, as was the case with the Benedictines. By the 1580s, Philip was forced to adapt his reform programme to the needs and conditions of particular congregations and accept a certain degree of papal intervention in monastic affairs. Some orders emerged strengthened from this process, the Carmelites, Trinitarians and Mercedarians (all founded as observant congregations following Trent) amongst them. The new and reformed orders (including the Society of Jesus, founded in 1540) took responsibility for revitalising educational, charitable, devotional and missionary activities, strengthening the Christian values of society through prayer, learning and example, in accordance with Tridentine objectives. The late sixteenth and early seventeenth centuries witnessed a dramatic growth in the size of these foundations – claimed to be excessive by some observers – as they became established within the pious framework of Spanish society (see Table 3.5). The effects on Spanish religious and cultural life of the renewed authority and vocation invested in the reformed orders were to be far-reaching. But, as with the secular clergy, the process was uneven: pockets of independence and intransigence persisted, even within those orders deemed to be fully 'reformed'. Ignorance, disorder and neglect continued to characterise observant religious communities of rural Catalonia, for example, towards the middle of the seventeenth century.[27] To be successful, reform had to combine spiritual renewal from within the congregation with an acceptance of the need for institutional adjustment and change, a process that could not be enforced under duress by the crown.[28]

Although the Discalced Carmelites undoubtedly left a deep imprint on the spiritual development of post-Tridentine Spain, the movement encountered considerable difficulties in the realisation of

Table 3.5 The growth in membership of male religious orders, 1591–1623

Examples of male orders	*1591 census for Castile*	*1623 estimate for Spain*
Franciscans	6 708	14 000
Dominicans	2 447	6 281
Augustinians	923	3 300
Carmelites (Calced)	747	2 710
Carmelites (Discalced)	187	1 730
Trinitarians	652	2 500
Mercedarians	*c*.400*	3 562
Jesuits	1 091	2 203
Totals	13 155	36 285

Sources: 1591: Felipe Ruiz Martín, 'Demografía Eclesiástica', in *Diccionario de Historia Eclesiástica de España*, vol. 2 (Madrid, 1972), pp. 718–19; 1623: Gil González Dávila, *Teatro de las Grandezas* (repr. Madrid, 1986), pp. 234–99. *1591 figure for Mercedarians has been taken from Bruce Taylor, *Structures of Reform: The Mercedarian Order in the Spanish Golden Age* (Leiden, 2000), Appendix III, p. 441.

its goals. The years of success of Carmelite reform (1562–76) were followed by years of conflict (1576–80) between its Calced and Discalced branches, exacerbated by jurisdictional tensions between the papacy and the crown over who had ultimate authority over the order. These tensions came to a head in 1578 when the papal nuncio, Felipe Sega, removed the apostolic visitor to the Carmelite community of Andalusia, Jerónimo Gracián, from his office, leading to a temporary cessation of the reform movement.[29] Gracián, a representative of the crown, was accused of exceeding his powers in the southern kingdom, where sensitivities among Calced friars ran high. In the same year, Juan de Yepes, the future Saint John of the Cross and founder of the male branch of the reform movement, was kidnapped and imprisoned by members of its unreformed branch. Following protests to Rome, Calced Carmelite rule was reinstated and its separation from Discalced authority was approved by Pope Gregory XIII in June 1580. Internal divisions within the reformed order continued after Teresa de Ávila's death in 1582 between those who wished to further its missionary role and those who sought to preserve its austere, contemplative character. The Carmelite reform movement encapsulated both the pious spirit and the reforming zeal of Trent, as well as the struggle the orders as a whole had in accommodating themselves to change.

Mercedarian reform was also hindered on a number of fronts,[30] firstly, by the conflict of interest and authority that existed between its two branches, one based in Castile and the other in the Crown of Aragón, linked to their respective outlooks on reform. While the Castilian province sought to build a new order, strengthened in its academic foundation and spiritual endeavour, the Aragonese grouping (including its Catalan parent body) wanted to preserve its traditional active apostolate in which lay and clerical interests were enshrined. Secondly, the crown's insensitive, authoritarian management of religious reform as a function of its *patronazgo* over the Spanish Church led it to underestimate the need to accommodate local and provincial rights invested in the Mercedarian order (especially in Cataluña) and to centralise its power in Castile. Philip eventually came to recognise that he had to separate out interests of state from those of reform in order to carry through his policy. By the end of his reign, the Mercedarians were emerging from a 30-year period of restructuring, culminating in the establishment of an observant, Discalced branch in 1603, and their contribution on a national level to raising the quality of spiritual life in early modern Spain. But, as with the Carmelites, the process of separation from the Calced community was a fractious one and the reconstruction of the religious life of the Mercedarians not without its limitations. The other side of the coin of Discalced reform, as Bruce Taylor has recently pointed out, was that 'such congregations were neither universally popular nor necessarily free of the ambition and worldliness which they excoriated in their parent orders'.[31]

Conclusion

The evidence currently available to historians suggests that, despite some significant advances made in the course of the sixteenth century, measures to raise the quality of spiritual and scholastic leadership in the early modern Spanish Church, and by extension improve the effectiveness of its mission, were only partially successful. As we have seen, conflicts of jurisdiction over the application of Trent emerged between the crown and the papacy at an early stage, which severely obstructed the process of reform. Philip II's vision of his role as the ultimate arbiter in the religious affairs of his kingdoms, which lay at the heart of this conflict, acted as a hindrance where the ambitions of the crown were placed before the needs of the Church. In addition, the breadth and pace of reform was severely restricted by vested institutional interests, especially those embodied in privileged cathedral chapters and the powerful mendicant orders, most notably the Dominicans, whose cautious reaction to Tridentine proposals and the influence they held with the crown as theological advisers shaped the conservative tendency within the Spanish Church. While some initiatives such as the raising of standards of recruitment to the Church hierarchy and the transfer of conventual religious foundations to observant rule were pursued with rigour, others, such as the establishment of regular church councils and synods and the erection of seminaries for the training of priests, all failed at an early stage. Divisions of authority at local level between lay and ecclesiastical patrons resulted in inconsistent patterns of clerical discipline and vocation. Reform was further hindered by the imbalances that lay within Spain's ecclesiastical infrastructure. There were too many clergy based in towns, too few in the countryside. While some lived in the lap of luxury, others struggled to maintain a living for themselves. Finally, there were fundamental differences in the practice of belief (and response to reforming initiatives) within the diverse geographical and regional complexity of Spain. Reform, as in most parts of Catholic Europe, was essentially an urban phenomenon. At local community level, ancient religious customs and traditions were not easily dislodged to make way for a centrally imposed and directed form of worship and belief. Huge areas of the peninsula remained beyond the disciplinary reach of reformers. The raising of the professional, pastoral and apostolic profile of the clerical estate in the post-Tridentine era was to be a long-term challenge for the leaders of the Spanish Church.

4 *The Church and the People*

Introduction

In order to assess the full impact of the Catholic Reformation in early modern Spain it is necessary to divorce it from the perspective of the Church authorities and attempt instead to understand it through the eyes of the ordinary man or woman. This task has recently been made easier by the publication of key sources of evidence – including fifteenth- and sixteenth-century synodal constitutions, the topographical surveys of Castilian rural communities (1575–80), as well as the 'trials of faith' from a number of provincial tribunals of the Spanish Inquisition – which collectively provide an insight into the essential features of Christian belief as practised by a representative section of the mass of the population. The religious experience of the Spanish people, in common with that of most other rural communities in mid-sixteenth-century western Europe, was in many respects far removed from that prescribed by the orthodox Church. While sacramental observance and participation in the official ceremonies and festivities of the church calendar were fundamental features of the lives of the faithful, religion meant much more than this. It provided an important bond of unity and identity in a society made up of diverse peoples and traditions. The practice of religion was intrinsically interwoven with patterns of work and leisure, as well as devotional habits. The village church was frequently a setting for both commercial and social activities – vigils, accompanied by singing, dancing and games – in addition to purely sacred ones. The Astorgan diocesan synod of 1553 saw fit to prohibit business activities, fairs, markets and council meetings, as well as eating and drinking, from being carried out in its churches.[1] In the remote rural regions of Spain, inadequately served by priests, a form of popular religious culture survived, linked to local traditions and agrarian rites. Saints, vows, chapels, shrines and holy relics were its essential components, providing the peasant farmer with a direct link with heaven beyond the formality of the institutional Church. While the latter remained a vibrant force at community level, the strength of popular faith cannot be underestimated. It was the formidable task of Spanish bishops in the post-Tridentine period, assisted by the Holy Office, to impose a level of conformity and discipline on a diverse range of religious customs, rites and beliefs at parochial level that in themselves constituted the colour and vitality of Spanish Catholicism in the sixteenth century. It is the purpose of this chapter to assess the impact of the reforms of Trent on the religious lives of the vast majority of the Spanish population who inhabited its rural landscape.

The Christianisation of the People

One of the fundamental objectives of the Council of Trent was that the Catholic peoples of western Europe should become more aware of doctrine and more diligent in their practice of the faith. A 'good Catholic' was characterised by his knowledge of the four essential prayers of the Church (the Lord's Prayer, the Apostles' Creed, the *Ave María* and the *Salve Regina*) and the Ten Commandments; his abstention from labour on Sundays and attendance at mass; his participation in Holy Communion and his confession of sins at least once per year during the season of Lent; his observance of the traditional feast days of the religious calendar; his receipt of the sacraments of baptism and marriage at the hands of the local priest; his recourse to the sacrament of extreme unction on the point of death; and his ordering of masses for the delivery of his soul.

How far did the majority of the Spanish population understand the basic concepts of Catholic belief and meet their sacramental requirements? Ignorance and illiteracy among the rural population, as well as a shortage of suitably trained pastors, severely hindered attempts to impose official orthodoxy on the Spanish people, even before the Council of Trent met. An elementary level of religious instruction had been provided in fifteenth-century Spain via the posting of a *tabla* or parchment letter in each church, which set out the Ten Commandments, the articles of faith, a list of the sacraments and the capital sins, to be read to parishioners every Sunday during Lent. In the pre-Tridentine rural environment the basic prayers of the Church were still taught in Latin, providing a further obstacle to understanding. Addressing his own diocesan synod in 1533, the Bishop of Sigüenza remarked that 'because priests do not set an example, we observe many men who do not know the Creed, or how to make the sign of the cross, or anything about Christianity'.[2] The post-Tridentine catechetical movement, which aimed at intensifying and deepening an understanding of the faith from the basic starting point of the *tabla*, built upon early sixteenth-century synodal initiatives. Priests were obliged to teach Catholic doctrine to children on holy days after noon and parents were urged to reinforce this learning. Trent's sanctioning of the translation of the Roman catechism into the vernacular, actively encouraged by the preacher and reformer Juan de Ávila, marked a major turning point in the movement to instruct the ill-educated masses. The Christianisation programme, accelerated in the years immediately following the closure of Trent in 1564, essentially fell to the priesthood to deliver, and it put their own teaching abilities to the test.

The Inquisition also played its part in enforcing the Christian faith. Having successfully cleansed Spain of what it identified as subversive spiritual and intellectual influences, from the middle of the sixteenth century it mounted a new offensive: to correct the behaviour and beliefs of the Old Christian community. So great was its concern about the level of religious awareness of the people that it incorporated a test of doctrinal knowledge into its interrogation procedures. From 1565, prisoners were asked to recite the four basic Christian prayers and make the sign of the cross. From 1570, they were required to provide evidence of their attendance at mass and the frequency of their participation in confession and communion. From 1574, a recitation of the Ten Commandments was also incorporated into the test. The archives of the Holy Office are thus able to provide the historian with an important insight into the orthodoxy of ordinary Spaniards brought before its tribunals in 'trials of faith'. Recent research by Jean-Pierre Dedieu into the doctrinal awareness of a sample of 747 witnesses interrogated by the Toledan tribunal reveals that in the pre-Tridentine period (before 1555) a cross-section of 40 per cent of the Old Christian community were able to successfully recite the four basic prayers needed for their salvation. After 1575, the success rate had almost doubled, to 72 per cent. By the turn of the century, it had reached 82 per cent (see Table 4.1).[3] A similar success

Table 4.1 Percentage of defendants of the Inquisition of Toledo able to recite their prayers successfully, 1550–1650

	Pater	*Ave*	*Credo*	*Salve*	*All four prayers*
Up to 1550	70	86	45	49	37
1550–4	73	85	49	54	39
1555–64	85	89	69	70	59
1565–74	90	93	78	71	69
1575–84	97	97	83	77	72
1585–99	90	90	83	70	68
1600–50	93	92	88	84	82

Source: Jean-Pierre Dedieu, '"Christianization" in New Castile', in *Culture and Control in Counter-Reformation Spain*, eds A. J. Cruz and M. E. Perry (Minneapolis, 1991), p. 15.

story is revealed by the findings of Sara Nalle in respect of defendants interrogated by the tribunal of Cuenca on their knowledge of the four prayers over the same period: 33 per cent satisfied the requirement in the pre-Tridentine period (1544–67), doubling to 66 per cent in the post-Tridentine period (1568–79).[4]

A knowledge of the Ten Commandments among prisoners also improved. A 40 per cent success rate was recorded by defendants interrogated by the tribunal of Toledo over the ten-year period 1565–74. This figure rose to 77 per cent over the period 1600–50. By the end of the sixteenth century, if the case studies of Toledo and Cuenca can be taken as reliable indicators, it would appear that a representative section of the adult male population of New Castile was equipped with the basic doctrinal knowledge required of them by the Catholic Church. However, while the ability to recite prayers and commandments was an all-important gauge of the success of the priests' instruction of the laity in the post-Tridentine period, we must remember that knowledge of the catechism at its basic level constituted a mere memory exercise and that the pedagogical initiatives of the Church highlighted by recent research were fundamentally central Castilian ones. In practice, the effects of the Spanish Church's mission were uneven.

Significant areas of Spain remained isolated from the basic currents of reform in the century after Trent. Doctrinal ignorance was a particular characteristic of those people who inhabited the mountains, the migrant population and those living beyond the geographical reach of priests. As we have seen, the uneven quality and distribution of pastoral leadership in the peninsula compounded the problem. Following a visitation of his new diocese made in 1613, the Bishop of Calahorra reported to the crown that 'the ministers [of the church] are incapable, of little virtue, and they are unable to teach their parishioners what they need to know for their salvation. As a result the people live like barbarians, not knowing their prayers or how to cross themselves'.[5] In a diocesan report of 1617, the Bishop of Ávila revealed that 'it is eight years since confirmation was last given, and in many villages because of their difficult terrain there is no record of any bishop ever having been or visited'.[6] The deep-rooted cultural, social and geographical boundaries that constituted Spain all limited the pace and effectiveness of the post-Tridentine campaign to re-Christianise the laity.

In an effort to reinforce the educational focus of the Church's post-Tridentine mission to instil respect for the sacraments and raise standards of lay discipline, the Inquisition sought to control the speech, thoughts and behaviour of all Spaniards. Having effectively eliminated the incidence of major heresy, the primary function of the Holy Office from mid-century became that of prosecuting cases of minor heresy. Popular ignorance and superstition now became criminal offences. Careless verbal outbursts concerning the Catholic faith were responsible for bringing many into contact with the Inquisition for the first time. Trials for blasphemy (irreverent utterances and acts of belligerence in matters of doctrine and discipline, which typically included denial of the power of the sacraments, disrespect of Mary and the saints, objection to tithe payments and a rejection of papal authority), and for the associated crime of 'propositions' (erroneous statements about aspects of the faith, reflecting a difficulty in assimilating official explanations), constituted a significant area of inquisitorial activity in the post-Tridentine period. Despite their obvious anti-religious overtones, such verbal outbursts were usually devoid of any real underlying heretical intent. They were most frequently uttered in anger, jest or simply out of habit, behaviour which now incurred the application of a fine, lashes, or, in the most serious cases, public penance or imprisonment. As a result, everyone was forced to watch their words carefully, as well as those of their neighbour. The high incidence of cases of blasphemy and propositions, which accounted for 34.6 per cent of all cases brought before Castilian and Aragonese tribunals in the period 1560–1614, however far removed they may have been from real heresy, is nevertheless indicative of a significant level of religious scepticism and idiosyncrasy in Spanish society. Nicholas Griffiths has recently suggested that the attempt to Christianise the masses, while outwardly successful, may in fact have unwittingly led the individual to distort or misinterpret doctrinal truths in the process of adapting them to his own experience and understanding, rather than adhering strictly to them.[7] A deliberate campaign was launched by the Holy Office to counteract popular religious deviance in post-Tridentine Spanish society. In Toledo, the percentage of trials for propositions and blasphemy fell from 46 per cent in the period 1560–1614 to under 20 per cent in the seventeenth century (see Table 4.2). In Galicia, the comparable figures were 56.6 per cent (1560–99) falling to 16.6 per cent (1600–1700).[8] By contrast, the tribunal of Zaragoza, heavily engaged with *morisco* dissidence, did not fully turn its attention to cases of religious deviance among Old Christians until after 1614.[9] From the evidence at our disposal it might be concluded that the educative programme

Table 4.2 Examples of cases of minor heresy brought before the Toledan tribunal of the Inquisition, 1551–1600

	Propositions + blasphemy		*Bigamy*		*Simple fornication*	
	no.	%	*no.*	%	*no.*	%
1551–5	256	68.6	23	6.2	–	
1556–60	230	62.8	21	5.6	–	
1561–5	142	49.6	20	7	17	5.9
1566–70	193	53.3	24	6.6	77	21.1
1571–5	137	45.9	5	1.7	45	15.1
1576–80	103	60.9	3	1.7	61	36.1
1581–5	110	55	6	3	66	33
1586–90	90	56.6	4	2.5	54	34
1591–5	46	26.1	10	5.7	17	9.7
1596–1600	28	19	5	3.4	9	6.1

Note: The figure is given as a percentage of all cases examined per five-year period.
Source: Jean-Pierre Dedieu, 'The Archives of the Holy Office of Toledo', in *The Inquisition in Early Modern Europe*, ed. G. Henningsen and J. Tedeschi (Illinois, 1986), pp. 180–1, and 'Le modèle sexuel: la défense du mariage chrétien', in *l'Inquisition Espagnole*, ed. B. Bennassar et al. (Paris, 1979), p. 327.

of the Church did not wholly satisfy the needs of the faithful, who struggled to understand and accept official doctrine. We might further question the extent to which the punitive measures take by the Inquisition actually served to change attitudes or simply temporarily silenced those who spoke out about their misgivings but whose fundamental doubts and misunderstandings remained.

Sacramental Observance

The overall success of the programme to raise standards of orthodoxy among the Spanish people, in which both the Church and the Inquisition participated, has to be measured in terms of the practice of their belief. As we have seen, regular attendance at mass, as well as a strict observance of the sacraments of baptism, marriage, confession and extreme unction, all became fundamental duties of the Old Christian in the post-Tridentine era. But how diligently did he adhere to them?

Attendance at mass on Sundays and days of obligation had long been an established feature of religious practice in Spain. But irregular mass provision led to the neglect and abuse of the official rite. Private and community votive masses were more regularly and enthusiastically attended than parochial masses. The diocesan synod of Mondoñedo of 1541 admonished parishioners for frequenting their local tavern rather than their church at the hour of the *misa mayor*.[10] In mid-sixteenth-century Oviedo, mass was often interrupted by violent disputes between members of the congregation! Clergy in Burgos were subjected to insults during mass, as reported in the archdiocesan constitutions of 1575:

> Sometimes it has happened that when priests or preachers are rebuking or speaking ill of vices or sins of the people, the persons referred to, or those that claim authority in the town, stand up and reply to him, and at times speak words that are rude, indecent, and unworthy of such a place.[11]

The Toledan Provincial Council of 1565–6 advised members of the choir to abstain from frivolous conversation and chatter that often disturbed divine services.[12] Trent's attempt to restore respect for the mass and place it at the centre of Catholic worship had to break through the barrier of popular ignorance and custom. The eucharistic sacrifice, performed by the priest during the mass ceremony, embodied the fundamental concepts of Catholic doctrine, hence the obligation on the part of the laity to hear mass in church and witness the divine presence in the transubstantiation of the bread and the wine. In post-Tridentine Spain, as in other Catholic countries of western Europe, the mass, officially conducted in accordance with the new Roman rite from 1569, remained essentially a priestly ceremony, delivered from the high altar in Latin, and largely unintelligible to the majority of the congregation. Although the evidence suggests that people attended mass (and observed the Sabbath and holy days) more frequently after Trent – a 75 per cent minimum compliance was recorded in Cuenca in the period 1564–80, rising to 85 per cent in the period 1581–1600[13] – they barely participated in it. Above all it was a social occasion. The Bishop of Mallorca's complaints of 1570 were typical of many others: his parishioners came to mass halfway through and left before it was finished, talking and discussing their affairs throughout![14]

Trent required Catholics to receive Holy Communion at least once a year, following their annual Lenten confession with their parish priest. The two sacraments were thus intimately linked. In order to take the Eucharist and benefit from its propitious effects, the communicant had to be free from sin. The findings of Dedieu indicate that 15 per cent of defendants brought before the Toledan tribunal during the Easter period between 1575 and 1599 surpassed this annual requirement; by 1600–50, this figure had reached 50 per cent.[15] In the intense atmosphere of popular piety that characterised post-Tridentine Spain, particular emphasis was placed on the act of confession. The 'penitential ethos' provided a powerful challenge to the Protestant rejection of confession as a means of obtaining God's grace, hence its promotion by Catholic reformers.[16] Penalties were imposed on those who did not meet their confessional obligation. The increased frequency with which the laity sought confession enhanced the role of the parish priest, who required a special licence from his bishop to carry out confessions. It also put his standards of morality and powers of discretion to the test.

Evidence provided by the constitutions of early sixteenth-century diocesan synods suggests that the average Spaniard did not adhere strictly to his other sacramental obligations, except where baptism was concerned. It was essential, given the intimate relationship between religion and national identity in early modern Spain, and the high incidence of infant mortality, that a newborn child be baptised as a Christian at the earliest opportunity. Trent insisted on parochial baptisms, as opposed to informal domestic ceremonies, often carried out by midwives when a child's life was known to be in danger. The Toledan Provincial Council of 1583 stipulated a maximum time of ten days between birth and the baptismal ceremony, a longer period than the three days recommended by Trent. An unbaptised child, so it was commonly assumed, would have little chance of a place in heaven, hence the urgency of confirming its entry into the Church and the civic community via the baptism service. Baptismal fonts were to be available in all churches serving communities of more than 15 households (*vecinos*) and kept under lock and key when not in use. A maximum of two godparents were to be nominated to look after the Christian education of the child. The importance attached to the sacrament of baptism was further reinforced by the obligation on the part of priests from 1555 to keep an official register of all baptisms (as well as marriages, burials and Easter communicants).

Trent sought to strengthen respect for the sacrament of marriage. It was common belief among peasantry in early modern Spain that for a man to engage in a sexual relationship with a woman, either inside or outside of marriage, was not a mortal sin. Thus acts of adultery and bigamy were not regarded as necessarily wrong. Prostitution was not a hidden profession. The frequenting of brothels was not made a public offence in Castile until 1623. Furthermore, promiscuity was not an activity exclusive to the laity. The lesser clergy were notorious for taking concubines and engaging in acts of solicitation in the confessional. Until 1561, when solicitation became officially recognised as an act of heresy, the Inquisition's jurisdiction in such cases had been limited by the authority of episcopal courts, renowned for their leniency in judging offending clergy. In 1567, Don Fernando Bazán, a canon of Toledo no less, was accused by the local tribunal of being a well-known womaniser (*público cazador*) and of causing great scandal by living in sin with Doña Juana de Vargas. He was condemned to six months' seclusion in the cathedral cloisters. In the same year, Alonso Díaz, a labourer from the Toledan village of Carpio, was forced to appear in penitence at an *auto de fe* for apparently being unaware that it was a sin to take a prostitute for payment.[17] Marriages frequently took place between close relatives in early sixteenth-century Tuy, while in late-century Toledo pre-Christian marriage rites were recognised as a common feature of the May festivals in an official visitation report: 'In many parts of this archdiocese it is the custom on the first of May every year for young men to climb up to the top of towers and other high places and, singing, to marry young lads and lasses of the area. Such [practices] are the cause of great scandal.'[18]

Trent sought to eradicate clandestine and casual marriages and to exercise much stricter control over the legitimacy of matrimonial alliances. In future couples were required to display an adequate knowledge of Christian doctrine prior to the official blessing of their union. Marriage was to take place in church, in the presence of a parish priest, following three official announcements of their intention to join in wedlock. The notion that marital status was preferable to that of celibacy, an idea promoted by the Protestant Church and provoked by the renowned licentious behaviour of certain lesser members of the clerical estate, was severely denounced. Following Tridentine recommendations, a rigorous campaign was launched to reinforce Catholic doctrine on the sacrament of marriage and sexual behaviour. The Church instructed and the Inquisition corrected.

In 1565, the Council of the Inquisition (known as the *Suprema*) ordered all tribunals to take a firm stand against bigamous practice. Accordingly, the number of bigamists brought before the tribunal of Toledo fell dramatically from 20 (1561–5) to 3 (1576–80). Attention then turned to eradicating sexual promiscuity, categorised as 'simple fornication', which became a punishable offence following its incorporation into the edict of faith in 1574. The Toledan tribunal once again took the initiative. Between 1576 and 1580, 36 per cent of prosecutions derived from this sphere of activity. By 1591–5, the figure had fallen to less than 10 per cent (see Table 4.2 above).[19] The message took longer to reach the more remote regions. Galician inquisitors acknowledged that they had an uphill struggle on their hands in seeking to eradicate the ignorance and moral laxity that prevailed in the peasant community and could only hope that fear of punishment would act as a deterrent.[20] While the Inquisition may have succeeded in suppressing public outbursts on the legitimacy of sexual relations outside marriage, it remains more difficult to gauge the extent to which private behaviour was modified as a result.

It was at the point of death – an ever-present reality in precarious times – that the sacraments of the Church and the services of the priest were most actively sought by the people. The elite classes were attended by a variety of ecclesiastics on their deathbeds, ranging from their personal confessors to the clergy and benefice holders of their parish church. Before receiving extreme unction, the dying person was expected to make a confession and receive absolution from a priest.

He or she was also under (theoretical) obligation as a Christian to make a will, an extremely important document that served both a legal and a spiritual function. Although a will could be prepared while one was still in good health, for the majority it was a task hastily carried out at the onset of death. The testament indicated how a person's income and estate were to be disposed of, including charitable donations as well as the religious devotions to be carried out on their behalf after death. A study of wills drawn up by Spaniards in the second half of the sixteenth century reveals how increasingly important it was for testators, the majority of whom belonged to the elite urban-based classes, to make detailed provision for their burial and, moreover, their needs in the afterlife. In arranging their funeral rites and rituals, the wealthier classes impressed their superior social status upon the ordinary citizen by requesting that members of their favourite religious order and/or confraternity take part in the procession from their deathbed to the place of burial, carrying lighted torches, and by ordering an ever-increasing number of masses (funeral and memorial) to be said for their souls. The redemptive function of the mass was actively promoted by Trent as a means by which the safe passage of the soul through purgatory could be facilitated. By vigorously reaffirming the value of post mortem devotions in contrast to the Protestant Church's rejection of them, the Counter-Reformation Church actively fostered recourse to intercessory prayer, hence the multiplication of suffrages for the dead recorded in post-Tridentine Spain. The practice also reveals Spaniards' increasing preoccupation with death and the insecurities surrounding the afterlife. Carlos Eire's recent study of wills drawn up in the city of Madrid in the sixteenth century reveals that an average 90 masses were being requested per individual in the 1520s, 200 in the 1550s, almost 500 in the 1570s, escalating to 777 in the 1590s. Over this period the cost of a simple mass doubled from 17 to 34 *reales*, while the cost of a special (sung) mass quadrupled from 17 to 68 *reales*.[21] According to Fernando Martínez Gil, in the city of Toledo requests for masses rose from an average of 106 per testator in the period 1575–1600 to 329 per testator in the period 1625–50, reflecting the ever-increasing concern of the individual to secure his or her salvation in heaven (see Table 4.3).[22] This pursuit of heavenly protection provided employment for a veritable army of ecclesiastics responsible for the saying of anniversary masses. In practice, only the wealthier classes could afford to make provision for the well-being of their souls, for the Church and its servants demanded substantial monetary remuneration for

Table 4.3 Increase in the number of devotional masses for the souls of the dead in Toledo, 1500–1700

Dates	*No. of masses requested*	*Percentage of all masses*	*Average no. per testator*
1500–25	10 967	5.5	127.52
1526–50	2 605	1.0	31.38
1551–75	17 825	9.0	178.25
1576–1600	9 362	4.5	106.38
1601–25	35 457	17.0	389.63
1626–50	30 338	15.0	329.76
1651–75	50 806	24.0	590.76
1676–1700	47 802	23.0	430.64

Source: Fernando Martínez Gil, *Muerte y Sociedad en la España de los Austrias* (Madrid, 1993), pp. 547–8.

their monopoly of the rites to ensure the spirit's salvation. A recent survey of funeral rites in Extremadura in the seventeenth century reveals that a simple funeral cost 216 *reales* – equivalent to two months' work for an average wage labourer (*jornalero*).[23] While the elite classes invested in lavish funeral ceremonies, endowed multiple masses for the redemption of their souls and built private chapels for their rest, the lower classes (of whom less than 20 per cent left a will and disposable income) had to rely on the charitable provision of their local church or confraternity to ensure that they received the last rites, were buried with dignity and had a safe passage through purgatory.

Forms of Popular Religious Culture

The religious horizons of the Spanish people, in common with much of the population of Catholic Europe, extended far beyond the confines of their parish church. For the typical peasant farmer, religion was intimately related to the natural world around him. It was a hostile, unpredictable and incomprehensible world that engendered a mentality ruled by fears and insecurities. Popular religious culture offered a safe passage, a means of explanation, protection and deliverance in times of hardship. The peasant farmer was primarily concerned to guard against disease and infertility, to protect his crops and livestock; human and material survival were at stake. He looked to God and to the divine order to attend to his needs. A strong sense of providence characterised the religious attitudes of the local people. The course of events was deemed to result directly from God's will, which could reward as well as castigate. The local community's familiarity with the physical environment led them to interpret many natural events as divine messages and to endow consecrated objects with miraculous properties, which could only be explained via the intercessory powers of God.

The veneration of the local saint personified the traditions, fears and aspirations of the rural community, reflecting its basic defencelessness when faced with the force of natural circumstance. Local saints were called upon to intercede on behalf of the community at times of difficulty or when special protection was required against natural phenomena such as severe weather conditions, pestilence and plague. Each met a special need. At times of great catastrophe, several saints might be called upon to provide deliverance. In the minds of the populace, the intercession of saints could influence a man's destiny. Their intervention could persuade God to divert the course of nature in response to the needs of the community. Saints were capable of bestowing both good and evil, hence the importance of

Table 4.4 The protective powers of local saints in New Castile, 1575–80

Saint	*Motivation of vow*	*No. of villages with advocations*
Sebastian	Plague, pestilence	241
Gregory of Nazianus	Vine pests	103
Anne	Plague	74
The True Cross	Drought, storms	71
Roch	Plague	59
Anthony	Cattle disease	46
Agatha	Climatic conditions	43
Pantaleon	Vine pests	42
Conception of Our Lady	Plague	42
Quiteria	Rabies	37
Augustine	Locusts	36
Blaise	Throat ailment	34
Catherine	Plague, pests, locusts	32

Source: Fernando Martínez Gil, *Muerte y Sociedad en la España de los Austrias* (Madrid, 1993), p. 260.

annual pilgrimages to the shrines of local saints, the celebration of a special mass in their honour, followed by acts of charitable devotion, all designed to venerate, as well as placate, their special patrons. It was confidently believed that acts of prayer, homage and repentance would restore God's grace and favour.

Vows were observed by villages to solicit their saint's protection against natural disaster. A vow was a promise of Christian devotion to a particular saint, enshrined in acts of charity or worship, who would then intercede on their behalf to obtain God's grace. Fear of death from disease prompted the saintly allegiance held by the villagers of La Fuente de Pedro Naharro in the province of Cuenca, as they recollected in their reply to the government survey of 1575: 'It all began when one morning, on Saint Agatha's day, three people died from an epidemic and it was decided to keep the Saint's day, to fast and give offerings on that day.'[24] There was a direct correlation in the minds of the populace between the observance of a particular vow and the promise of deliverance being fulfilled, as recorded by the residents of Calzada de la Calatrava in Ciudad Real: 'There was a great need for water at the time the vow was taken out, which was a Friday, and on the Saturday the land was saturated with water.'[25] Failure to keep a vow could result in the recurrence of the evil force. The villagers of Usanos in the province of Guadalajara recalled the dramatic consequences of neglecting their offerings to Saint Barbara: 'and it is said that one year these [offerings] ceased and on this very day in the afternoon, a thunderbolt struck the church tower and burnt three or four people. Since then the offerings have always been made and the Saint's day observed.'[26] Shrines, hermitages and chapels

Table 4.5 Number of votive festivals celebrated in New Castile, 1575–80

Province	*Total no. of festival days*	*Average no. per village*
Ciudad Real	261	4.3
Cuenca	126	3.4
Guadalajara	611	4.2
Madrid	318	3.8
Toledo	382	2.8

Source: F. J. Campos y Fernández de Sevilla, *La Mentalidad en Castilla la Nueva en el siglo xvi* (Madrid, 1986), p. 76.

were built to honour local saints and were administered by charitable confraternities, who also helped to organise the celebration of local votive feast days, processions and pilgrimages. While most small communities had an average of two chapels dedicated to their village saints, larger ones could have five or even six each.

Votive festivals, held in honour of local saints, were also an opportunity for merrymaking, a means of release from the order and convention of daily life. Having attended to their spiritual devotions, local people would engage in dancing, drinking, eating, acts of role reversal and social satire. It was reported from Fuentelaencina, Guadalajara, that:

> Saint Anne's day has been vowed in this village for a very long time, it being the principal festival that is celebrated and on that day there is great rejoicing and merriment both on foot and on horseback; there is dancing and performances are put on, and, when they were allowed, bulls were run, all at the expense of the town council; according to the old folk, the vow was taken out to guard against locusts.[27]

These popular community events characterised the part-sacred, part-profane nature of the practice of local religion in late sixteenth-century Spain. They formed the essential manifestations of the cultural experience of the ordinary Spaniard. While the rich diversity of devotional activity at local level helped strengthen ties of community solidarity, it clearly posed a threat to the authority of the mother Church. One of the main priorities of Tridentine reform thus became the extension of ecclesiastical control over these independent elements of popular belief.

Trent encouraged the legitimate veneration of the biblical, martyred saints of universal acclaim, whose lives and works might serve as salutary examples for the faithful. It strongly condemned idolatrous devotion, which characterised some aspects of popular religious culture. The Toledan Provincial Council of 1565–6 urged preachers in their sermons to 'remind people of the traditions, rites and ceremonies of the Holy Catholic Church, of the mysteries enshrined within and all that concerns the salvation of souls. They should refrain from their [excessive] belief in fabulous stories, but not from [their devotion to] those saints and martyrs commonly acknowledged by the mother church'.[28] In the closing decades of the sixteenth century, saintly devotions and cults took on a new importance in peoples' lives as they became victims of the acute economic crisis that paralysed the kingdom of Castile (see Chapter 6). Sara Nalle has shown that in post-Tridentine Cuenca people increasingly sought the protection of stronger, more powerful patrons of universal renown in response to prevailing conditions, as opposed to their local ones. The chapel dedications of 84 communities in the region, surveyed between 1583 and 1645, reveal an increase in the number of rural shrines (from an average of 2.4 to 2.9 per community) but a sharp 33 per cent reduction in the broad range of patronal advocations. By the mid-seventeenth century, eight patrons commanded two-thirds of all chapel devotions, the most popular being Mary, the Holy Family and Christ.[29] The cult of the Virgin Mary – promoted as a symbol of orthodox piety by Catholic reformers – served as a particularly powerful link between the local and the universal Church. She was the premiere patron, the supreme protectress of mankind. Images, chapels and churches honouring the Virgin, especially those associated with the Passion, proliferated in the post-Tridentine period. Marian chapel devotions accounted for 65 per cent of all those reported as in existence by New Castilian towns who responded to the government questionnaire in 1575–80.[30] Images of the Virgin Mary or a favourite saint were often associated with miraculous events and cures. It was reported from Auñón in Guadalajara in 1575 that a young child who had fallen on rocky ground adjacent to the shrine of Our Lady was restored to good health following a mass celebrated before her image. The village of Illescas boasted in its survey return of 1575 that Philip II had visited the miraculous shrine of Our Lady of Charity, accompanied by Queen Anna of Austria and Princess Juana, demonstrating their respect for local symbols of devotion. The cult of relics ran parallel to the veneration of saints. The miraculous properties of relics were used to ward off storms, as well as to bring the rains and cure illnesses. Philip II was an avid collector and worshipper of religious relics, gathering over 7000 specimens in the Escorial. Relics were perquisites of power. When the body of Saint Eugène (the first Spanish primate) arrived in Toledo in 1565, Philip helped carry it to its resting place in the cathedral. He and his daughter Isabel were also in the city for the festivities marking the return of the body of the Spanish martyr Saint Leocadia to Toledo from Flanders in 1587.[31]

The celebration of official alongside local religious festivals, which could be both spectacular and modest in dimension, embodying community pride, Catholic ritual and popular piety, increased in Counter-Reformation Spain.[32] The winter cycle of festivals culminated at Easter when Lent and Holy Week processions took place in major towns. They gave way to the summer cycle, incorporating the liturgical feasts of Ascension, Corpus Christi and the Assumption, celebrated alongside local patron saints' days, concentrated in the months of August and September. Special events such as the beatification and canonisation of Spanish saints prompted further celebrations. In late sixteenth-century Castile, up to one day in every four was devoted to a religious feast. These were public holidays when people were obliged to abstain from their labours and engage in processions, special masses and rituals. Crosses, candles and torches were carried through the streets, accompanied by singing, chanting and praying. For the Castilian peasant farmer such regular events became ever more burdensome as agriculture entered into a period of severe recession. The economic repercussions of strict adherence to the religious calendar could threaten livelihoods, as reported in the proceedings of the Burgos archdiocesan synod of 1575:

> In many places in our archdiocese, in addition to Sundays and holy days that the Holy Mother Church orders observed, there are many other days that the villagers out of their devotions or council vows promise to keep; and afterwards . . . they encounter considerable difficulties. For since many of these days fall at harvest time or grape-gathering time, when there is much necessity to bring in the wheat and wine and dig around the vines, and sow, many work and go against their vows; and other poor folk, because they, their wives and children are unable to work, die of hunger.[33]

A compromise solution was reached which allowed for a rationalisation of devotional practice. It was decreed that once the members of the community had honoured their local saint and fulfilled their vows they were free to return to their labours.

The post-Tridentine Church authorities also sought to remove all pagan or superstitious elements from religious celebrations. The transformation of the feast of Corpus Christi from a predominantly secular festival, in which giants and dragons participated, to one of the major feast days of the ecclesiastical calendar, serves as an example of the successful propaganda effort of the Counter-Reformation Church to glorify the Holy Sacrament – carried through the streets under a pallium – and demonstrate the triumph of ecclesiastical discipline and Catholic doctrine over popular variants of belief. Corpus became one of the most magnificent of the summer religious festivals, incorporating a procession, pageant and drama. Religious drama had long been a feature of pre-Tridentine Corpus celebrations in Spain, as in other Catholic countries of western Europe. Popular liturgical drama (known as the *representación, farsa, juego* or *auto*), organised by the local guilds, was criticised by the church authorities for its display of ignorance and irreverence. However, its value as a teaching mechanism was clearly recognised. In the post-Tridentine period, the *auto sacramental* became an official part of Corpus celebrations. Professional performances replaced amateur ones. The *auto* reinforced the sacramental ethos of the Corpus feast. All plays were performed in the presence of the Holy Sacrament and in front of the most important members of the local Church and municipal authorities. In the second half of the sixteenth century, the writing of dramatic allegories to honour the Eucharist became a major function of professional playwrights and shaped the development of Spanish theatre. Félix Lope de Vega (1562–1635) and Pedro Calderón de la Barca (1600–81) were to become the great masters of the *auto* in seventeenth-century Spain. Corpus Christi celebrations combined pomp and ceremony with dogma and doctrine in such a way as to glorify the image of Spain's Catholic supremacy, which the Church sought earnestly to project, while at the same time satisfying the needs of popular entertainment.[34]

The Universal Brotherhood of Believers

The holy brotherhood, or *cofradía*, was a lay body with a religious function, well established within the pious framework of each community, big and small. It was largely through the work of holy brotherhoods that Spanish Catholicism maintained and extended its popular roots. The confraternity had originated in medieval times as a voluntary group of people, often linked by their trade or profession, who joined together in devotion to a particular saint or cult with charitable aims. They formed centres of religious practice which often competed with the parish, organising and participating in local processions and feast day celebrations; they gave alms to the poor and provided burial rites for their fraternal kinsmen; they maintained their own chapels, chaplains and shrines; they scheduled masses to honour their patron saints and in remembrance of fellow *cofrades*. Their influence on the shaping of local religion was exceptionally strong. The confraternity offered an alternative spiritual life to its members, and one that increasingly operated independently of church control.

The divine favours that the confraternities cultivated via their devotions to local saints and cults prompted civil authorities to seek their aid in times both of national crisis and of triumph. Confraternal processions not only served to foster national pride and convey joy in communal solidarity but also to circulate news among the population. In Toledo, the Brotherhood of the True Cross held devout and ordered flagellant processions 'whenever appropriate for the health of royalty and princes, for victories, or for the common good'.[35] The religious corporations of Zamora welcomed the closing of the Council of Trent in 1563 with a general parade, and in November 1571 they celebrated the victory of Lepanto in procession with city officials and church prelates. In 1588, Philip II ordered all Spanish bishops to organise processions of holy brotherhoods for the successful outcome of the Armada against England.[36]

The number of holy brotherhoods increased dramatically in Spain during the second half of the sixteenth century in response to the religious needs of society. Although confraternities were predominantly urban-based, most small communities (with an average of 100 households) supported at least one. Here the *cofradía* might well be the only religious organisation in the vicinity other than the parish church, hence its capacity to shape religious identity and influence the practice of belief. Holy brotherhoods proliferated in major towns. Valladolid had an estimated 100 for a population of 30 000. Neighbouring Zamora held the highest concentration – 150 in a community of under 9000 residents. The government survey of the city of Toledo conducted in 1576 revealed a total of 143 *cofradías* serving a population of some 60 000, equivalent to one per 84 households.[37] The majority were well established in the city; 28 new brotherhoods were set up between 1549 and 1576. They fell into three main categories, each serving a different level of society: (a) those associated with professional bodies who offered mutual aid to their fraternal kinsmen, and were much criticised for their engagement in secular rather than spiritual pursuits; (b) those parochial brotherhoods of charitable concern, dedicated to aiding the poor and the sick and providing for their needs at death; and (c) those that specifically advocated the Tridentine cults (the holy sacraments, souls in purgatory, Christ's passion and the sorrowing Virgin). This third category of brotherhood, which operated under direct clerical control, was among the most numerous and prestigious in the city. The growth in their popularity was an indication of the success of the Counter-Reformation's promotion of the Eucharistic and penitential cults. The Brotherhood of the Holy Sacrament (*Santíssimo Sacramento*), whose function was to revere the Eucharist, was established in 23 out of 27 Toledan parishes. Souls in Purgatory (*Las Ánimas del Purgatorio*) was the fastest-growing Toledan confraternity, specifically dedicated to meeting the needs of souls in purgatory via the collection of alms, the celebration of mass and prayer. Holy Charity (*La Santa Caridad*) was the most prestigious Toledan brotherhood, attracting a distinctly elite membership, joined in charitable purpose, including distinguished nobles and intellectuals, canons and magistrates. Luis de Hurtado, the parish priest of San Vicente in Toledo, responsible for replying to the government survey of the city undertaken in 1576, noted that 'The people of Toledo are punctilious in celebrating the feasts of Our Lady, the Holy Sacrament, and the Souls in Purgatory in order to show the splendour of their faith against the three principal errors of the Lutherans'.[38] However, while some confraternities were clearly serving the needs of the community by providing burials, masses and vigils for the dead, supporting hospital provision and encouraging pious devotions, others amassed funds under false pretences. Furthermore, by administering the sacraments and arranging local forms of worship, they came close to challenging the authority of Catholic clergymen in the same way as the Protestant notion of universal priesthood did. A delegation of Spanish clergy wrote to Pius IV in 1556 complaining that confraternities violated their authority and enjoyed exclusive privileges. 'Many persons of sinful personal habit and others who owe many debts enter these confraternities wishing to protect themselves with ecclesiastical jurisdiction', they alleged.[39] The close supervision of holy brotherhoods thus became a priority of Tridentine reform.

The Council of Trent sought to bring confraternities under the strict supervision of the ecclesiastical authorities. Decrees were approved in the final session aimed at reducing confraternal independence. New foundations were to be restricted to those of purely penitential purpose; the lax moral behaviour of members was to be disciplined; their financial affairs and welfare programmes were to be subject to much closer scrutiny. Post-Tridentine synods set out to reinforce these requirements at diocesan level. The task was greatest in those urban centres, such as Toledo, with a heavily embedded confraternal structure. It was reported from the city in 1576 that brotherhoods carried out 'spiritual works that should be exercised by clerics...and they treat clerics like apprentices'.[40] The Toledan Provincial Council of 1582–3 sought to limit the size of confraternities 'since they have grown to such an extent that they are capable of great harm'.[41] The crown itself intervened in the reform process. A policy aimed at the replacement of private sources of charity, such as that provided by the brotherhoods, with government-supported projects, centred on hospitals, was finalised between 1581 and 1583. It led to some reduction in the confraternal system, but not its total abolition, as recommended by reformers.

In practice, the restrictions designed to limit both the independence and the following enjoyed by confraternities did little to lessen their popular appeal. Although the economic recession late in the century reduced pious donations to brotherhoods, they nevertheless retained the spiritual allegiance of the local people, who continued to employ their services in burials and anniversary mass cycles – deemed to be of immeasurable benefit in securing the personal delivery of the soul from the torment of purgatory – in the decades immediately following Trent. In Madrid, 66 per cent of testators requested the presence of confraternities at their funeral in the 1560s, 58 per cent in the 1570s and 59 per cent in the 1580s, after which their popularity as escorts to heaven declined.[42] In the neighbouring city of Toledo an even higher number of holy brotherhoods were represented at funerals held in the post-Tridentine period (83 per cent in the period 1551–75), followed by a gradual reduction in their presence (69 per cent in the period 1601–25) as attempts to restrict the size and influence of the confraternal system took effect.[43] Maureen Flynn has shown that in Zamora, although confraternities were forced to conform to official notions of orthodoxy and allow the church hierarchy to assume control over the transmission of grace and the pardoning of sin, the people continued to place their trust in their private confraternal associations.[44]

Conclusion

How far did Trent succeed in regulating the religious lives of the majority of the population and in enforcing a uniform Catholic culture upon them? Research carried out thus far on the impact of the Counter-Reformation in Spain suggests that, at least within the context of central Castile, the Church, aided by the Inquisition, was successful in raising standards of doctrinal awareness among the people, in promoting adherence to the sacram[illegible] ing clerical control over the practice of belief an[illegible] morality at local level and in focusing their attentio[illegible] symbols of piety, notably those promoting Christ and [illegible] Virgin.

However, the same evidence also suggests that Trent di[illegible] wholly succeed in removing long-established variants and symbols of belief and popular expressions of piety, as embodied in the work of holy brotherhoods, which carried just as much significance for the typical Spaniard as those promoted by the orthodox Church. Popular forms of piety were reinforced in the late sixteenth century by the renewed emphasis placed by the Church hierarchy on acts of penitence, mercy and charity, which had for centuries been emblematic of community faith. The attempt made by reformers to centralise the practice of local religion on the parish and formalise its delivery failed to take account of the need of the ordinary man or woman to be able to see, hear, feel and touch the fundamental elements of their belief system. Religious festivals, which combined ceremony with entertainment, continued to give external expression to the people's faith in a visual, dramatic and colourful representation of Catholic ritual. For all the efforts of post-Tridentine clergy and inquisitors to impose a uniform religious culture on society, Spanish Catholicism retained its diverse and popular roots.

5 *The Church in the New World*

Introduction

On 3 August 1492, seven months after the victory of Christian forces at Granada, a Spanish fleet of three small ships, captained by Christopher Columbus, set out on the first voyage of discovery across the Atlantic. This historic journey was to culminate in the colonisation and evangelisation of territories in central and southern America and inspire Spaniards with a powerful sense of global mission. Few contemporaries were willing to doubt the notion that God had elevated Spain to such greatness in order to further his cause on earth by upholding and extending the Christian faith to its farthest ends. The crown seized the opportunity afforded by the discovery of a vast overseas empire of pagan tradition to capitalise on its Christianising mission and build a church in the New World, modelled on that in Spain, subject to its own will and direction.

The bull *Inter caetera divinae*, issued by Alexander VI on 4 May 1493, set the framework for royal rights of patronage over the Church in the Indies by authorising the Crown of Castile to undertake both the conquest and the Christianisation of the newly discovered lands.[1] The political and spiritual submission of the Indians to the Christians went hand in hand, as did the interests of the Spanish Church and state. Further papal concessions were to follow. In 1501, the crown acquired the right to collect tithes and first fruits from the natives in perpetuity in order to finance what was to become the vast organisation of the Church in the New World. The seal was set on royal direction of ecclesiastical affairs in the Indies by the bull *Universalis ecclesiae regimini*, issued by Pope Julius II on 28 July 1508, which effectively institutionalised the *Patronato Real de las Indias*.[2] The bull made reference to the success of the Spanish monarchy in establishing the Church in Granada and to the progress already made in the New World. It invested in the crown the right to erect and maintain all cathedral, collegiate and parish churches, to found convents, monasteries and hospitals and to nominate to all clerical offices – in effect, to draw up the ecclesiastical map of Spanish America. The royal prerogative also extended into the area of ecclesiastical jurisdiction and discipline: all papal bulls and edicts had to be approved by the crown, via the Council of the Indies, before publication; they could be suspended if they appeared to infringe on the authority of the crown. There was no system of appeal to Rome; in fact no papal nuncio ever set foot in the Indies. By the death of Ferdinand in 1516, royal patrimonial rights over the colonial Church were fully established, investing in the crown a degree of control that exceeded that provided by the Granada *Patronato* and was unparalleled in the pre-Reformation European world. In the Americas, it was the Spanish monarchy rather than the papacy that acted as the supreme head of the Catholic Church. However, despite the absolute nature of the crown's ecclesiastical power base in the New World, the missionary enterprise faced multiple challenges.

The history of the establishment of the Church in Latin America has traditionally been told from an institutional perspective and largely through the experience of missionary friars. Modern historians have begun to redress the balance by exploring some of the social and ethical issues surrounding the whole process of cross-cultural contact between Christian and Indian civilisations. Their findings suggest that the programme of evangelisation in the New World generated many conflicts of interest and tradition, some of which also underpinned the organisation and practice of Catholicism in the motherland, bringing into focus both its strengths and its weaknesses. This chapter aims to draw an objective assessment of the success of Spain's religious endeavour in the Americas on the basis of this broad evidence.

Colonisation and Evangelisation: the Jurisdictional Debate

The discovery and conquest of the New World initiated a vigorous and wide-ranging debate within Spanish society regarding the rights and duties of the conquering nation over the native Indian population.

The participants in the debate included humanist scholars, political theorists and mendicant friars, some of whom had experience as colonisers and left valuable written records of their experiences. The legitimacy of the Spanish crown's claim to temporal jurisdiction over its Indian subjects and its readiness to use force in pursuit of its Christianising mission were brought into question, as was the whole issue of how the spiritual aims of conquest could be reconciled with the inherent material gains. The public debate, which extended over much of the first half of the sixteenth century, by challenging the foundations of colonial rule, marked a major stage in Spain's religious and political development. It revealed the disquiet felt by many Spaniards, clergy as well as laity, at the methods employed to spread Christianity, and it led them to give serious consideration to their colonial responsibilities in the New World, and, by implication, to their role as militant defenders of Catholicism in the Old World. At the same time, the fundamental conflict of interests exposed in the parallel exploitation and evangelisation of the Indian community was seized upon by contemporary critics of Spain's mission abroad as evidence of its underlying hypocrisy. It was a debate of historic proportions since it raised issues that touched on the whole ethos of Spanish imperialism.

The empire in the Indies was regarded as a divine gift; it was thus the sacred duty of Spaniards to propagate Christianity within it. The military and political conquest of America, by means of which land, people and their possessions were brought under Castilian control, prepared the way for its spiritual conquest. In order to Christianise, it was first necessary to civilise and subdue. The functions of Church and state were thus mutually dependent upon one another in the colonial enterprise. However, that dependency also bred conflict. In the subjugation of the Indians to their secular and spiritual will, were Spaniards not stepping over the bounds of natural law which conferred certain mutual rights and duties on civilised and non-civilised societies alike? Such fundamental questions exercised the minds of many leading intellectuals of the day, members of the Dominican order prominent among them.

The instigator of the jurisdictional debate was the Dominican friar Antonio de Montesinos, one of the first missionaries to arrive on the island of Hispaniola. In December 1511, he delivered an historic sermon at Santo Domingo in the founding church of the Christian mission in New Spain. Speaking to a congregation of Spanish settlers and officials – the beneficiaries of Indian labour and tribute under the semi-feudal institution known as the *encomienda* – he caused major public scandal by openly attacking their inhuman treatment of the indigenous population: 'Tell me, by what right or justice do you keep these Indians in such a cruel and horrific servitude? On what authority have you waged a detestable war against these people, who dwelt quietly and peacefully on their own land? ... Are these not men? Have they not rational souls? Are you not bound to love them as you love yourselves?' he protested.[3] Fellow Dominican friars took up the cause. Having failed to shake the settlers' consciences, Montesinos returned to Spain to appeal directly to the crown. As a result of his initiative, the Laws of Burgos – a detailed code of practice regulating settlers' treatment of the Indian population – were published in December 1512. The laws marked the first attempt to incorporate a sense of justice into the colonisation of the New World. Meanwhile the intellectual debate gathered momentum.

Opinion was divided into two main groups. On the one hand there were those who regarded pre-conquest Indian society as a valid one, despite its ignorance of Christianity, and wished to protect the indigenous population from exploitation and safeguard their spiritual welfare. On the other, there were those who looked upon the Indians as inferior, defective human beings who needed to be subjugated to the will of the conquerors and coerced into accepting their belief system. The Dominican friar Francisco de Vitoria, a distinguished humanist scholar, professor of theology and founder of international law, gave a series of lectures on the subject of Spain's legal title to the Indies at Salamanca in the late 1530s. In his lecture entitled *Relectio de Indis*, delivered in 1539, he raised a series of fundamental doubts as to the foundation and exercise of power by the Emperor in the New World. He argued that all communities, whether Christian or non-Christian, possessed legitimate rights to their own property and to self-governance. The law of nations (*jus gentium*), so he claimed, gave every nation the right to engage in peaceful commercial and missionary interchange with other nations. Only if resistance was offered to either of these activities could war justifiably be waged. Despite this concession to the legitimacy of Spanish rule, Vitoria remained deeply sceptical: 'I personally have no doubt that the Spaniards were compelled to use force and arms in order to continue their work there; although I fear that measures were adopted in excess of what is allowed by human and divine law', he confirmed.[4] His bold public opinions on Spain's right to reduce the native peoples of America to its will by force, although silenced by the Emperor, Charles V, soon prompted an explosion of treatises on the subject.

Bartolomé de Las Casas was perhaps the most outspoken critic of Spanish colonialism in the New World.[5] In August 1514, after personally witnessing first as a *conquistador* and then as an *encomendero* in Cuba the tyranny under which the Indian population lived, he publicly denounced the treatment of the natives by the colonists and renounced his temporal responsibilities. He was to spend the remaining 52 years of his life combining his role as a combative Dominican friar in the New World with that of a powerful politician at the Spanish court, passionately defending the rights of the Indian community to retain their own property and be governed by their own rulers, rights which he believed had been usurped by the Spanish settlers. In 1516, Las Casas was officially proclaimed 'Protector of the Indians' in recognition of his humanitarian efforts in respect of the native population. He had great faith in the ability of the Amerindians to adapt to the customs of civilised society, as he reflected in his will: 'I have had no other interests but this: to liberate [the Indians] from the violent deaths which they have suffered and suffer... through compassion at seeing so many multitudes of people who are... so well equipped to receive our Holy Catholic Faith.'[6] He recommended that their conversion to Christianity be directed exclusively by mendicant friars. He held the Indians in deep personal affection and his controversial interventions on their behalf were inspired by a genuine humanitarian concern for their welfare. In 1542 he wrote *A Brief Account of the Destruction of the Indies*, in which he described with great passion the atrocities committed by Spaniards against innocent Indians and prophesied that such actions would lead to the conquering nation's own destruction. When *A Brief Account* was published ten years later, it provided Spain's Protestant enemies with precisely the evidence they needed to further the 'Black Legend' campaign. A stereotypical image of the barbarity and bigotry that underpinned Spanish imperialism thus became impressed upon the minds of future generations of Europeans.

Las Casas's philosophy was underlined by his political objection to the *encomienda* system, by means of which Spanish settlers acquired the right to exact taxes and service from a settlement of Indians in return for providing them with protection and religious instruction. Las Casas believed that the *encomenderos*, as semi-feudal overlords, were directly responsible for the brutal exploitation and maltreatment of their Indian serfs. 'The reason the Christians have murdered on such a vast scale and killed everyone in their way is purely and simply greed. They have set out to line their pockets with gold and to amass private fortunes as quickly as possible so that they can then assume a status quite at odds with that into which they were born', he claimed.[7] He urged the crown, as the ultimate defender of justice and the Christian faith, to reclaim its authority over its Amerindian subjects, so liberating them from their rapacious oppressors. His arguments opened up the underlying rivalry between the settler community, supported by members of the Council of the Indies, who regarded the native population as their slaves, and mendicant missionaries, who by contrast looked to their spiritual salvation. A *Junta*, set up by the Emperor, produced legal proposals in 1542 for abolishing *encomenderos*' right to demand personal service of their Indian serfs who would become instead vassals of the king. The Indians were to be recognised as equals of the Spaniards in human dignity and status. The 'New Laws', as they were known, produced a hostile response from the *encomenderos* in the Indies and their lobbyists in government, who soon found powerful allies in the religious orders. Although opposed to the barbarous treatment of the Indians, the mendicants increasingly found it more beneficial to work with rather than against the colonists in protecting their own privileged positions which were increasingly threatened from mid-century as the secular clergy became engaged in regaining some of the ground they had lost to the mendicants during the initial stages of conquest. Las Casas's idealism, in part, fell victim to these changing circumstances.

The opposition to Las Casas's policy of pacific persuasion was led at court by one of the most learned men of the age, the Aristotelian scholar, jurist, theologian and royal historian, master of Latin and Greek Juan Ginés de Sepúlveda.[8] In 1542, as Las Casas wrote his *Destruction of the Indies*, Sepúlveda (who, by contrast, had no first-hand knowledge of the New World) penned his famous treatise *Democrates Alter*, in which he set out his theory on the legitimacy of the *conquistadores* waging war on the Indian population in pursuit of their civilising aims, given the naturally inferior, barbaric status of the native population. Spain, as the superior nation, was perfectly justified in subjecting heathen races to its will since they were, in his words, '[peoples] who require by their own nature and in their own interests to be placed under the authority of civilised and virtuous princes and nations, so that they may learn from the might, wisdom and law of their conquerors to practice better morals, worthier customs and a more civilised way of life'.[9] This tutelar role, according to Sepúlveda, would best be performed by members of the settler community, the people whom Las Casas so despised.

In 1548 Sepúlveda's treatise, alternatively titled *The Just Causes of War against the Indians*, was scrutinised on behalf of the crown by two leading Dominican theologians from the University of Salamanca, Melchor Cano and Bartolomé de Carranza. They recommended that no royal licence be granted for such an inflammatory work. In April 1550 the Emperor, Charles V, in view of the controversy unleashed by the increasingly bitter debate over the ethics of conquest, was forced to suspend temporarily all missionary expeditions, known as *entradas*, in the New World. Sepúlveda, angered by the rejection of his work, pressed to have his case heard. Four months later, in August 1550, he and Las Casas were called to Valladolid to put their arguments forward before a panel of theologians, jurists and government officials. The stage was set for potentially one of the greatest intellectual combats of the early modern era in which the pacifist, Las Casas, met the militant, Sepúlveda, to determine the rules of imperial conquest. In practice there was no head-on clash between the two participants. Despite their differences of opinion over the treatment of the native population, they were at one in acknowledging the primacy of Spain's Christianising mission and the just use of force in the face of resistance. No final verdict was ever issued. This was a measure, perhaps, of the strength of complementary arguments put forward on both sides and the risk that an open condemnation of colonial policy might have had a deleterious effect on the crown. The intellectual debate between those sceptical of the ethical foundation of Spain's overseas mission and those who supported the imperial ambitions of the crown ran parallel to that current in Spanish society, where, as we have seen, the advocates of spiritual and intellectual freedom interacted with theologians of strictly orthodox tradition. Unofficially, Charles V was clearly more predisposed towards the ideals of Las Casas, supporting as they did the superior jurisdiction of royal as opposed to settler authority over his distant subjects. Sepúlveda was refused a licence to publish his *Democrates Alter*, but nevertheless retained his official position at court as royal historiographer. Over 20 years later, in 1573, Juan de Ovando, President of the Council of the Indies, published the *Ordenanzas sobre descubrimientos*. These new laws determined that Spaniards were in future to be sent on missions of 'pacification' to the Indies, rather than of 'conquest'. Las Casas's lifelong mission, to prove that 'all peoples of the world are men', was belatedly acknowledged in government policy. As the new rules were issued and the debate subsided, the successful age of colonial expansion and missionary enterprise in the New World had effectively run its course.

Missionary Euphoria

The Church in the Indies was originally conceived as a missionary Church, within which the religious orders were to play a leading role. The propagation of the Christian faith was regarded as a serious undertaking by the first Spanish colonisers. Columbus acknowledged his primary religious purpose (an extension of the campaign to eradicate all traces of Jewish and Moorish belief from the Spanish kingdoms) in the journal of his first voyage:

> Your Highnesses, as Catholic Christians and princes devoted to the Holy Christian Faith and the furtherance of its cause, and enemies of the sect of Mohammed and of all idolatry and heresy, resolved to send me, Christopher Columbus, to the said regions of India to see the said princes and the peoples and lands and determine the nature of them and of all other things, and the measures to be taken to convert them to our Holy Faith.[10]

As each new settlement of Indians was discovered, conquered and subdued, its members were formally required, as subjects of the Crown of Castile, to submit to the superior spiritual authority of the Church of Rome. They were to be gently persuaded to abandon their worship of pagan idols and to allow missionaries to instruct them in the ways of Christianity. The evangelising role of the early friars was to become equal in importance to the military role of the first *conquistadores* in establishing a Spanish presence in the New World. As the work of colonisation advanced, however, the spiritual and secular functions of conquest were to enter increasingly into conflict with one another.

The initial enterprise was characterised by a genuine spirit of optimism and euphoria. Mendicant friars, drawn principally from the Franciscan, Dominican and Augustinian orders, undertook the formidable task of establishing a Christian civilisation in the New World within half a century of its discovery. Their achievement was all the more remarkable given the unknown nature of the lands in which they worked and the complexity of their unfolding task. They were faced with the challenging task of confrontation with alien societies and belief systems upon which they sought to impose what they considered to be the only acceptable definition of doctrinal and behavioural civility, that based on the 'superior' Old Christian and European model. Part of the success of their mission can be attributed to the energy and dynamism that underpinned the pre-Reformation Church in peninsular Spain, of which they were the product. The missionary enterprise had been prepared well in advance within the framework of Ferdinand and Isabella's ecclesiastical reform programme, incorporating a 'root and branch' reform of the religious orders. Cardinal Cisneros's eradication of licence and liberty within the conventual branch of his own Franciscan order and his promotion of piety and learning within its observant body paved the way for the expansion of a highly trained, disciplined and dedicated 'spiritual militia' of mendicant friars, ready to undertake the campaign of conversion in newly discovered overseas territories.

The majority of early missionaries and prelates of New Spain were schooled in the humanist tradition, which had exercised such a profound influence on the intellectual climate of northern Europe in the opening decades of the sixteenth century. But while humanism was quickly suppressed in Spain, it flourished in the New World. Imbued with the spirit of reform and inspired by the ideals of Renaissance humanism, the founding generation of missionaries took on the challenge of delivering Christianity to the primitive peoples of the New World with great enthusiasm. The apparent ease and willingness with which the Indians flocked to hear the Christian message and submitted to baptism provided them with convincing evidence of the rebirth of the early church of the apostles in the American continent. The Franciscan friar Juan de Zumárraga, the first Archbishop of Mexico (1527–48), was influenced by the teachings of Erasmus and Sir Thomas More, as well as by the example of Archbishop Talavera in Granada, in seeking to build a perfect Christian society among the native Aztec population of New Spain. In 1547 he published a *Doctrina breve* – a manual for use by the Mexican clergy – and a *Doctrina cristiana* – a catechism for Christianised Indians – works of Erasmian inspiration. At the Colegio de Santa Cruz at Tlatelolco in Mexico City, founded in 1536, Zumárraga supported a programme for the translation of the Scriptures into native Indian languages and the training of native clergy. His work incorporated the full application of Christian-humanist ideals to the American mission.

The earliest missionaries were Dominicans, but it was the Franciscans, armed with papal privileges and autonomous powers, who were responsible for much of the early evangelisation of New Spain. Cortés himself wrote to the Emperor to request their assistance. A papal bull of 1522 (known as the *Omnímoda*) charged the Franciscans with the Mexican mission. Furthermore, it allowed them to carry out their pioneering work of conversion free from episcopal control. A symbolic group of 12 friars of the province of San Gabriel journeyed across the Atlantic in 1524, under the leadership of Fray Martín de Valencia, to begin their mission within the heart of the former Aztec empire. They were joined by Dominican friars in 1526 and by Augustinians in 1533. It was reported that the Franciscan missionaries were responsible for baptising a million Mexicans in the period up to 1531 and that by 1536 a further four million had been baptised, evidence of the realisation of the Franciscans' millenarian mission. The virtues of the Indian – his simplicity and relative poverty, together with his obedient, docile nature – accorded with the Franciscan order's own ideals and helped foster a close relationship between them. By mid-century there were over 800 friars in New Spain, forging a 'golden age' of mendicant evangelical enterprise.[11]

In order to convert or 'reduce' the native Indian population to Christianity their existing belief systems had to be dismantled.[12] This proved to be a difficult task since practice varied within each community. While cannibalism and human sacrifice were characteristics of certain native Amerindian religions, idolatry and a belief in cult heroes were prominent features of others. The language barrier was initially overcome by the use of interpreters and sign language. Missionaries soon took it upon themselves to learn native tongues in order to reach out directly to the people. Given the small number of friars available, Indians were encouraged to resettle in segregated, self-sufficient urban communities (known as *reducciones de indios*) rather than in their scattered rural habitats, so that the preaching of Christianity and mass baptisms could be carried out more effectively and their spiritual development be closely supervised. Initial religious instruction was very simple. It was later supplemented by catechism training, consolidated through the use of music, drama and mime. Missionary friars developed an insight into Indian psychology, which enabled them to adapt the ritual and ceremonial of native religious culture to that of Christian worship. All the prominent devotional features of orthodox practice in Counter-Reformation Spain were transferred to the New World. The veneration of saints and devotions to souls in purgatory were promoted as a substitute for the worship of pagan gods and ancestral idols (known as *huacas*). Crosses were erected in newly conquered areas to extinguish old non-Christian loyalties and re-sanctify Indian society. The building of churches and chapels using Indian labour served to channel energies and replace the splendour of lost pagan temples. In the period up to 1576, some 270 churches were established in New Spain. At the height of the missionary enterprise there were less than a thousand mendicants in New Spain ministering to several million Amerindians. The early stages of the evangelisation process were conducted with military-like precision. The friars' success was aided by the political and ethnic divisions to be found within Indian society. As a result, the native population was more ready to accept change. During the first half of the sixteenth century the mendicant friars, favoured by the first two viceroys of New Spain and by the Archbishop of Mexico, Juan de Zumárraga, exercised a completely free hand in shaping the development of the Christian Church in the New World and in ensuring its allegiance to the will of the crown. However, their supremacy in the evangelical mission was soon to be challenged by that of the secular clergy. At the same time, evidence began to emerge of spiritual and moral backsliding among the newly converted native population, resulting in a growing sense of disillusionment within the missionary community at the capacity of the Indian to embrace Christianity fully. This change of attitude coincided with the optimistic view of human nature current in Renaissance Europe giving ground before a renewed emphasis on the innate sinfulness and depravity of man, which was fostered by Counter-Reformation teachings. When a *Junta* of Mexican clergy met in 1532, they insisted on the spiritual and intellectual capacity of the native Indian. Just over 20 years later, delegates at the first Mexican Provincial Council of 1555 drew attention to their intellectual weakness, their inconsistency and their natural inclination to vice. By the time the third Mexican Council met in 1585, it was being argued that since Indians were of base and imperfect character, 'they should be ruled, governed and guided to their appointed end by fear more than by love'.[13] The paternalistic approach gradually gave way to one of mistrust and contempt.

A Clash of Cultures

During the second decade of the Mexican mission, it was discovered that many Indians, baptised into the Christian faith, were continuing to practise their pagan rites clandestinely. The millenarian optimism was fading. The theory of the primeval innocence of the Indian was rapidly being replaced by a growing awareness of the influence of the devil in indigenous cultures. In a letter to Charles V, Fray Toribio de Motolinía (who had initially shared the millenarian optimism of the early evangelists) confirmed that the Indians were guilty of concealing their idols 'at the foot of crosses or beneath the stones of the altar steps, pretending they were venerating the cross, when they were in fact adoring the devil'.[14] Idolatry was deemed to be so widespread that in 1571 Juan de Zumárraga, whose humanist outlook had so inspired early evangelisation initiatives in New Spain, felt it necessary in his capacity as Inquisitor General to implement the first inquisitorial investigations against the practice of idolatry among the indigenous population. In the pre-Reformation period there had been considerable scepticism over the extent to which the devil could influence human will. There was widespread confidence in the power of the Church to defeat diabolism. Attitudes changed following the Council of Trent's endorsement of the Ten Commandments as indicative of the moral obligations of Christians and their insistence that idolatry was a primary offence against God and nature. It also served the interests of the crown's imperial policy to stress the diabolic nature of Indian religions and their subverting influence, thereby justifying its brutal condemnation of them. 'Under the guise and appearance of religion, they dealt with their own rites, giving cult to the Devil and plotting against our Christian religion', observed Friar Pedro de Feria in his *Revelación sobre la reincidencia en sus idolatrías de los Indios de Chiapa después de treinta años de Cristianos* of 1584.[15] The Jesuit historian and missionary José de Acosta took a more sympathetic approach in his *Historia natural y moral de las Indias* (the first ambitious attempt to describe the behaviour, patterns of belief and past history of the American Indian), published in 1590. He stressed the natural goodness of Indian cultures and their need to preserve those elements of indigenous belief systems that did not conflict with their practice of Christianity.[16] In Acosta's opinion, the Indians were not necessarily submitting to the whims of the devil by their reluctance to abandon their ancestral rites and ceremonies. Rather, their behaviour was not far removed from that of the majority of the Castilian peasantry whose local saints were regarded as resident patrons of their communities in the same way as tutelary gods were revered by the indigenous peoples of Central America. But Acosta's objective explanation and acceptance of religious intermixture soon gave way to scepticism and fierce condemnation. Once he came face to face with the Indian, he recognised the invincible supernatural force of the devil that lay at the heart of their inverted religious practices. Diabolism was to become a major preoccupation of the Mexican and Peruvian Inquisitions in the seventeenth century.

The disillusionment that characterised the spiritual conquest of New Spain in the second half of the sixteenth century was duplicated, if not intensified, in that of Peru. The progress of evangelisation was slower in the Andes in comparison to the Mexican mission on account of geographical constraints. In addition, the Peruvian missionary enterprise, which was led by the Jesuits from 1569 (the last of the major religious orders to undertake missionary work in the Americas), met with a mixed response. Practice varied from place to place and from individual to individual. Christianity was neither wholly accepted nor wholly rejected. Many Andean Indians, baptised into the Catholic Church, continued to practise their old rites and ceremonies within their own communities, as was the case with Spain's own New Christian community. The practice of 'syncretic religion' (simultaneous belief in the Christian God and the pre-Conquest deities) was commonplace. This ambivalent approach prompted one of the pioneer Jesuit missionaries to exclaim in despair that the Amerindians 'were like the Moors of Granada, in that all, or most of them, have only the name of Christians and practice only the outward ceremonies'.[17] Such admissions, which revealed the growing intolerance of churchmen towards the native population, led to a questioning of the efficacy of the missionaries' methods and the ethics of reducing Indians to an alien form of belief and way of life without any real understanding of their culture or regard for the social and psychological consequences of their actions. Early missionaries had adopted the model of conversion by persuasion. Subsequently, convinced that Andean peoples were inferior and therefore could not sustain an understanding of Christianity, they opted for religious coercion. Missionary campaigns began with the physical destruction of ancestral stone idols known as *huacas* (central features of pagan culture) and the break-up of local rural communities. This policy gave rise to a mutual distrust between natives and friars. It led, furthermore, to a much-diluted form of religious instruction being offered to the 'simple-minded' Indian that failed both to eradicate indigenous belief systems and to foster a lasting conviction of the truth of Christianity. The so-called 'idolatry campaigns' of the early seventeenth century, conducted in the style of inquisitorial investigations, revealed that in many areas the worship of pagan gods continued.

By seeking refuge in their ancient culture, the Peruvian Indians demonstrated their alienation from that of their conquerors. The removal of bodies from Christian cemeteries and their reburial next to their ancestors in traditional burial grounds was part of an overall reaffirmation of their non-Christian values and traditions. While the ostensible aim of the idolatry investigations was to induce the natives to return to the fold of the Christian faith via preaching and instruction, in practice the pedagogical objective often took second place to efforts to punish and humiliate Andean spiritual leaders and denounce their pagan values. The rigorous persecution of popular religious practice (which forced the Jesuits to withdraw their cooperation from the exercise in the 1650s) effectively cancelled the corrective purpose of the campaigns. Instead they spread a form of resentment and hatred which gave way to the survival of forms of 'religious intermixture' and a strong aversion to what was heralded as official Christianity.[18] Sabine MacCormack has observed that Spanish missionaries 'were never able to translate Christianity into native terms: that is, to separate Christianity from its European cultural, sociological, and even political framework'.[19] Hence there were effectively two civilisations and two Churches in post-conquest Peru: those of the Indians and those of the Spaniards. There are clear parallels to be drawn here between the vain attempts by the Spanish Church in the motherland to integrate fully Jewish and Moorish converts into the Christian faith and their punishment at the hands of the Inquisition for religious backsliding.

The failure to produce a native priesthood was a consequence of the failure properly to integrate the indigenous population into the Christian fold. The *Patronato de las Indias* had made no reference to the exclusion of native clergy from the Church. Rather it was envisaged that, with appropriate education and training, Amerindians would eventually be admitted to minor orders and welcomed into the priesthood, where they would help strengthen acceptance of Christianity among the indigenous population. But by the middle of the sixteenth century, the kind of prejudice characteristic of the Spanish Church's relationship with *conversos* and *moriscos* was duplicated in its attitude towards the admittance of native clergy into the American Church. The first (1555) and second (1556) Mexican Provincial Councils denied Amerindians admission to holy orders. The post-Tridentine period saw some relaxation of this ethnocentric policy, but in practice the exclusion order was retained. There was, as we have seen, a growing attitude of mistrust emerging within colonial society towards the native population, whom they regarded as inferior beings in terms of their race, intellect and civility. In 1599, the Mercedarian friar Gregorio de Mendieta reinforced this notion in his *Historia Eclesiástica Indiana*, in which he wrote: 'The majority of them are not fitted to command or rule, but to be commanded and ruled. I mean to say that they are not fitted for masters but for pupils, not for prelates but for subjects, and as such they are the best in the world.'[20] The seventeenth century witnessed some attempt to redress the balance. In 1618, the Franciscans of New Spain allowed for Spaniards and Creoles (born in the Indies of Hispanic parentage) to be admitted alternately as members of the order. At the same time, Creoles began to be accepted into the episcopate. In 1668 the Archbishop of Quito, Fray Alonso de la Peña Montenegro, published a guide for parish priests in Spanish America. In it he argued forcefully that Amerindians should be allowed to take holy orders, contradicting much crown and colonial legislation on the matter. He also supported the ordination of *mestizos* (those of mixed Spanish and Amerindian origin) provided they were of legitimate birth and appropriate training. His remained a lone cry for the formation of an indigenous clergy in the New World. The Spanish American Church was to remain overwhelmingly peninsular in its outlook and composition until the second half of the eighteenth century.

Divisions of Authority

The colonial Church in the New World became fully established during the second half of the sixteenth century under firm episcopal administration and direction. Bishops, their authority reaffirmed via the decrees of Trent and further strengthened by their colonial responsibilities, were to be instrumental during this period in transferring the pastoral mission from the privileged mendicant orders to the secular clergy, thus altering the whole balance of authority within the colonial Church. Amidst conflict and struggle, the energetic involvement of a new influx of university-trained clergy – the product of post-Tridentine initiatives to professionalise the clerical estate – charged with the spiritual direction of the Amerindian community and their submission to the social and political order, was eventually to replace the dwindling enthusiasm of the missionary friars.

Dioceses were set up immediately after the colonisation of a new region. The first to be established was that of Santo Domingo in 1512, soon to become the primate church of the Indies. By 1550, when most of the pioneering work of military and missionary conquest was complete, there were 22 dioceses in Spanish America. A further 9 sees were created in the period 1551–77, and only 5 more were added in the course of the seventeenth century. Theologically trained bishops were preferred in appointments made during the period 1516–1620, the majority originating from the Dominican (31 per cent), the Franciscan (23 per cent) and the Augustinian orders (10 per cent).[21] The diocese was to become a vital centre of ecclesiastical activity and initiative, from which the consecration of clergy, the training of priests and the carrying out of missionary work were all coordinated. Following Tridentine recommendations, 25 diocesan synods were held in the period 1555–1631, implementing legislation approved at provincial church level. New World bishops also exercised an important civil function, taking responsibility for the execution of laws and directives from the secular authorities.

During the second half of the sixteenth century, the mendicant friars found their semi-autonomous status placed under ever-increasing threat by the ascendancy of the secular clergy. In the context of the Church in the New World, the secular clergy were initially regarded by their regular counterparts as lesser churchmen, unsuited to undertaking the spiritual direction of the Indian peoples – a task exclusively entrusted to the mendicants during the height of the missionary enterprise of New Spain. This situation was set to change from mid-century as a result of two factors. Firstly, in settled areas the missionary role of the mendicant friar had effectively become obsolete once the spiritual conquest was complete. Following successful missions, friars took on a pastoral role, establishing *doctrinas* (parish-like centres for Christian instruction). Secondly, the episcopal hierarchy, armed with increased powers following Trent, sought to place secular rather than regular clergy in newly created parishes, their charge being to impose the revised definition of orthodoxy that had emerged from the council on the Spanish American Church. Prominent among New World prelates was Fray Alonso de Montúfar, the second Archbishop of Mexico (1554–71), who openly clashed with Franciscans, Augustinians and liberal members of his own Dominican order. The mendicants, some of whom exercised spiritual and temporal powers over the natives, staunchly resisted any challenge to their position, going so far as to discourage the Indian population from paying the tithe – a vital source of financial support for the diocesan and parochial clergy. Philip II, who retained his preference for secular over regular clergy in all aspects of ecclesiastical administration, sought to settle the widening rift between the two branches of the colonial Church by approving legislation that defined their respective roles. The royal *Ordenanza del Patronazgo* of 1574 effectively subordinated the role of the regular clergy in the New World by removing their now anomalous privileges and subjecting them to strict episcopal control. Each bishop now had direct authority over the movement and employment of friars in his diocese. Although they were now second choice candidates in presentations to livings, members of the religious orders continued to be actively employed in frontier zones. Once they had completed their task of 'pacifying' border regions and had converted the Amerindian community (a process which could take ten years or more), they were expected to pass on their responsibilities to secular priests.

The clash of interest and ideology to be found in the Spanish American Church between the idealistic fervour prominent within the religious orders, the product of pre-Reformation initiatives within the Church, and the strict orthodoxy embodied in its secular clergy, schooled in the post-Tridentine tradition, continued beyond the new legislation of the 1570s. This struggle had its counterpart in Spain where, as we have seen, different 'voices' within the Church adopted varied and sometimes conflicting approaches to reform. It was also part of a wider power struggle within the ruling hierarchy. Beneath the success of Spain's colonial enterprise there existed a network of competing interest groups. In the same way that *conquistadores* and *encomenderos*, viceroys and members of the *audiencia* worked both with and against one another in carrying out their designated roles, so mendicant friars struggled to preserve their missionary function in the New World against the rising competition of a new generation of ecclesiastical administrators drawn from the secular clergy.

Conclusion

The history of the colonisation and the evangelisation of New World territories is a history of tension and conflict between two different civilisations with competing ideologies, cultures and traditions. The extraordinary concentration of temporal and ecclesiastical authority in the hands of the Spanish crown blurred the dividing line between Church and state policy in the New World. It opened up the controversial debate over how the spiritual objectives of colonial rule could be reconciled with its secular aims, in particular the exploitation of the Indies for material gain. There was also a clash of authority and approach within the New World Church between the Renaissance–humanist ideals of the early missionary friars and the more rigid orthodoxy that emanated from the Council of Trent, promoted by the secular clergy. The initial euphoria generated by the prospect of establishing a utopian civilisation among the indigenous peoples of the New World soon gave way to pessimism and despair. By their own admission, the conquerors only succeeded in imposing a superficial level of belief on the native population, many of whom continued to practise their pagan cults under the influence of the devil. The Christianisation of the New World, for all its outward success, was never as complete or as effective as the missionary friars had intended it to be. The conquering nation imposed an alien set of spiritual beliefs and secular values on the Amerindian peoples. They were unable to cross the cultural boundary and accept any compromise between their European view of the world and the non-European experience of their colonial subjects. As a result there remained a huge gulf between the theory and practice of Christian belief where the majority of Indians in post-conquest Mexico and Peru were concerned.

Table 5.1 A chronology of the conquest and evangelisation of the New World, 1492–1575

1492	Columbus's first voyage of discovery
1493	Bull *Inter caetera divinae*
1494	Columbus's second voyage of discovery
1498	Columbus's third voyage of discovery
1501	Nicolas de Ovando nominated Governor of the Indies
1502	Columbus's fourth voyage of discovery
1503	Foundation of the *Casa de Contratación* in Seville
1506	Death of Columbus
1508	Bull *Universalis ecclesiae regimini*, establishing royal rights of patronage over the Church in the Indies. Diego de Colón nominated Governor of the Indies
1510	Arrival of the Dominicans on the island of La Española
1511	Anti-settler sermon of Antonio de Montesinos
1512	Law of Burgos: regulation of *ecomiendas*. First Bishop, Alonso Manso, arrives in the Indies
1513	Discovery of Florida by Juan Ponce de León
1514	Evangelisation of region of Cumaná by the Dominicans

Table 5.1 (*continued*)

1515	Discovery of Río de Plata by Juan Díaz de Solis
1516	Bartolomé de Las Casas named 'Protector of the Indies'
1519	Major epidemic in New Spain
1520	Discovery of Straits of Magellan
1521	Hernán Cortés conquers Mexico. Beginning of construction of primate cathedral of Santo Domingo
1522	Cortés made Governor and Captain General of New Spain. Franciscans invited to undertake Mexican mission (*Omnímoda*)
1523	Expeditions to Central America by Pedro de Alvarado. Council of the Indies established
1524	Franciscans arrive in New Spain and begin mass conversion programme
1525	Dominicans arrive in New Spain
1526	Fray Juan de Zumárraga (OSF) nominated as first Bishop of Mexico
1533	Augustinians arrive in New Spain. Pizarro enters Cuzco
1534	Discovery of silver mines of Taxco
1539	Francisco de Vitoria's lectures at Salamanca on Spain's legal title to the Indies (*Relectio de Indis*)
1542	Las Casas writes *A Brief Account of the Destruction of the Indies*. Sepúlveda writes *The Just Causes of War against the Indians* (*Democrates Alter*)
1545	Discovery of the silver mines of Potosí in Peru
1546	Creation of archbishoprics of Santo Domingo, Mexico and Lima
1547	Discovery of mines at Guanajuato
1550	Debate in Valladolid between Las Casas and Sepúlveda
1551	Discovery of mines at Pachuca near Mexico. First Church Council of Lima
1555	First Mexican Church Council
1556	Second Mexican Church Council
1569	Arrival of the Jesuits in Peru
1570	Establishment of first tribunal of Inquisition in Lima
1571	Establishment of second tribunal of Inquisition in Mexico
1573	*Ordenanzas sobre descubrimientos*: missions of pacification, not conquest
1574	*Ordenanzas de Patronazgo*: regular clergy subject to episcopal authority

Source: *Historia General de España y América*, vol. 7 (Madrid, 1982), pp. 802–17.

6 *Crisis and Resilience in the Early Seventeenth-Century Spanish Church*

Introduction: Crisis in Castile

The death of Philip II and the accession of Philip III provided the opportunity for Spaniards in general, and for Castilians in particular, to reflect upon the current condition of their kingdoms and assess their prospects for the future. As one century drew to a close and another began, their fortunes indeed looked bleak. They observed around them the catastrophic level of human devastation wrought by hunger and contagious disease. Between 1596 and 1602, some 600 000 Castilians (9 per cent of the kingdom's population) fell victim to the virulent bubonic plague which swept through the peninsula from the north, striking hardest in Old Castile and leaving in its wake a considerably weakened society. Castilians also bore the consequences of an acute agrarian crisis, provoked by a series of poor harvests and worsening climatic conditions, which led to severe food shortages and the spiralling of grain prices. The so-called 'flight from the land', which took place in the closing decades of the sixteenth century as a result of the increasing unprofitability of Castilian agriculture, led to the import of foreign grain to meet domestic needs. Furthermore, Castilians were subject to escalating fiscal pressures, prompted by the high cost of foreign warfare and the crown's heavy debts. From 1590, a new direct tax, known as the *millones*, was levied in Castile on basic foodstuffs; although it was a universal subsidy to which the privileged estates were also subject, it nevertheless further increased the tax burden of the masses, already victims of the prevailing subsistence crisis, and sharpened divisions between the 'haves' and the 'have nots'. The severe crisis which society faced at the end of the old century, demographic and economic in its broad dimensions, was set to intensify as the new era dawned.[1]

In the later years of his reign, Philip II was inundated with advice on how to regenerate the health and wealth of his kingdoms. This trend continued under his successor. The opening decades of the seventeenth century, in particular the period 1615–25, saw the publication of an unprecedented volume of writings focusing on Spain's ailing condition. The debate was led by a heterogeneous group of commentators, collectively known as the *arbitristas* – including economists, theologians, political and moral philosophers – who put forward diverse remedies (*arbitrios*) for curing the ills afflicting the body politic. Their arguments were also taken up by members of central and local government, as well as by foreign observers, academics and literary figures. When viewed collectively, they provide historians with a unique insight into how Spaniards perceived their own predicament. The deep sense of depression felt by contemporaries at the condition of their country inevitably led them to distort and exaggerate the gravity of the prevailing situation. In our appreciation of their writings, therefore, we need to distinguish between the factual, the impressionistic and the polemical.[2]

The early seventeenth-century Spanish Church found itself in the peculiar position of contributing to and at the same time profiting from the prevailing crisis, rather than being on the receiving end of it. Its privileged role in society ensured that it weathered the storm much more successfully than did other sectors. As a result, it naturally became the focus of much criticism. But, as we shall see, those who attacked the Church often included those who patronised and protected it. This chapter will attempt to explain the anomalies that underpinned the Church's position in early seventeenth-century Spanish society. It will examine the critical evidence and evaluate the Church's response to it.

Arbitrismo and the Church

The *arbitristas* focused considerable attention on the contribution of the Church to the crisis in which the country found itself. They were motivated by a number of common concerns. The excessive growth of the clerical estate, so they argued, had created a demographic imbalance, seriously reducing the size of the potential labour force. As a profession, the Church encouraged idleness and a disinterest in economically productive activities. The exemptions and privileges enjoyed by the clergy were regarded as having a polarising effect on society, elevating those of clerical status and accentuating the plight of those who carried the burden of service and tribute. Contemporaries observed that a disproportionate amount of wealth had been absorbed by the clerical estate, instead of being channelled into more productive areas of investment. At certain levels, the Church had also allowed itself to succumb to corrupt practices of preferment. The fundamental perception that many people held of the Church, beyond the small *arbitrista* circle, was that of an institution responsible for taking away the potential force and vitality of an ailing nation, for widening the contrast between privilege and poverty in society, and for readily accepting the ill-prepared into its ranks. The publication of anticlerical views of this sort was of course not a new phenomenon, nor was it exclusively a lay activity. However, it acquired a special intensity in early seventeenth-century Castile, where criticism of the Church was not necessarily incompatible with dutiful devotion to its teachings. It was paradoxical that controversial opinions in respect of the Church were allowed to enter into public debate at a time in Spain's history when Catholicism held such political as well as ideological sway.

Many *arbitristas*, significantly, were members of the clerical profession itself. Sancho de Moncada was a priest and professor of theology at the University of Toledo. In his *Restauración Política de España* of 1619, he presented a series of proposals designed to increase Spain's prosperity. He drew a direct parallel between the harshness of economic circumstance and the increase in clerical recruitment. 'So many people enter the Church', he wrote, 'because they cannot survive in these times, and thus it is the poverty of the kingdom that forces them to become priests or religious, for they cannot pursue any other course and that is where the fault lies.'[3] According to Moncada, an ecclesiastical career was the only available means of survival for many. Reiterating the recommendations of Trent on clerical reform, he urged that a stricter control be exercised on the educational qualities of those seeking entry to the priesthood; likewise, only those with a true sense of vocation should join the religious orders. These measures, he argued, would serve to restore the social and fiscal imbalance, providing more people to engage in labour, commerce and agriculture, thus reducing the tax burden of the masses and raising royal revenues.

Licenciado Jerónimo de Ceballos, a Toledan lawyer and local councillor (*regidor*), published his *Discurso sobre el Remedio de la Monarquía Española* in 1620 – a treatise addressed to the monarch on how he might arrest Spain's decline, including a recommendation to reduce the size of the clerical estate. In it he referred to the privileged status a career in the Church could provide, irrespective of the worthiness of its members for office. 'Let us consider the large number of people who daily join the ranks of the clerical estate; with a mere sackcloth cassock on their backs they acquire honour and benefits with all the ease in the world, and obtain the licence to receive from everyone, but to give to no one',[4] he wrote. Ceballos took a more overtly critical line than Moncada, arguing that the Church provided easy immunity from civil justice, as well as the opportunity to escape social denigration in menial occupations. There was an ironic personal twist to his arguments. In 1625, following two unsuccessful applications, Ceballos was preferred to a prestigious New Kings chaplaincy within Toledo Cathedral – an honorary appointment reserved for loyal Toledan citizens. Despite his views on the lack of sincerity of many of those entering the profession, he eventually became a beneficiary of ecclesiastical office himself.

The Cistercian friar and university professor Ángel Manrique published a discourse in 1624 (entitled *Socorro del Clero al Estado*) in which he criticised the crown for encouraging the disproportionate growth of the clerical estate in relation to the needs of secular society. Too many clergy were being ordained and too many monasteries being founded, he argued. Ambition, greed and social vanity were all identified by Manrique as being motivating forces. 'Having a priest as a son turns a peasant into a nobleman; the office of canon transforms a merchant into a knight and if anyone reaches the heights of becoming a bishop, he brings unparalleled distinction to his lineage',[5] he noted. Here was a very direct criticism of the distorted honorific value attached to ecclesiastical office, coming from within its own senior ranks. Manrique became Bishop of Badajoz in 1645.

The canon of Santiago, royal chaplain and secretary Pedro Fernández de Navarrete published a treatise on the state of the monarchy in 1626 (*Conservación de Monarquías*), in which he criticised the Church for accepting men of little talent into the profession. Over 60 years after Trent's recommendations on ecclesiastical reform, Navarrete felt that church offices were still being dispensed too freely, without proper regard for the calibre or commitment of candidates, resulting in a lowering of moral and educational standards within its ranks. 'Many enter the Church without sufficient learning or qualifications..., without adequate benefices or income to support themselves; consequently one observes such a large number of mendicant clergy who bring shame on a profession, the reputation of which depends, if not on wealth, at least on sound background',[6] he observed. He called for a reduction in the foundation of religious houses and a more thorough examination of all those seeking admittance into holy orders. He also observed that while the Church amassed wealth in the form of land, property and vassals, it gave very little back in the form of charity. It thus represented a negative form of investment and contributed to the stagnation of the economy. These were harsh judgements that reveal something of the internal dilemmas that existed within the ecclesiastical estate over its own condition, reinforcing those concerns raised in the public debate.

Alongside the publication of *arbitrista* literature, criticism of the Church also surfaced from within the heart of government, where professional rivalries between churchmen and statesmen were often fought out. The *Junta de Reformación*, a sub-committee of the Council of Castile, was commissioned by the crown in 1618 to make recommendations on how to resolve the crisis affecting the kingdom. It was to place the reduction in size of the clerical estate high on the political agenda. In its famous *consulta* of 1 February 1619, the *Junta* expressed its concern at the growing number of churchmen residing unnecessarily at court, neglecting their pastoral obligations. It remarked upon the dangers of excessive recruitment to the religious orders and how this inevitably led to a relaxation of their rule, thereby overturning the objectives of reform. In its judgement, 'more people enter [the orders] fleeing from poverty and out of a desire for the sweet pleasures of a leisurely life, than out of a genuine sense of vocation'.[7] Attention was also drawn to the growth of inalienable Church property in contrast to the increasing hardships endured by lay society. In short, according to the 1619 report, the Church bore considerable responsibility for the demographic and economic stagnation of Castile.

These various critical viewpoints reveal a fundamental disquiet within both the clerical and lay sectors of society at the protection – legal, fiscal and professional – that membership of the Church offered, which not only cushioned it from the worst effects of the crisis but also allowed it to ignore its long-standing reforming obligations. The qualitative judgements of contemporary commentators now need to be examined in relation to the factual evidence.

The Clericalisation of Spanish Society

The *arbitristas* were commonly concerned about the clericalisation of Spanish society. A close examination of the 1591 fiscal census drawn up for the kingdom of Castile (and whose general trends can be applied to the Aragonese territories) suggests that these concerns may well have been exaggerated.[8] At the end of the sixteenth century there were 91 000 secular and regular clergy in Spain, 74 000 or 81 per cent of whom were concentrated in the kingdom of Castile and 17 000 or 18.6 per cent in the crown of Aragón. The ecclesiastical estate made up just over 1.1 per cent of the total population – hardly an exceptional figure. In broad geographical terms there was one member of the clerical estate for every 88 inhabitants. However, their regional distribution was distinctly uneven. The northern coastal areas of Galicia, Asturias and the Basque Lands, together with parts of the kingdom of Aragón, had the lowest proportion of clergy relative to inhabitants: a figure of up to 1 per cent. In the central Castilian provinces of León, Ávila, Cuenca and Segovia, as well as Valencia and Cartagena in the south-east, the concentration of clergy was slightly higher. Here they represented between 1 and 1.5 per cent of the population. In Catalonia, Extremadura, Salamanca, Toledo and Seville, the size of the clerical component of society exceeded 1.5 per cent. In the majority of diocesan capitals this figure was further surpassed. Around 75 per cent of clergy were based in towns whereas well over 80 per cent of the population lived in the countryside. Overall there was a slightly higher presence of clergy, both secular and regular, in the southern half of the kingdom of Castile than in the northern half. The following century witnessed a considerable alteration in the balance between the clerical and non-clerical components of Spanish society.[9]

A recurrent series of demographic catastrophes devastated the Spanish kingdoms during the first quarter of the seventeenth century, beginning with the great plague of 1596–1602. Close on 1 million Spaniards (some12.5 per cent of the total population) fell victim to epidemic disease, pestilence, expulsion and warfare during this period. The kingdom of Castile was worst affected by this crisis, set to intensify in the second quarter of the century in the wake of crop failures and famine, while a further wave of plague (1647–52) severely affected the Andalusian and Levant regions. The Castilian lay population is estimated to have fallen from around 6.5 million inhabitants in 1591 to 5 million in 1665, while that of Spain as a whole decreased from

Table 6.1 The clerical population of Castile and Aragón in 1591

Clergy	*Castile*		*Aragon*		*Spain*	
	No.	*%*	*No.*	*%*	*No.*	*%*
Secular	33 087	0.50	7 512	0.49	40 599	0.50
Regular (m)	20 697	0.31	4 748	0.31	25 445	0.31
Regular (f)	20 369	0.31	4 672	0.31	25 041	0.31
Total	74 153	1.12	16 932	1.11	91 085	1.12
Total number of inhabitants	6 534 098	100	1 503 086	100	8 046 184	100

Source: Felipe Ruiz Martín, 'La población Española al comienzo de los tiempos modernos', *Cuadernos de Historia*, vol. 1 (1967), pp. 189–202, and *idem*, 'Demografía Eclesiástica', *DHEE*, vol. 2 (Madrid, 1972), pp. 682–733.
Note: A coefficient of 5 inhabitants per household was used to calculate the size of the lay population.

around 8.5 million to 6.5 million over the same period. Against this background, the clerical estate underwent a rapid expansion in its size. By the mid-1660s there were an estimated 160 000 clergy in Spain, making up 2.5 per cent of the population. Each member of the clerical estate now served an average of 40 members of secular society. These calculations suggest that there were now more than twice as many clergy in relation to laity in mid-seventeenth-century Spain as there had been at the end of the sixteenth century.

No detailed census of the clerical estate equivalent to that drawn up for Castile in 1591 was available to early seventeenth-century contemporaries. They sensed growth rather than having actual numerical proof of it. Their calculations thus provide us with a somewhat speculative interpretation of clerical demography. In his treatise of 1619, Sancho de Moncada suggested that between a quarter and a third of Spain's population was made up of clergy. This was clearly a grossly exaggerated estimation (in 1591, as we have seen, the figure stood at just over 1 per cent). Fray Ángel Manrique wrote in 1624 of a doubling in the size of the clerical estate, an increase that more accurately refers to the period between 1591 and 1665. He also referred imprecisely to a tripling in the number of monasteries and convents. There was a total of 1326 religious communities (841 male and 485 female) in Castile at the end of the sixteenth century. By 1623 there were reported to be 2141 in Spain as a whole; this figure may have risen to 3000 by 1700.[10] Observers clearly had little or no conception of the relationship between secular and clerical demographic trends, nor were they apparently aware of the diversity affecting the geographical distribution and structural composition of the Church's membership. Their generalisations, therefore, have to be treated with some caution in the absence of more accurate data. Furthermore, we should also be aware that the peninsula's clerical population 'peaked' in the mid-1660s, after which lay society began to recover its losses. By 1700 Spain had a population – once again on the increase – of some 7 million, while the number of clergy had stabilised at around 150 000. Taking into account all these variable factors, the statistical evidence currently available to historians seems to confirm the broad opinion held by contemporaries that the growth in size of the clerical estate registered over the first half of the seventeenth century was excessive and unnecessary, far outstripping the needs of society. Nevertheless, this blanket viewpoint needs refining. Certain sectors of the Spanish Church grew, while others remained stable in size.

Gil González Dávila, a priest and prebendary of Salamanca and court historian to Philip III, acknowledged in 1619, 'I am a priest, but I fear that there are more of us than is necessary'.[11] The expansion of the ecclesiastical estate, to which he and other contemporaries referred, was not a general phenomenon, but rather one specific to its lower reaches. As far as the secular clergy were concerned, there was no major increase in the size of their professional body of senior stipended clergy (archbishops, bishops, cathedral and collegiate clergy) during the first half of the seventeenth century. Nor does there appear to have been any significant new recruitment of parish clergy. Indeed, there were continued reports of a shortage of priests in some remote parts of Galicia and Granada and in those areas worst affected by depopulation. In the diocese of Barcelona, 4502 men received the tonsure – the first grade of clerical status – over the period 1546–70, but only 284 entered the priesthood (an average of 11 priests per year). In the later period 1635–1717, the number of priests being ordained declined to an average of 7 per year.[12]

It was at the lesser, supernumerary levels of the secular branch of the clerical estate that the most rapid expansion occurred. Although the statistical evidence still remains patchy, the number of assistant priests, chaplains, prebendaries and minor beneficiaries (without care of souls) in Castile is likely to have at least trebled during the course of the seventeenth century (from an estimated figure of 15 000 to one of 45 000), after which it levelled off.[13] The majority of these simple benefice holders, although classified as clergy, were either unordained or merely tonsured clerics, who exercised a part-time, non-professional clerical function (for which they generally received meagre recompense) alongside a lay one. Simple benefice holders, the majority of whom were appointed by lay patrons, gained a reputation – difficult to substantiate from the evidence available, but widely accepted by contemporaries – for being of limited talent and questionable vocation. It is likely that a proportion sought the privileges associated with ecclesiastical office, however minor the post, and the opportunity it afforded to escape the pressures of everyday existence. Many *arbitristas*, Sancho de Moncada, Jerónimo de Ceballos and Pedro Fernández de Navarrete among them, were part of this semi-professional expanding branch of the clerical estate. There was a common misunderstanding among contemporaries of the difference between a simple tonsured cleric and a priest who had risen through the professional career structure of the Church to acquire a benefice with care of souls, leading to a distortion of what each category actually constituted in terms of size.

The Growth of the Religious Orders

The dramatic expansion in size of the lesser ranks of the secular clergy in post-Tridentine Spain was accompanied by a parallel growth in membership of the religious orders as they underwent reform and renewal. There was a total of 41 066 regular clergy in the late sixteenth-century kingdom of Castile. Over half lived in the large cities of New Castile and Andalusia (housing between 2000 and 5000 families) where favourable economic circumstances encouraged charity and patronage. According to the 1591 census, six of the most heavily populated towns in Castile each held on average 1400 members of the religious orders (see Table 6.2). Here regular clergy predominated over secular clergy by an average ratio of 3:1. It was in urban settlements such as these that early modern Spain acquired the reputation for being excessively 'clericalised'. But it may have been a false impression given the uneven distribution of the religious orders throughout the peninsula as a whole. While major cities such as Toledo, Seville, Granada and Valladolid were overpopulated with religious, their presence was scarcely felt in small villages of under 300 families where over 43 per cent of lay society lived. The much criticised growth of the regular clergy to which contemporaries referred needs to be

Table 6.2 Secular and regular clergy in six major Castilian towns, 1591

Town	*No. of families*	*No. of secular clergy*	*No. of regular clergy*
Toledo	10 933	793	1 942
Seville	18 000	1 047	1 666
Córdoba	6 257	313	1 505
Madrid	7 500	418	1 011
Granada	8 200	450*	1 207
Valladolid	8 112	350	1 140

* Estimated figure.
Source: Based upon *Censo de la Corona de Castilla de 1591: Vecindarios* (Madrid, 1984); Eduardo García España and Annie Molinié-Bertrand (eds), *Censo de Castilla de 1591: Estudio Analítico* (Madrid, 1986), pp. 736–7; Felipe Ruiz Martín, 'Demografía Eclesiástica', *DHEE*, vol. 2, p. 717.

set within the context of these late sixteenth-century trends. It was essentially an urban phenomenon resulting from the establishment of new and reformed orders in major towns in the post-Tridentine period.

Madrid provides a prime example of this phenomenon. The re-establishment of the court in Madrid in 1606 profoundly affected the city's development. One of the key features of its growth was the foundation of religious houses in the city by prominent members of the nobility, as well as by the crown itself, as a means of further enhancing their status in society and of ensuring their place in heaven. As the friar Sebastián de Bricianos observed:

> Gentlemen and those of noble stock, out of vanity, to add status to their possessions, and to emulate their equals, have introduced the idea of owning a monastery or several of them; and this is their objective, alleging the founding of so many monasteries (especially those of the barefooted order, being the cheapest) to serve only for their good.[14]

At the end of the sixteenth century, as Philip III succeeded to the Spanish throne, Madrid had a population of 83 000 inhabitants, including some 1000 friars and nuns housed in a total of 18 communities. Both the new king and the Duke of Lerma, his powerful favourite, were renowned patrons of the orders, notably the Capuchins – a reformed branch of Franciscan friars – who first established

Table 6.3 Religious foundations in the city of Madrid, 1556–1665

Reign	*Monasteries*	*Convents*	*Total*
Philip II (1556–8)	11	7	18
Philip III (1598–1621)	6	7	13
Philip III (1621–65)	7	5	12
Totals	24	19	43

Source: Gil González Dávila, *Teatro de las Grandezas de Madrid* (facs. edn, Madrid, 1986), pp. 234–99; José Antonio Álvarez de Baena, *Compendio de las Grandezas de Madrid* (facs. edn, Madrid, 1978), pp. 98–182.

themselves in the capital in 1609 and whose influence subsequently spread rapidly through Castile and Andalusia. A total of 12 new religious houses (six convents and six monasteries) were founded in Madrid between 1606 and 1618 (the period immediately following the revival of its capital status), eight of which were of Discalced (Barefooted) rule. By the end of Philip III's reign, Madrid's lay population had almost doubled, to 150 000. There was a total of 31 monasteries and convents in the city housing just over 2500 friars and nuns. Philip IV was to establish a further 12 new religious foundations in the capital, three with the aid of royal patronage. The Franciscans were now the most heavily represented religious order in the city, owning a total of ten houses, followed by the Carmelites with five. Alongside the 2615 religious in Madrid, there were 1000 secular clergy based in the capital, serving the needs of churches, chapels and the royal court.[15]

Despite their deep piety, Spaniards were forced to draw distinctions between the spiritual and economic needs of the nation. Via their representatives in the Castilian Cortes, the urban population regularly voiced their concerns at the excessive growth in size of religious communities and the burden they placed on an already impoverished society. In 1607 they called upon the crown to prohibit new religious foundations, especially those of mendicant rule, which were heavily dependent on charity, for the next ten years:

> Every day the number of monasteries increases, especially those of the mendicant orders, resulting in much suffering, for the people of these kingdoms cannot support them as they would wish; thus we plead with Your Majesty that for a period of ten years no licence is given to allow the foundation of any new monastery.[16]

An attempt by the Cortes to link the concession of the regular fiscal subsidy known as the *servicio* to a restraint being placed on the licensing of new monasteries failed to materialise. From the deliberations of the 1633 Cortes, it is clear that dispensations were still being granted for new foundations and the resulting strains this placed on the social order ignored:

> The size of the religious orders has increased so much ... at a time when these kingdoms are ever more depopulated and impoverished, with the income that is assigned to these foundations further reducing the wealth of the lay population and being insufficient to maintain so many religious.[17]

Despite the many criticisms raised of this sort, a policy of religious protectionism, supported by the crown and legitimised by the intensely pious nature of public life, prevailed against the prudent advice of observers. New foundations of reformed habit, however genuine their goals, continued to emerge, absorbing money and potential manpower, until at least the end of the seventeenth century, by which time their number had well surpassed the spiritual needs of society.

The Temporalities of the Spanish Church: Pressures and Survival

Ecclesiastical wealth was commonly regarded as excessive by early seventeenth-century observers, providing a sharp contrast with the poverty that afflicted the masses. It was reported to Philip IV at the beginning of his reign that 'The ecclesiastical estate is without any doubt the most powerful in terms of its riches, rents and possessions; and, I fear, not only is it the wealthiest [estate], but it is set to bring all the resources of these kingdoms under its control'.[18] In 1630, the fixed wealth of the Castilian Church (derived mainly from its ownership of land, its property and financial investments, as well as its material possessions) stood at some 10 million ducats, a figure which approximated to the crown's annual income from taxation and silver receipts for the year 1623. Its regular annual income (as much as 75–80 per cent of which derived from its tithe entitlement) averaged just less than 1 million ducats. In this same year, the total regular income of the 115 titled members of the Spanish aristocracy amounted to some 5 million ducats.

The traditional sources of regular ecclesiastical income (tithe payments, land and property rents and returns from mortgaged assets), which had more than doubled in value during the course of the sixteenth century, were declining in worth in early seventeenth-century Spain as a result of prevailing economic circumstances. At the same time, the fiscal pressures being placed upon the clerical estate by the crown were steadily increasing. Nevertheless, the Church managed to survive the acute period of economic crisis that cut across the turn of the century. We need to examine the reasons behind this apparent contradiction more closely. Two crucial factors had a bearing on the rental income of the Church: agricultural production and price inflation. Both directly affected the size and value of the tithe – a 10 per cent tax on the agricultural product – worth in the region of 9 million ducats in early seventeenth-century Spain. Approximately two-ninths of the proceeds of the tithe was retained by the Church and principally went to pay for the upkeep of senior (and some lesser) clergy, the remainder being divided between the crown and lay beneficiaries.

Between about 1580 and 1630, Castilian cereal production (especially that of wheat and barley) fell by an average 40 per cent in the kingdom as a direct result of poor harvests, adverse weather conditions and the flight from the land, all of which prompted an increase in grain prices.[19] The grain price index reached its highest point between 1598 and 1601. The highest level of monetary inflation was recorded in Castile between 1615 and 1630, following the debasement of the coinage and the manipulation of the face value of coins. Using early seventeenth-century Castilian episcopal rents as a reliable source of data that can be charted over an extended time period, it is possible to analyse the effects of these fluctuating economic circumstances on a significant proportion of the regular income of the Spanish Church (see Table 6.4).

In the northern region of Galicia, the value of the tithe declined by approximately 15 per cent between 1615 and 1645 – a less dramatic fall than that experienced in some regions. An investment in maize production along the coastal strip from mid-century helped to revive agricultural fortunes. Santiago felt the early benefits of this crop diversification programme: its archiepiscopal income, directly linked to tithe returns, fell by under 10 per cent between 1615 and 1630 and recovered quickly thereafter. In Orense, where maize was not planted until the 1670s, diocesan rents fell by 23 per cent during the first half of the century, a figure slightly above the decline in value of the tithe.[20]

Table 6.4 Episcopal rents in early seventeenth-century Castile (in ducats per annum)

Bishopric	c.*1615*	*1630*	*1650*	c.*1665*
Santiago	50 000	43 150	46 150	45 880
Astorga	12 400	8 000	8 000	9 600
Ávila	14 700	13 000	11 300	14 980
Badajoz	11 000	19 100	14 500	7 220
Ciudad Rodrigo	7 500	7 000	6 000	6 000
Coria	21 000	21 300	18 600	20 500
Lugo	6 500	6 200	5 000	4 600
Mondoñedo	4 000	4 200	4 000	4 000
Orense	7 250	5 600	5 650	4 000
Plasencia	41 000	47 700	38 600	35 600
Salamanca	21 000	16 000	14 400	17 200
Tuy	9 000	7 000	8 000	7 000
Zamora	16 800	16 500	13 450	14 600
Totals	222 150	214 750	193 650	191 180
Burgos	29 600	30 000	38 620	38 620
Calahorra	18 000	17 000	17 000	22 100
Pamplona	20 000	23 000	20 000	22 000
Palencia	20 000	15 300	13 500	15 400
Totals	87 600	85 300	89 120	98 120
Toledo	225 000	225 000	240 000	240 000
Cartagena	22 000	15 000	15 000	16 600
Córdoba	41 800	40 000	42 200	33 740
Cuenca	43 000	38 700	33 750	33 750
Jaén	34 800	36 000	31 000	30 350
Osma	20 900	17 600	18 800	20 200
Segovia	20 600	17 600	17 670	24 990
Sigüenza	46 700	34 000	34 160	41 000
Valladolid	11 000	12 000	14 430	14 430
Totals	465 800	435 900	457 010	455 060
Seville	87 000	88 000	100 000	100 000
Cádiz	10 100	14 000	12 200	12 200
Canaries	14 000	15 500	18 000	23 800
Málaga	36 400	40 000	45 500	45 100
Totals	147 750	157 500	175 700	181 100
Granada	31 600	40 500	32 000	32 000
Almería	2 700	4 800	4 500	5 300
Guadix	6 000	6 000	5 000	6 000
Totals	40 300	51 300	42 300	44 100

Exempt sees				
León	12 300	13 000	13 120	13 120
Oviedo	11 300	9 400	13 000	19 300
Totals	23 600	22 400	26 120	32 920
Grand totals	986 950	967 150	983 900	1 002 980

Sources: *AHN*, *Consejos Suprimidos*, Legajos 15220–15293 (1615–65) (figures based on diocesan estimates submitted on the vacation of see, with *subsidio, excusado* and other charges deducted); Antonio Domínguez Ortiz, 'Las rentas de los prelados de Castilla en el siglo xvii', in *Estudios de Historia y Social de España* (Granada, 1987), pp. 223–60.

The repercussions of the agrarian crisis were most severely felt in Old Castile. In 1632, the cathedral chapter of Valladolid reported a considerable decline in the value of its rental income. It gave as its reasons 'the lowering of interest levels and the difficulty in recovering income from mortgaged investments, the reduction of tithe returns due to depopulation, the decline of agriculture and land rents and the burden of old and new fiscal demands'.[21] The city's population declined by 63 per cent between 1591 and 1646, falling from 8112 to 3000 *vecinos*. The Valladolid chapter suffered a corresponding 47.5 per cent reduction in its rental income derived from tithes of wheat and barley during the first half of the seventeenth century. Bread tithes in the Segovia region fell by 30 per cent over the ten-year periods 1590–9 and 1630–9, with catastrophic consequences for the rental income of the diocese (see Table 6.5). Segovian cpiscopal rents underwent a dramatic 50 per cent decline in their value over this same period (falling from 34 000 ducats per annum in 1590 to 17 600 ducats in 1630), a decline partly attributable to the reduction in the rent levied on the propertied assets of the cathedral chapter, which fell by 30 per cent during the first half of the seventeenth century.

A different picture emerges from central and southern Castilian dioceses. In the archbishopric of Toledo, average returns from the wheat and barley tithe declined by 30 per cent over the periods 1583–91 and 1628–36, but without adversely affecting archiepiscopal rents which remained steady at just over 200 000 ducats. The archbishopric's non-tithed assets helped cushion the temporary financial setback. It was mid-century before crisis overtook the southern region, where a series of poor harvests and a rampant rise in wheat prices followed in the wake of the second great plague (1647–52) in which some 600 000 Andalusians lost their lives. The wheat tithe of the Sevillian

Table 6.5 The value of the Segovian tithe set against diocesan income, 1590–1659 (calculated in *fanegas* of cereal production and ducats per annum)

Year	*Value of tithe*	*Index 1590–9*	*Diocesan income*	*Index 1590–9*
1590–9	3 104	100	34 000	100
1600–9	2 910	93.7		
1610–19	2 869	92.4	20 600	60.5
1620–9	3 401	109.5		
1630–9	2 198	70.8	17 600	51.7
1640–9	2 934	94.5		
1650–9	2 915	93.9	17 600	51.7

Source: Tithe figures taken from Ángel García Sanz, 'El sector agrario durante el siglo xvii: depresión y reajustes', in *Historia de España Menéndez y Pidal*, vol. 23 (Madrid, 1989), pp. 166–7. I have used a different index to that used by García Sanz to equate with the height of diocesan income in conjunction with tithe returns.
Notes: (a) a *fanega* was a measure of bulk, equivalent to 1.6 bushels; (b) a ducat (*ducado*) was a unit of account, equivalent to 375 *maravedís*.

archbishopric fell by 37.5 per cent, from 120 000 *fanegas* in 1640 to 75 000 *fanegas* in 1645–50. Sevillian wheat prices plummeted to between 647 and 782 *maravedís* per *fanega* in 1650, but rose dramatically to 3400 *maravedís* in 1652 as a result of the scarcity of supply. In its administration of the bread tithe the Church became a direct *beneficiary* of these higher resale values. As in the case of Toledo, Sevillian archiepiscopal rents thus survived the relatively short-lived crisis, rising from 88 000 ducats in 1630 to reach 100 000 ducats in 1650.

The evidence examined here suggests that although the Castilian Church as a whole was in receipt of a reduced quantity of tithed produce during the worst years of agricultural recession, this was partly compensated for, especially in the more densely populated and more fertile central–southern areas, by setting an increased resale value for the grain tithe at times of bread scarcity. The total value of regular episcopal income in Castile, principally derived from the tithe, underwent no appreciable decline during the crisis years, remaining steady at just under a million ducats. Those dioceses suffering losses of rental income as a result of the agrarian and monetary crises had begun to regain their former values by mid-century, the peripheral regions recovering their economic strength more quickly than the central areas, in line with demographic trends. Price inflation and monetary devaluation – both of which crippled the consumer – paradoxically aided the recovery of the Castilian Church's rental income. Diocesan rents as a whole recovered from their losses between 1640 and 1665.

The Fiscal Burden

The Spanish Church's capacity to ride out short-term economic crises contrasted with its long-term battle to evade the fiscal burden. The crown had a direct interest in protecting, even encouraging, the accumulation of wealth by the ecclesiastical estate. Had it not been able to tap these resources, its own revenues would have been considerably depleted. Royal prerogatives over ecclesiastical income were many. Apart from its two-ninths share of the tithe (worth 2 million ducats in 1623), the crown also extracted three main subsidies from the Church with papal sanction, known as the three graces (*tres gracias*), which together raised around 1.4 million ducats for the crown at the beginning of Philip IV's reign (13.3 per cent of the crown's gross annual income). The *cruzada*, originally raised to help finance the crusade against the Moors of Granada, was a tax levied on the sale of papal indulgences, sold under the auspices of the Church, and yielded 800 000 ducats annually. The *subsidio*, which took the form of a subsidy on clerical incomes, was first sanctioned in the early 1560s to assist the crown in its Mediterranean struggle with the Turk and was worth 420 000 ducats per year. The *excusado*, the tithe from the richest estate in each parish, was granted by the Pope to the crown in 1567 to help finance the wars against Protestants and rebels in the Low Countries. It raised 250 000 ducats a year. Each of these contributions continued to be collected by the crown long after the periods of religious warfare which they helped to finance had ceased.[22] The crown also enjoyed the right to extract between one-third and one-quarter of the gross value of the most lucrative episcopal incomes to offer as pensions to long-serving churchmen. In practice, a large percentage of ecclesiastical pensions, which were worth around 250 000 ducats annually, fell to the benefit of those in civil and political life. In March 1622, the crown received 575 petitions for pensionable income, worth a total of 50 800 ducats, from cardinals of Rome, counsellors and government ministers, members of the aristocracy,

Table 6.6 Examples of direct deductions from episcopal incomes (in ducats per annum)

Bishopric	*Year(s)*	*Gross income*	*Pension*	Subsidio + escusado	*Residual income*
Ciudad Rodrigo	1598–1600	8 956	810	730	7 416
León	1602–6	13 400	3 400	2 800	7 200
Segovia	1607–11	20 970	5 650	3 825	11 495
Burgos	1612	40 000	8 500	6 000	25 500
Zamora	1612–14	16 800	4 200	3 250*	9 350

* Estimated figure.
Source: *Archivo General de Simancas, Patronato Eclesiástico*, Legajos 135–136; *AHN, Consejos Suprimidos*, Legajo 15.217.

the religious orders and the royal household.[23] Heavy pension charges were a considerable burden for some prelates, as illustrated in Table 6.6 above. In 1615, the Bishop of Zamora complained that 'the income of this diocese belongs more to those with a claim on its pensionable income than to me'.[24] Pension claims were now depriving him of the majority of his episcopal living following the 33 per cent decline in the rental income of his see (from 24 400 ducats in 1590 to 16 800 in 1615) as a result of the fall in value of the bread tithe.

The Bishop of Zamora's was not a lone voice. At the beginning of Philip IV's reign, the crown was accumulating over 3.6 million ducats of revenue per year from ecclesiastical sources in the form of direct or indirect levies, equivalent to a third of its overall income (see Table 6.7). Although the majority of churchmen lived a lot more comfortably than the mass of the population, the demands on ecclesiastical incomes (including the considerable cost of financing reforming initiatives) and the fluctuation in their real value were probably far greater than contemporaries acknowledged.

The strength of collective opposition that surfaced within the Church to the extraordinary fiscal impositions (over and above the regular ones) made by the later Habsburgs on ecclesiastical incomes was to represent a serious obstacle to the realisation of royal policies, including the application of Tridentine reforms. Senior clergy with the highest incomes were those most heavily burdened. At the end of the sixteenth century, the ecclesiastical estate fiercely objected to its

Table 6.7 Royal income, 1621

Source	*Amount in ducats*	%
Ecclesiastical		
Royal tithe	2 000 000	18.6
Three graces	1 430 000	13.3
Ecclesiastical pensions	250 000	2.3
Secular		
Millones	2 000 000	8.6
Servicios	400 000	3.7
Alcabalas	900 000	8.3
*Maestrazgos** + trade taxes	2 420 000	22.5
Indies fleet	1 100 000	10.2
Casual sales	250 000	2.3
Total	10 750 000	

* Tax levied on lands of military orders.
Source: Adapted from I. A. A. Thompson, *War and Government in Habsburg Spain, 1560–1620* (London, 1976), Table A, p. 288.

non-exemption from payment of the *millones* tax on basic foodstuffs (set at 9 million ducats in 1590, payable over six years, and increased to 18 million in 1601). Of the 2 million ducats raised by the *millones* tax in 1621, one-third (650 000) is estimated to have come from ecclesiastical sources. Additionally, it became customary for extraordinary payments, known as *décimas eclesiásticas*, to be demanded of the Church (subject to papal approval) with increasing regularity to help finance the major military enterprises of the crown. In 1632, a *décima* worth 600 000 ducats was sanctioned by the papacy to assist the crown in the war effort in central Europe. Further *décimas* were granted in subsequent years: 550 000 ducats in 1648 to suppress the revolt of Naples and 800 000 in 1662 to support the military campaign to reconquer Portugal.[25]

As American silver remittances began to stabilise from the mid-1640s and measures to raise additional revenues failed to produce adequate returns, the crown was forced to suspend payments to its creditors in the summer of 1652. The Church, via the power of the pulpit, voiced the widespread grievances of society in respect of the economic chaos in which the country found itself. Clergy were at the forefront of serious popular disturbances in Andalusia in 1652 over the rise in the cost of a standard measure of grain (the *tasa de trigo*) to unprecedented levels as a result of crop failures (from which the Church, as we have seen, drew certain financial benefits). These riots followed in the wake of the second onslaught of the plague, which swept into the region from the Levant in 1648, resulting in major human devastation. Friar Pedro de Tapia, in his capacity as Bishop of Córdoba (1649–52), felt deep sympathy for the oppressed masses and wrote to the President of Castile blaming the local government for the crisis through their mismanagement of grain supplies.[26] Andalusia was again a scene of popular disturbance in the mid-1650s, this time in response to new tax impositions approved by the Castilian Cortes of 1655–8.

Tapia, promoted to the archbishopric of Seville in 1652, soon emerged as a major proponent of fiscal disobedience amongst the Castilian clergy. He fiercely objected to a renewal of the *millones* tax being imposed on the ecclesiastical estate by the crown without the required papal sanction having been received.[27] The diarist Jerónimo de Barrionuevo, himself a clergyman, reported daily on the growing rift between the two camps. The Archbishop led a strike of churchmen (described as a *huelga eclesiástica*), inciting the Bishops of Segovia (Francisco de Arauz), Osma (Juan de Palafox) and Málaga (Diego Martínez de Zarzosa) into opposition. The Primate, Baltasar de Moscoso y Sandoval, added his voice of protest to the assault on clerical immunity, threatening to resign over the matter. Allegations of fiscal fraudulence were hurled at the Church by ministers, provoking a heated response from Bishop Arauz of Segovia in which he vigorously defended the position of the clergy, whom he claimed were only just able to survive from their incomes, attributing the poor state of royal finances to the maladministration of government. Bishop Arauz's resignation from office in October 1656 stands as testimony to his exasperation over the matter.[28] The king and his ministers stood firm in the face of this outburst of clerical recalcitrance. Tapia threatened to take the case to Rome rather than to agree to churchmen becoming taxpayers. The Council of Castile discussed removing him from office. In December 1656 the newly elected Pope Alexander VII conceded a renewal of the *subsidio* and *excusado* subsidies, but in July 1657 he was still refusing to approve the renewed levying of the *millones* tax on the Church. Tapia's death in August must have helped defuse some of the tension. Within a year, Rome had retreated from its position and issued the required sanction. The clergy, so valuable to the crown as its allies, proved formidable as its opponents.

A Crisis of Religious Conscience in Society

The debilitating series of crises faced by their country in the late sixteenth and early seventeenth centuries prompted educated Spaniards to examine their own consciences in search of an explanation. They began to question the validity of established values and, in particular, to reflect upon the whole nature of their relationship with their multi-cultural past. Was the basic philosophy of society, founded on the supremacy of the Old Christian, the orthodoxy of his faith and his dedication to the Catholic cause, which, according to official propaganda, had raised Spain to such greatness, still relevant in changing times? There was a strong and influential body of lay and ecclesiastical opinion that questioned the exclusivity of religious policy and the justification of methods employed to keep Spain free from the contamination of those of alien creed and blood. This led to a review of attitudes and prejudices in society, in particular those surrounding the purity of blood statutes. Many contemporaries recognised the injustice inherent in a code of practice which discriminated irrationally and was perhaps even becoming an obsolete requirement in the century after the expulsion of the Jews from Spain. A crisis of religious conscience was about to unfold.

The controversy came to a head in 1599 when Fray Agustín Salucio, a prominent Dominican theologian, published (without royal authority) a scathing attack on the purity of blood statutes.[29] He drew attention to the widespread scandal and abuse surrounding investigations into the background of supposed *conversos* which had resulted in a 'State divided into two factions ... as in a civil war'.[30] Such was the extent of malpractice involved that the statutes had lost all validity. He urged that 'Old Christians and *moriscos*, and *conversos* should all come to form one body and all be secure Christians'.[31] Salucio argued that unless genealogical investigations were limited to 100 years, it was likely that every generation in Spain would display some signs of impure blood in their ancestry. How many people could really be sure about the purity of origins of their four grandparents and eight great-grandparents? There was no longer the same need to prove *limpieza* as there had been a century ago when Jewish descent was still an identifiable feature of many genealogical lines. *Conversos* were just as good New Christians as non-*conversos* were Old Christians. In short, the statutes (as they existed) had effectively outlived their purpose. His argument was not that *limpieza* should be totally abolished but that its scope of inquiry be restricted and the abuse within the system eradicated. Salucio's discourse was 'revolutionary' insofar as it dared to raise questions about the whole philosophy of society upon which Spain had built its pride and reputation. By extension, it seemed to cast a shadow over the Inquisition itself as the institution responsible for instigating the ruthless persecution of religious minorities. There were many influential figures of *converso* extraction, prominent in ecclesiastical and secular life, who privately welcomed the proposed relaxation of the statutes and could well have brought their influence to bear on the debate via the likes of Salucio.

Salucio's treatise sparked off a heated debate within the heart of the Spanish Church and state. It was supported by senior ecclesiastics, including the Cardinal Archbishop of Toledo and the Archbishops of Valencia and Burgos, as well as the future Duke of Lerma, whose own tolerance of *conversos* may have derived from his family connections with the Society of Jesus. Deep discord emerged within the Inquisition over the issue. In 1599, the *Suprema* voted by a majority to ban Salucio's discourse as a work of subversion. However, in August of the following year Niño de Guevara, the newly appointed Inquisitor General (1599–1602), wrote to Lerma expressing his approval of Salucio's treatise, praising him as 'a very learned friar to whom the whole Catholic Church and particularly the Holy Office owe a great deal',[32] thus adding his weight to those advocating reform. His views supported those of the Cortes of Castile, which had met in a special session of January 1600 to discuss the matter of the statutes. Reporting to the king in February, the procurators of the Cortes recommended a thorough reform of the application of *limpieza*, drawing attention to the serious anomalies that now existed in society as a result of their influence. They foresaw the danger of the established nobility having their role and status challenged by the self-created 'pure blood' nobility of plebeian origin. As a result, they claimed, 'we esteem a common person who is *limpio* more than an *hidalgo* who is not *limpio*'.[33] The higher honour of *hidalguía* was effectively being displaced by that of *limpieza*, itself often dependent on nothing more than popular opinion. The exercise of such irrational criteria, so they argued, was having a detrimental effect on the calibre of the professions, discouraging the talented but tainted *hidalgo* from competing for office where rigorous genealogical proofs were required. The Cortes agreed with Salucio that *limpieza* investigations should be limited to a period of 100 years. Beneath the rhetoric the nature of the argument had been fundamentally transformed. What concerned those in authority was not the unnecessary assault on the religious sincerity of the *converso* and the purity of his racial origins, but the risk to social rank and status inherent in *limpieza* investigations from which not even an Old Christian could claim to be immune. The debate over purity of blood reflected the deep concern of the Spaniard for his reputation in society. The underlying fear of Salucio, Niño de Guevara and the members of the Castilian Cortes was that the traditional honour of the old nobility (who now feared the outcome of investigations into their lineage) was being undermined by the continued rigid adherence to the code of *limpieza* which produced a rival pure-blooded 'factitious nobility' of plebeian origin.

The debate continued into the reign of Philip IV. In February 1623, the *Junta de Reformación* proposed the unacceptability of verbal evidence in purity of blood investigations and that a candidate should be confirmed as eligible for employment following three positive proofs of his clean lineage, thereby avoiding endless trials.[34] The Count-Duke of Olivares, himself of *converso* blood via his paternal grandmother, was naturally sympathetic to the call for greater racial tolerance within society. He expressed his personal views on the matter at a meeting of the Council of State in November 1625: 'The law prohibiting honours is unjust and impious . . . Without crime, without sin of offence against God, they find themselves – even when they excel all others in virtue, sanctity and scholarship – condemned not only without being heard, but without the possibility of being heard . . . .'[35] In 1626, Pedro Fernández de Navarrete argued that the policy of excluding all but those of Old Christian origin from public office had driven New Christians in desperation back to their former religious roots. If they adopted Christianity they knew they would never escape the infamy attributed to the race of their forefathers.[36] The same year saw the publication of a report by the Holy Office, endorsed by Inquisitor General Andrés Pacheco, which effectively called for the abolition of the statutes. According to the *Suprema*, the application of *limpieza* was based on an anomaly: 'Today no one can be found who persists in error . . . It follows, then, that since what gave rise to the statutes has wholly ceased it would be civic and political prudence that at least the rigour of their practice should cease.'[37] It was at this crucial juncture, as inquisitors began to question the necessity of the *limpieza* laws and by implication to challenge the future *raison d'être* of their own institution, that the debate began to lose some of its momentum. In 1628 Antonio de Zapata y Mendoza, the Inquisitor General (1627–32), issued a *consulta* which completely overturned the opinions expressed by the *Suprema* two years earlier.

'We are convinced', he argued, 'that the observance of the statutes of *limpieza* in any community is both just and praiseworthy, and they have been of great benefit in these Your Majesty's realms.'[38] Other inquisitors individually came to the defence of the statutes. It is possible that this *volte-face* was prompted by the fractious internal politics of the Holy Office as it fought to maintain its authority and status within the secular administration. One of the last voices to be raised in the *limpieza* controversy, significantly, belonged to a member of the Society of Jesus, which had fought hard to avoid excluding New Christians from its company. In 1632 Fernando de Valdés, the rector of the Jesuit college of Madrid and a censor of the Inquisition, published a *memorial* addressed to Philip IV in which he reinforced all the arguments in favour of abolishing the statutes, whose influence in society he likened to that of a disease. 'What plague could destroy a state more than this matter has destroyed the conscience of our Spain?' he wrote.[39] Despite this desperate call for the reality of the situation to be acknowledged, for prejudices and false conceptions to be put aside – fundamental arguments which permeated the deliberations of the *arbitristas* – the problem remained an intractable one. The contradictions inherent in the application of the laws of *limpieza* lay unresolved. By the late 1630s, although the proposals of the 1623 *Junta* had in theory been rejected, belief in the validity and necessity of the statutes had in practice been seriously, if not permanently, undermined.

Conclusion

The Spanish Church survived the pressures and criticisms it was subjected to at the beginning of the seventeenth century in response to its excessive size, wealth, and its endorsement of a rigid discriminatory code, by virtue of the extensive spiritual, temporal and ideological power base it held in society. Although the traditional sources of ecclesiastical income were declining in face value as a result of the economic recession and the heavy fiscal demands being placed on members of the clerical estate, there was an increase in the quantity of money, goods, property and real estate being bequeathed and donated to the Church by private benefactors. In 1623, Jerónimo de Ceballos advised the readers of his *Arte Real* to 'take account of the *juros* [investment bonds] that are held by religious communities; look at their inheritances, properties, lands and tributes . . . and you will find that it amounts to much more than is held by the lay sector'.[40] Despite the rigours of the economic crisis, there were still sufficient resources available within society to maintain the Church in the traditional opulence and splendour that was so often commented on by early seventeenth-century observers. The dramatic rise in the mortality rate prompted more money to be spent by the surviving population on 'heavenly protection'. The need to secure one's place in heaven by one's actions on earth – a fundamental message of the Counter-Reformation Church – led to a heavy investment, both human and material, in the least productive sector of society and the perpetuation of the social and economic imbalance this created. By joining the lesser ranks of the ecclesiastical estate or by making a pious bequest in his will, the average Spaniard, notwithstanding the strength of his commitment to Catholicism, was taking out a form of religious insurance policy. While the contradictions inherent in the combination of the Church's spiritual role with its accumulation of temporal wealth and its over-recruitment of ill-equipped lesser clergy were readily identifiable by contemporaries, the intensely sacred nature of public life seemed to justify and legitimise it. Similarly, the Spaniard's concern for his reputation and honour took priority over attempts to resolve the anomalies he recognised as operative within society's code of values. As long as the Church, with its essentially Old Christian mentality, retained its commanding authority over the Spanish people, these paradoxes would prevail.

Conclusion

In March 1586, El Greco was commissioned to paint *The Burial of the Count of Orgaz* for the Toledan parish church of Santo Tomé to commemorate a miraculous event which took place at the burial of a local aristocrat in the early fourteenth century. According to legend, as the body of Don Gonzalo Ruiz de Toledo, the Count of Orgaz, was being placed in his tomb, Saint Stephen and Saint Augustine came down from heaven to offer their assistance and bless the Count's soul on its passage to salvation in recognition of his Christian charity and piety. El Greco depicted the legend as if it were a late sixteenth-century phenomenon, including portraits of elite members of Toledan society among the line of mourners: regular and secular clergy performing their official funereal duties alongside intellectuals and noblemen paying their last respects. Toledo, the spiritual capital of Spain, had a reputation for being a profoundly Catholic and rigidly orthodox city, dominated by churchmen who emphasised the necessity for a strict observance of the central doctrines of the Tridentine Church. The message of the painting is clear: the priests, friars and nobles who engage in the burial ritual are by their presence endorsing the good Catholic behaviour of the deceased Count – a valued benefactor of the local church – and at the same time confirming their submission to the Old Christian values of Spanish society. The painting invites the viewer to live and die in the service of God and the Church, just as the Count of Orgaz did. Art was used by the Counter-Reformation Church as a powerful medium of instruction, inciting the faithful to venerate Christ, Mary and the saints (present in the celestial section of the painting), to marvel at acts of piety, charity and mercy (via the person of the Count of Orgaz) and to rule their lives according to the examples set before them. *The Burial of the Count of Orgaz* projects a model of holiness and obedience that accorded with the teachings of the Tridentine Church. Here was an image of the perfect Catholic society, an image upon which Spain so prided itself both at home and abroad. But how far was this a universal reflection of Toledan society's predicament, and by extension that of Spain as a whole, at the end of the sixteenth century?

Spain's commitment to orthodoxy, discipline and regulation in religious life was a principal feature of its identity in the early modern period, but it is also true that there were flaws and inconsistencies in the practical application of these ideals. Toledo can be used to illustrate the paradox. The primate city of the Spanish Church, renowned in medieval times for its atmosphere of racial and religious harmony, was set to become in the early modern period a major centre of intolerance. It was in Toledo that the doctrine of *limpieza de sangre* was first instituted in 1449 and where the Spanish Inquisition set up one of its most active tribunals in 1485. But from the proceedings of the Toledan Inquisition, the constitutions of synods and church councils, as well as the surveys conducted of local rural communities, all of which were used in the preparation of this study, it is evident that diversity of religious belief and practice prevailed among Toledo's Old Christian community, while much of its New Christian population was only nominally Catholic. The capital of the Spanish Church did not remain totally free from doctrinal deviation or spiritual dissent. In the early sixteenth century, it was home to the *Alumbrados* and to humanist thinkers, including Archbishop Alonso de Fonseca and the ecclesiastical scholar Juan de Vergara, as well as alleged Lutherans. Following the arrest of Archbishop Carranza in August 1559 at the hands of the Inquisition, placards were found posted up first on houses in the city and later in five chapels of the cathedral itself, accusing the Catholic Church of being 'an assembly of evil people . . . not the Church of Jesus Christ but the Church of the devil and of Antichrist his son, the Antichrist pope'.[1] The culprit was found to be a local priest, Sebastián Martínez, who was burnt at the stake for his heresy. In the second half of the sixteenth century, Toledo's leadership of the movement to reform the Church from within and raise standards of religious observance in society, in accordance with the recommendations made at the Council of Trent, met with a number of obstacles. In the first instance, while Carranza remained in inquisitorial custody (1559–76) it had no resident archbishop, allowing the cathedral chapter to vigorously oppose attempts to remove its privileges. Secondly, Toledo's endeavours were restricted, as we have seen, by the crown's insistence on personally directing religious policy and its reluctance to concede to papal recommendations. The Toledan Church, led by Archbishop Quiroga from 1577 – the same year in which El Greco arrived in the city – was essentially an unreformed one in which abuses, dissension and enmity were rife. His intention was to make Toledo into an ideal archdiocese – an example for the rest of the Church to follow. It was within this context that El Greco was commissioned to undertake the painting of religious themes and images designed to communicate Tridentine doctrine. Via the Toledan synodal constitutions of 1583, Quiroga set about reinforcing the austere, disciplined brand of Catholicism that faithfully followed the prescriptions of the Council of Trent. Despite the Archbishop's determined efforts and the example he set through donations to charitable and educative foundations, the whole process of implementing Catholic reform and modifying the practice of popular piety was of limited impact. In practice, as we have observed, there remained a huge gulf between the Catholicism practised by the elite urban classes (as depicted in *The Burial of the Count of Orgaz*) and the religion of the people. A report prepared for Quiroga's successor as Archbishop, Albert of Austria, nephew to Philip II, in 1595 revealed that many Toledan village parishes continued to offer little or no instruction in the basic foundations of Catholic belief to their flock. Rural priests were still collecting fees for baptisms, marriages and burials, in contravention of Quiroga's synodal decrees. Popular religious practice that did not correspond with the orthodox teachings of the post-Tridentine Church prevailed in many local communities.[2] In 1601, two years after the appointment of Cardinal Bernardo de Sandoval y Rojas to the primatial see, a new set of synodal constitutions were published which underlined the need for 'the reform of customs, the correction of abuses, and the extirpation of vices'.[3] The new Archbishop gained a reputation for his generous commitment to works of charity alongside his opportunism in appointing close relatives to rich capitular benefices, a practice which aroused tensions within the chapter and provoked an appeal to Rome. By the turn of the century, as depopulation hit the city and the local economy suffered a severe recession, Toledo had become overpopulated with religious, many of whom were thought to be entering the clerical profession more out of physical need rather than spiritual devotion – as pointed out by the Toledan jurist and local councillor Jerónimo de Ceballos in

his treatise of 1620 – thereby counteracting attemp
calibre of churchmen and restore respect for their ro
The case of Toledo illustrates some of the contradiction
in this study, inherent in early modern Spain's identific
Catholicism.

In drawing up a balance sheet of the relationship between the Church, religion and society in early modern Spain, we need to assess both the strengths and weaknesses of the correlation between them. This study has demonstrated that the spirit of *convivencia* survived alongside a rigid intolerance of those of non-Christian blood or creed; that while conservative values predominated, innovative trends in religious scholarship continued to flourish; that there was only a partial acceptance and application of reforming initiatives within the Church; that popular religious culture continued to shape the lives of rural communities; that the missionary enterprise overseas met with more resistance than those who championed Spain's Catholic crusade acknowledged; and that the Church had its critics as well as its worshippers. Spain's religious heritage in the early modern period is distinguished as much by its abiding diversity as by the rigorous drive for conformity.

Profiles of Church Leaders and Reformers

The following profiles are arranged in chronological order of birth.

Pedro González de Mendoza (1428–95) Archbishop of Toledo under Ferdinand and Isabella; a warrior prelate

1428	Born in Guadalajara, fifth son of Marquis of Santillana; uncle Archbishop of Toledo 1442–5.
1438	Curate of Hita (aged 10).
1446–52	Studied canon law at University of Salamanca.
1448	Archdean of Guadalajara (aged 20) – one of the richest benefices in Spain.
1458	Became leader of Mendoza family.
1453	Bishop of Calahorra.
1467	Bishop of Sigüenza (until 1482).
1473	Confirmed allegiance to Isabella in War of Succession (1469–79).
1473	Cardinal of Rome.
1474	Archbishop of Seville.
1476	As Captain General of Royal Army, fought opposite Alfonso Carrillo at battle of Toro.
1478	Supported establishment of Holy Inquisition.
1482	Archbishop of Toledo and Patriarch of Alexandria.
1484	Founded Colegio Mayor of Santa Cruz, Valladolid, and Hospital of Santa Cruz, Toledo.
1492	Present at entry of Catholic kings into Granada. Endorsed expulsion of Jews from Spain.
1495	Died in Guadalajara, aged 67.

Hernando de Talavera (OSJ) (1428–1507) First Archbishop of Granada; an advocate of conversion by persuasion

1428	Born in Talavera de la Reina, Toledo, of poor parents. One of maternal grandparents was a Jew. Relatives included Fray Alonso de Oropesa, General of the Jeronimites (1457–68).

1463–6 Held chair of moral philosophy at Salamanca.
1466 Took religious habit of Saint Jerome (OSJ).
1470 Prior of Valladolid. Preaching talents acknowledged.
1475–6 Confessor to Queen Isabella and member of Royal Council.
1478 Participated in National Church Council of Seville.
1486 Bishop of Ávila (a resident bishop).
1493 First Archbishop of Granada. Moorish community subjected to a policy of conversion by persuasion.
1499–1500 Forced conversions provoked Albaicín uprising. Talavera intervened to restore calm.
1505 Accused of being a Judaizer by Holy Office.
1506 Case absolved on appeal to Rome.
1507 Died in Granada (14 May), aged 79.

Francisco Jiménez de Cisneros (OSF) (1436–1517) Archbishop of Toledo under Ferdinand and Isabella; a militant defender of orthodoxy

1436 Born in Torrelaguna, the disinherited son of noble family. Educated at Alcalá (grammar) and Salamanca (canon and civil law). Patronised by Cardinal Mendoza of Toledo (1482–95).
1471 Archpriest Uzeda.
1480 Chaplain Sigüenza.
1484 Joined observant branch of the Franciscan order (OSF).
1492 Confessor to Queen Isabella. Supported expulsion of Jews.
1495 Provincial of OSF and entrusted with reform of order.
1495 Archbishop of Toledo and Grand Chancellor of Castile.
1499–1500 Rapid conversion tactics provoked first Alpujarras revolt.
1506 Regent of Castile (upon death of Archduke Philip).
1507 Cardinal of Rome; Inquisitor General.
1508 Founded University of Alcalá and initiated Polyglot Bible project.
1509 Took part in the Conquest of Oran.
1516 Regent of Castile (upon death of Ferdinand).
1517 Died in Roa, Burgos (8 November), aged 81.

Bartolomé de Las Casas (OSD) (1474–1566) Dominican defender of Indian rights in the New World

1474 Born in Seville, the son of a merchant who accompanied Columbus on his first journey to the New World.
1502 Held preaching responsibilities in Santo Domingo for a *repartimiento* of Indians.
1510 Ordained as a priest. Spent two years as a preacher in La Concepción.
1513 Served Diego Velázquez in conquest of Cuba. Obtained an *encomienda*.
1514 Horrified at exploitation of Indian community. Renounced his temporal responsibilities and dedicated his life to the defence of the Indian.

1515	Returned to Spain. Council of the Indies opposed his proposals.
1516	Given the title 'Protector of the Indians' by Cisneros.
1517–20	Pressed his case successfully at the court of Charles I.
1522	Entered the Dominican order (OSD). Spent eight years in monastic seclusion.
1526	New rules on discovery and conquest issued in Spain.
1527	Began writing his *Historia de las Indias*.
1531	Presented *Memorial* to Council of the Indies on treatment of Indians.
1542	Wrote *Brevísima Relación de la Destrucción de las Indias*.
1542	The New Laws, heavily influenced by Las Casas, introduced to release native population from servitude.
1543	Refused bishopric of Cuzco. Elected Bishop of Chiapa. Little residence.
1547	Left the Indies for the last time and returned to Spain.
1550	Resigned bishopric.
1550	Engaged in debate with Juan Ginés de Sepúlveda at Valladolid to discuss the legality of conquest and rights of Indian population.
1551	Resident of San Gregorio, Valladolid.
1552	Publication of *Brevísima Relación de la Destrucción de las Indias*.
1559	Intervened to support Archbishop Carranza following his arrest.
1562	Increasingly alienated from court.
1566	Died in Madrid, aged 92.

Fernando de Valdés (1483–1568) Inquisitor General at time of Protestant discoveries and arrest of Carranza. A ruthless and ambitious ecclesiastical administrator

1483	Born in Salas, Asturias.
1512	Studied at Colegio de San Bartolomé, Salamanca.
1515	Rector of college. Obtained degree in canon law.
1517	Collaborated with Cisneros in production of New Constitutions of University of Alcalá.
1520	In Flanders with Juan de Vergara to inform Archbishop Croy on religious developments in Spain.
1527	Present at Valladolid Congregation as inquisitorial adviser.
1528	Dean of Oviedo (until 1533).
1529	Bishop of Elna.
1530	Bishop of Oviedo (1533: synod; 1535: visitation of diocese).
1535	President of Chancellery of Valladolid.
1539	President of Royal Council.
1539	Bishop of León (May).
1539	Bishop of Sigüenza (October). Undertook four visitations of diocese.
1546	Archbishop of Seville. Governed archdiocese via 'vicars general'. In residence 1549–50.

1547 Inquisitor General.
1558 Discovery of 'Protestant' cells in Valladolid and Seville announced.
1559 Orchestrated arrest and imprisonment of Archbishop Carranza (principal adversary of Valdés).
1559 Produced Spanish Index which fiercely condemned spiritual literature.
1565 Increasingly out of favour at court. Replaced as Inquisitor General by Diego de Espinosa.
1568 Died in Madrid (9 December), aged 85.

Juan Martínez de Siliceo (1486–1557) Archbishop of Toledo under Charles V; instigator of Toledan *limpieza de sangre* statute

1486 Born in Villagarcía, Badajoz. Parents were poor farm labourers from Extremadura.
1502 Began education in Valencia (Dominican convent) and continued in Paris (Sorbonne).
1516 Studied arts and theology at Salamanca. Appointed to chair in Mathematics and Natural Sciences.
1525 Magistral canon, Coria.
1534 Tutor to Prince Philip.
1540 Bishop of Cartagena (aged 54).
1543 Appointed senior royal chaplain.
1546 Archbishop of Toledo (aged 60).
1547 Introduced *limpieza de sangre* statute into the cathedral chapter of Toledo. Strongly opposed by aristocratic canons who believed they had a birthright to office.
1551 Jesuits prohibited from preaching, administering the Eucharist and delivering mass within limits of archdiocese. *Ejercicios Espirituales* withdrawn from circulation by Siliceo.
1555 Cardinal of Rome.
1556 Royal ratification of *limpieza* statute.
1557 Died in Toledo (31 May), aged 71.

Ignatius of Loyola, SJ (1491–1556) Founder of Society of Jesus and writer of the *Spiritual Exercises*

1491 Born in Guipúzcoa, the youngest son of a powerful aristocratic family of Old Christian origins. Attracted to a military career, influenced by the experience of his elder brothers.
1517 Participated in the quelling of the Comuneros revolt.
1521 Wounded in the defence of Pamplona against French attack. Influenced by the reading of devotional literature during his convalescence to take up the life of an ascetic.
1523 Set out on a pilgrimage to Rome. Spent a year in prayer and penitence at Manresa. Began to write the *Spiritual Exercises*.
1524 A student of theology at Barcelona.
1526 A student at Alcalá and a member of Erasmian circles, combining his studies with his role as a proselytiser. The Inquisition

	launched an investigation into his spiritual methods and activities. Arrested in April and released in June.
1527	Fled to Paris to avoid further persecution. Met with six other scholars who shared his apostolic ideals.
1534	At Montmartre the founder members of the Society of Jesus (SJ) took their vows of poverty, chastity and obedience.
1540	The Society of Jesus received official papal sanction and soon became the international cornerstone of the Counter-Reformation's education mission.
1553	*Spiritual Exercises* suspected of Illuminist content and withdrawn from circulation in the 1559 Index. The Dominicans led the opposition to the Society in Spain, accusing it of Illuminist and *converso* infiltration.
1556	Died in Rome (31 July), aged 65.
1622	Canonised.

Juan de Vergara (1492–1557) Humanist scholar at court of Charles V and friend of Erasmus

1492	Born in Toledo, mother of Jewish descent, brother Bernardino Tovar an *alumbrado*.
1512–16	Educated at Alcalá, protected by Cardinal Cisneros. Undertook the Greek translation of the Polyglot Bible.
1516–17	Doctor of theology and professor at University of Alcalá. Secretary to Cardinal Cisneros. Acquired canonry of Alcalá, plus other benefices.
1518	Appointed secretary to Guillermo Croy, Archbishop of Toledo (1517–21).
1520	Travelled to Bruges to meet Croy at court of Charles I. Became friend and admirer (*amigo y aficionado*) of Erasmus.
1521	Attended Diet of Worms. Not inspired by Luther.
1522	Appointed court chaplain to Charles V in Spain.
1523	Appointed secretary to Archbishop Fonseca.
1525	Erasmus's *Enchiridion* translated into Spanish.
1529	Erasmian scholars from Alcalá began to be hounded by Inquisition.
1530	Inquisition began collecting evidence against Vergara, denounced by the *beata* Francisca Hernández as an alleged Lutheran.
1533	Vergara arrested, accused of being a *luterano, alumbrado y erasmista* and of suborning the work of the Inquisition.
1535	Vergara condemned at an *auto de fe* held in Toledo. Accused of triple heresy and ordered to abjure *de vehementi*. Confined to monastic seclusion for one year and fined 1500 ducats.
1537	Freedom granted. Resumed post as canon of Toledo but health and career affected by trial.
1547	Opposed introduction of *limpieza de sangre* statute into Toledo Cathedral.
1557	Died in Toledo (20 February), aged 65.

Juan de Ávila (*c*.1499–1569) A pre-Tridentine religious reformer and writer

c.1499	Born in Almodóvar del Campo, Ciudad Real, of *converso* family origins.
1520–3	A student at Alcalá, where he was tutored by Domingo de Soto. Influenced by Erasmian philosophy.
1526	Ordained as a priest. Worked as a popular preacher in Seville, where he enjoyed great success, attracting a large number of devotees. Noted for his views on the lack of vocation within the priesthood and the misery of the poor.
1531	Inquisition began to investigate the suspect content of Ávila's sermons.
1532–3	Ávila imprisoned, accused of *alumbrado* tendencies, of favouring mental over vocal prayer. He began writing *Audi, filia* – a commentary on Psalm 44.
1533	Case against Ávila absolved.
1534–6	Worked as a preacher in Córdoba and Granada. He developed around him a sacerdotal school of New Christians, who engaged in apostolic missions. He established colleges for the training of priests, soon to become model seminaries.
1559	*Audi, filia*, published in 1556, condemned by Valdés's Index as a work of heterodoxy and withdrawn from publication.
1569	Died in Montilla, Córdoba (10 May), aged 70.
1894	Beatified by Pope Leo XIII.
1970	Canonised.

Pedro Guerrero (1501–76) A pre-Tridentine reformer and principal Spanish delegate at Trent II and III

1501	Born in Leza del Río, Logroño.
1513	Studied Latin grammar at Sigüenza where his uncle was a Jeronimite monk.
1520s	Studied arts at University of Alcalá. Met Juan de Ávila, 1520–6.
1529	Studied theology at Salamanca, San Bartolomé.
1531–5	Held two professorial chairs in theology at Salamanca: Santo Tomás (1531–2) and Durando (1532–5).
1535	Held professorial chair at Sigüenza (Prima de Teología) and magistral canon of cathedral.
1546	Archbishop of Granada: a pre-Tridentine reforming prelate. Restored the Colegio de San Cecilio, established by Talavera, as a seminary (Colegio Eclesiástico) and prepared Constitutions (1547).
1551–2	Trent II. Interventions on the Eucharist, the sacrament of penance and the order of priesthood.
1553	Returned to archdiocese to implement reform.
1561–3	Trent III. Took a major role in debates on residence and the primacy of papal authority. Inspired by religious ideals and initiatives of Vitoria and Ávila.
1565–6	Held Provincial Council of Granada. Met with considerable difficulties in application of Tridentine ideals.

1568–71	Supported rigorous campaign against the *moriscos* leading to second Alpujarras revolt.
1572	Held diocesan synod.
1576	Died in Granada (2 April), aged 75.

Bartolomé de Carranza y Miranda (OSD) (1503–76) Archbishop of Toledo under Philip II; imprisoned by Inquisition for 17 years on a charge of heresy

1503	Born in Miranda de Arga, Navarra, of poor, *hidalgo* parents of Old Christian origin.
1520	Joined Dominican order. Studied at Salamanca and Valladolid.
1533	Professor of theology, San Gregorio, Valladolid.
1545	Attended first session of Council of Trent where he gained a reputation as a distinguished theologian and supporter of church reform.
1547	Published treatise on clerical residence.
1550	Confessor to Prince Philip.
1551–2	A delegate at Trent II. Produced a tract (*Speculum pastorum*) on the responsibilities of the ecclesiastical hierarchy.
1554	Accompanied Philip to England as his religious adviser.
1557	Appointed Archbishop of Toledo by Philip II, absent in Low Countries.
1558	Sent to Flanders to investigate clandestine literature. Took a rigid stance on extirpation of heresy in the Netherlands. *Comentarios sobre el catechismo cristiano* published in Antwerp. Entered Toledo (October) and began his visitation of archdiocese.
1559	Arrested at Torrelaguna (22 August). Philip arrived at Laredo on 29 August.
1559–66	Imprisoned in Valladolid. Trial began in 1561.
1566	Fernando de Valdés removed as Inquisitor General.
1562	*Catechismo* approved by Council of Trent.
1567–76	Imprisoned in Rome. Released April 1576, accused of being 'highly suspect of heresy'. Required to retract certain suspect propositions from his writings and forbidden to return to his archdiocese for five years.
1576	Died in Rome (2 May), aged 73.

Melchor Cano (OSD) (1509?–1560) Dominican scholar, delegate at Trent, religious adviser to Philip II, fiercely opposed to reformist ideas and innovation in religious life

1509?	Born Tarancón, Cuenca.
1524	Entered Dominican order, San Esteban, Salamanca.
1527–31	Studied arts and theology under Francisco de Vitoria at Salamanca.
1531	Completed studies at San Gregorio, Valladolid.
1536	Obtained chair in theology at San Gregorio (Cátedra de Vísperas) where Carranza held a rival chair (Cátedra de

	Prima). Divisions between *carrancistas* and *canistas* began to emerge.
1542	In Rome for General Chapter of Dominican Order.
1543	Chair in theology (Santo Tomás) at University of Alcalá de Henares.
1546	Chair in theology (Prima de Teología) at Salamanca (upon death of Vitoria).
1550	Present at debate between Las Casas and Sepúlveda held at Valladolid.
1550	Present at Dominican Provincial Chapter (with Carranza its President) – the scene of doctrinal disputes between scholars with ideologically opposed views. Cano attacked Jesuit philosophy for its Illuminist leanings.
1551	Trent II (with Carranza): two of the most well-respected theologians at Trent.
1552	Appointed Bishop of Canaries.
1553	Renounced see (already rejected by Carranza). His ambitions went beyond the Canaries.
1556	Cano called to Roman curia to explain support for Philip II in tensions between royal court and the papacy.
1556	Provincial of OSD (unconfirmed by Rome). Adviser to king on various juntas. Censor to Inquisition. Collaborator in compilation of 1559 Index.
1557	Prior of San Esteban.
1560	Died in Toledo (30 September), aged 51.

Francisco de Borja, SJ (1510–72) Duke of Gandía; third General of Society of Jesus

1510	Born in Gandía, Valencia, into a distinguished aristocratic family. First son of Juan de Borja, third Duke of Gandía, and Juana de Aragón. A great-grandson of Pope Alexander IV via the paternal line and of Ferdinand the Catholic via the maternal line.
1520	Educated in Zaragoza (letters, music, arms) where his uncle was archbishop. Entered into royal service as a page to the sister of Charles V, Catalina, betrothed to John III of Portugal.
1529	Married Leonor de Castro, Portuguese lady of honour to Empress Isabel.
1530	Nominated master of the hunt and master of the horse to Empress Isabel. Birth of first son, Carlos.
1539	Profoundly affected by unexpected death of Empress Isabel. Appointed Viceroy of Catalonia. Began his own spiritual journey which brought him into contact with the Jesuits.
1542	Inherited the title Duke of Gandía following death of father. Continued service for Charles V at court.
1546	Death of wife Leonor in March contributed to decision to enter Society of Jesus in June.
1547	Founded Jesuit college in Gandía, soon elevated to university status by Pope Paul III.

1548	Formally admitted into Society with papal approval.
1550	Doctor in theology. Visit to Rome: Jesuit status confirmed.
1551	Renounced secular titles and possessions in exchange for religious habit. Ordained as a priest. Dedicated himself to preaching and the writing of spiritual tracts.
1554	Nominated *Comisario General* for Spain and Portugal by Loyola. Charged with establishing Jesuit colleges.
1555	Called to Yuste to be at bedside of Charles V in his dying days. Executor of his will.
1559	Borja's *Obras del Cristiano* expurgated in Valdés's Index of prohibited texts. Deeply wounded by this affront to his name.
1561	Left Spain for Rome, called to serve Pope Pius IV.
1565	Nominated third General of Society of Jesus in succession to Laínez.
1570	New edition of *Constitutions of Society* published under Borja's direction.
1572	Died in Rome (30 September), aged 62.
1624	Beatifed by Pope Urban VIII.
1671	Canonised by Pope Clement X.

Gaspar de Quiroga (1512–94) Archbishop of Toledo under Philip II. A distinguished ecclesiastical statesman whose career spanned 50 years

1512	Born in Madrigal, Old Castile. Parents of lower noble origins. Brother Rodrigo treasurer to Juan de Tavera, Archbishop of Toledo.
1531	Studied at Colegio Mayor, San Salvador de Oviedo, Salamanca.
1536	Studied at Colegio Mayor de Santa Cruz, Valladolid.
1538	Doctor in canon law.
1540	*Vicario General* of Alcalá de Henares.
1543	Master of Schools, Alcalá de Henares. Excommunicated by Rome for refusal to publish papal bulls prejudicial to royal jurisdiction over Spanish Church.
1545	Canon of Toledo. Supported enforcement of *limpieza de sangre* statute.
1554	Auditor on the Council of Rota, Rome. Earned papal absolution.
1558	Inspector of monasteries in Naples and Sicily.
1558	Councillor of Castile.
1566	Councillor of Inquisition. Inspector, Council of Crusade.
1567	President of Council of Italy.
1572	Bishop of Cuenca (aged 60). Supported programme of religious reform.
1573	Inquisitor General.
1574	Councillor of State.
1577	Archbishop of Toledo (aged 65), charged with carrying forward the work of the Counter-Reformation in Spain. Refused presidency of Council of Castile.

1578	Cardinal of Rome.
1582–3	Led 12th Toledan Provincial Council.
1583–4	Index of prohibited texts published: part 1 prohibitory, part 2 expurgatory.
1584	Authorised the commissioning of *The Burial of the Count of Orgaz* by El Greco for the Church of Santo Tomé, Toledo.
1594	Died in Toledo (3 December), aged 82. Residue from his estate (1 500 000 ducats) bequeathed equally to Holy See, Philip II and to pious undertakings.

Teresa de Ávila (OCarm) (1515–82) Founder of Discalced Carmelite order and renowned Spanish mystic

1515	Born in Ávila into a Toledan family of *converso* blood via the paternal line.
1535	Entered the Carmelite convent of La Encarnación, Ávila.
1536	Entered the Carmelite order (aged 21).
1538	Influenced by her reading of the *Tercer Abecedario* to take up mystical prayer and meditation.
1540s	Experienced a 'divine revelation'.
1550s	Further experiences of mystical union with God.
1560	Met Pedro de Alcántara in Ávila. Began to write *Libro de la Vida*. Determined to reform Carmelite order.
1562	Founded Convent of St Joseph, Ávila, under primitive rule.
1562–82	16 female and 14 male Discalced Carmelite convents founded with aid of John of Yepes (John of the Cross).
1562–7	Wrote *Camino de Perfección* and *Meditaciones sobre los Cantares*. Publication of *Libro de la Vida* deferred.
1576–80	Conflict between the reformed and unreformed Carmelites.
1576	Denounced to the Inquisition of Seville on account of suspicions surrounding her spiritual methods. Suggestion of her connection with the *alumbrado* movement in Seville.
1582	Died in Alba de Tormes (4 October), aged 67.
1614	Beatified by Pope Paul IV.
1622	Canonised by Pope Gregory XV.

Luis de León (OSA) (1527–91) Augustinian poet, philosopher, liberal theologian and hebraist scholar of *converso* origin

1527	Born Belmonte, Cuenca.
1544	Entered the Order of Saint Augustine (OSA).
1546–51, 1552–5	Studied theology at Salamanca.
1551–2, 1555–7	Studied theology at Alcalá.
1561	Translated the Song of Songs from Hebrew.
1561	Elected to Thomas Aquinas chair in theology at Salamanca.
1565	Elected to the Durando chair in theology at Salamanca.
1568	Entered into dispute over authority of Vulgate Bible with León de Castro.

1571 Denounced to Inquisition. Charged with 17 suspect propositions.

1572 Arrested and imprisoned for $4\frac{1}{2}$ years. Wrote *De los nombres de Cristo*.

1576 Released from imprisonment without charges and resumed his lecture with the words '*dicebamus hesterna die*' ('As we were saying the other day').

1578 Elected to chair in moral philosophy, Salamanca.

1579 Elected to chair of Holy Scripture, Salamanca.

1582 Subject to further Inquisitorial inquiry.

1584 Case against him absolved under Archbishop Quiroga.

1588 Edited the work of Teresa de Jesús.

1591 Elected Vicar General and Provincial of OSA.

1591 Died at Madrigal, Ávila (23 August), aged 64.

Benito Arias Montano (1527–98) Liberal biblical scholar, compiler of new Polyglot Bible

1527 Born in Extremadura of poor, *hidalgo* parents. Father a notary to the Holy Office.

1548 A student of biblical scholarship at Alcalá and a highly proficient linguist.

1560 Entered the Order of Santiago as a priest.

1562 Accompanied Bishop of Segovia, Martín Pérez de Ayala, to the third session of the Council of Trent where he made important speeches on marriage and communion.

1566 Appointed royal chaplain with pension of 200 ducats.

1568 Sent to Netherlands to supervise new Polyglot Bible project, patronised by Philip II.

1572 Publication of new Polyglot ratified by Pope Gregory XIII. Sent to the Netherlands as political counsellor to Philip II.

1574 Luis de Castro launched attack on Montano for his liberal interpretation of the Latin Vulgate Bible.

1576 Congregation of Cardinals approved the new Polyglot, although judged to contain many inaccuracies.

1576 Montano appointed curator of the royal library of the Escorial, charged with the classification and expurgation of suspect texts.

1577 Juan de Mariana defended the publication of the new Polyglot as a scholarly work that did not conflict with doctrinal principles.

1586 Retired increasingly to monastic seclusion in Seville, where he dedicated himself to his writing.

1598 Died in Seville (6 July), aged 71.

Juan de Ribera (*c*.1532–1611) Archbishop and Viceroy of Valencia. A reforming prelate, increasingly intransigent towards *morisco* community

c.1532 Born in Seville. Possibly bastard son of Don Pedro Enriquez y Afán de Ribera y Portocarrero and Dona Teresa de los Pinelos.

1536	Obtained dispensation from papal nuncio to pursue church career.
1534	Aged 12 received tonsure as priest in Church of San Esteban, linked to Ribera family.
1544–61	Studied canon law, arts and theology at University of Salamanca (Domingo de Soto and Melchor Cano among masters). Also influenced by liberal thinkers (Juan de Ávila, Luis de Granada) and semi-Protestant trends (e.g. Constantino, Carranza).
1557	Graduated in theology.
1562	Bishop of Badajoz (with dispensation for being below canonical age). Intent on carrying forward reform in his bishopric. A model pre-Tridentine bishop.
1568	Rewarded for his exemplary pastoral work by Pius V with title of Patriarch of Antioch.
1568	Elevated to office of Archbishop of Valencia, a seat of heavy *morisco* influence. Initially daunted by the task. Heard Lenten confessions of clergy. Celebrated seven synods. Undertook visitation of archdiocese. Erection of seminary (Colegio del Patriarca).
1573	Discussed with local clergy ways of better integrating *morisco* population, including plan to extend parochial infrastructure.
1599	Instructed by Philip III to continue with preaching mission and publication of new catechism for New Christians.
1601–2	Wrote to king advocating expulsion of *moriscos* as only possible solution.
1602–4	Viceroy of Valencia.
1609	Delivered a speech justifying expulsion on religious grounds.
1611	Died in Valencia (6 January), aged 79.
1796	Beatified by Pope Pius VI.
1960	Canonised by John XXIII.

Juan de Mariana, SJ (1536–1624) Jesuit historian, theologian and writer

1536	Born in Toledo, the illegitimate son of Juan Martínez de Mariana, archdeacon of Talavera, and Bernardina Rodríguez. Began studies in Talavera, then transferred to University of Alcalá where he obtained a masters degree in arts.
1554	Joined Society of Jesus. Took noviciate in Simancas (under direction of Francisco de Borja). Continued studies at Alcalá, specialising in Latin and Greek.
1561–5	Studied at Colegio Romano, Rome. Master in theology and classical studies.
1562	Ordained as a priest.
1564	Doctor in theology.
1565–7	Rector, Loreto. Continued with preaching and teaching role.
1567–9	Prefect of studies and professor at Messina.
1569–74	Lecturer in theology (Summa, Santo Tomas) at Colegio de Clermont, Paris. Returned to Spain, suffering from illness.
1574–1624	In Toledo, writing and continuing with his ministry. Worked with Archbishops Quiroga and García de Loaysa.

1577	Issued a favourable judgement on Montano's Polyglot Bible.
1582	Attended Toledan Provincial Synod.
1583	Helped compile censorship Index.
1592	Produced his *Historia General de España* in Latin (Castilian edition 1601).
1609	Wrote a tract critical of the rule by favourite (*valimiento*) of the Duke of Lerma (*Del cambio de la moneda*).
1624	Died in Toledo (16 February), aged 88.
1640	Mariana's work expurgated by Inquisitorial censors.

Bernardo de Sandoval y Rojas (1546–1618) Archbishop of Toledo under Philip III; a voice of opposition to *valimiento* of his great-nephew

1546	Born in Aranda del Duero, Burgos. Second son of family of nine children. Uncle: Cristóbal de Rojas y Sandoval, Archbishop of Seville (1571–80); nephew: Francisco Gómez de Sandoval y Rojas, Duke of Lerma.
1555	Received tonsure as priest (episcopal palace, Oviedo).
1567	Degree in arts, University of Alcalá de Henares.
1567	Degree in theology, University of Salamanca.
1574	Canon of Seville, Archdeacon of Ecija, Governor of the archbishopric of Seville.
1586	Bishop of Ciudad Rodrigo
1588	Bishop of Pamplona. Held synod and undertook visitation of diocese. Clash with members of chapter over elevation of his relatives (*criados*) to cathedral office.
1596	Bishop of Jaen.
1599	Cardinal of Rome (upon recommendation of Duke of Lerma).
1599	Archbishop of Toledo and Councillor of State.
1600	Wrote a critical account of the itinerancy and extravagance of the court and the exercise of favouritism in appointments.
1602/3	Refused office of Inquisitor General.
1604	Established the Chapel of Nuestra Senora del Sagrario in Toledo Cathedral.
1608	Accepted office of Inquisitor General.
1615	Cervantes acknowledged his patronage in the prologue to Part II of *Don Quijote*.
1618	Died in Madrid (7 December), aged 72.

Source: *Diccionario de Historia Eclesiástica de España*, ed. Quintín Aldea et al., 4 vols (Madrid, 1972–5), and Suplemento I (Madrid, 1987).

Notes

Notes to Chapter 1: The Breakdown of Spain's Multi-Cultural Heritage

1. Philippe Wolff, 'The 1391 Pogrom in Spain: Social Crisis or Not?', *Past and Present*, 50 (1971), pp. 4–18.
2. Francisco Cantera Burgos, 'Fernando del Pulgar and the *Conversos*', in *Spain in the Fifteenth Century*, ed. J. R. L. Highfield (London, 1974), p. 347.
3. See Albert A. Sicroff, *Los estatutos de limpieza de sangre* (Madrid, 1985), pp. 51–6.
4. Angus MacKay, 'Popular Movements and Pogroms in Fifteenth-Century Castile', *Past and Present*, 55 (1972), pp. 33–67.
5. On the establishment of the Inquisition, see Henry Charles Lea, *A History of the Inquisition of Spain*, vol. 1 (London, 1922), chap. 4; Henry Kamen, *Inquisition and Society in Spain in the Sixteenth and Seventeenth Centuries* (Bloomington, 1985), chap. 3.
6. Cited by J. N. Hillgarth, *The Spanish Kingdoms, 1250–1516*, vol. 2 (Oxford, 1978), p. 424.
7. Burgos, 'Fernando del Pulgar and the *Conversos*', p. 339.
8. Kamen, *Inquisition and Society*, p. 42.
9. Ibid., pp. 33–4.
10. Alonso Fernández de Madrid, *Vida de Fray Fernando de Talavera* (facs. edn, Granada, 1992), p. lvi.
11. Kamen, *Inquisition and Society*, pp. 35–6.
12. Ibid., p. 55.
13. Hillgarth, *The Spanish Kingdoms*, vol. 2, p. 413.
14. Ibid., p. 414.
15. John Edwards, 'Religious Faith and Doubt in Late Medieval Soria, *c.*1450–1500', *Past and Present*, 120 (1988), pp. 3–25.
16. Jaime Contreras and Gustav Henningsen, 'Forty-four Thousand Cases of the Spanish Inquisition (1540–1700): Analysis of a Historical Data Bank', in *The Inquisition in Early Modern Europe: Studies in Sources and Methods*, ed. Gustav Henningsen and John Tedeschi (Illinois, 1986), p. 117.

17. H. C. Lea, *A History of the Inquisition of Spain*, vol. 2 (London, 1922), p. 91.
18. Hillgarth, *The Spanish Kingdoms*, vol. 2, p. 443.
19. Jerónimo de Zurita, *Historia del rey Don Hernando el Catholico*, 6 vols (Zaragoza, 1610), vol. 1, fol. 9*v*, cited by Henry Kamen, 'The Expulsion: Purpose and Consequences', in *Spain and the Jews*, ed. Elie Kedourie (London, 1992), p. 83.
20. Pilar León Tello, *Judíos de Toledo*, 2 vols (Madrid, 1979), vol. 1, p. 347.
21. Andrés Bernáldez, *Memorias del reinado de los reyes católicos* (Madrid, 1962 edn), chap. cx, p. 251.
22. Kamen, 'The Expulsion: Purpose and Consequences', p. 85.
23. John Edwards, 'Jews and *Conversos* in the Region of Soria and Almazán: Departures and Returns', in *Religion and Society in Spain, c.1492* (Aldershot, 1996), article IV.
24. Jaime Vicens Vives (ed.), *Historia Social y Económica de España y América*, vol. 2 (Barcelona, 1988), pp. 362–3.
25. L. P. Harvey, *Islamic Spain, 1250 to 1500* (Chicago and London, 1990), p. 316.
26. Peggy K. Liss, *Isabel the Queen: Life and Times* (Oxford, 1992), p. 171.
27. M. A. Ladero Quesada, *Mudéjares de Castilla* (Valladolid, 1969), doc. 148.
28. Geoffrey Woodward, *Spain in the Reigns of Isabella and Ferdinand, 1474–1516* (London, 1997), p. 83.
29. Mercedes García-Arenal, *Inquisición y moriscos: los procesos del tribunal de Cuenca* (Madrid, 1978), especially chap. 3 on religious customs.
30. Cited by J. H. Elliott, 'The Discovery of America and the Discovery of Man', in *Spain and its World, 1500–1700* (New Haven and London, 1989), p. 53.
31. Louis Cardaillac, *Moriscos y Cristianos: un enfrentamiento polémico (1492–1640)* (Madrid, 1979), pp. 111–12.
32. Kamen, *Inquisition and Society*, p. 106.
33. Albert W. Lovett, *Early Habsburg Spain, 1517–1598* (Oxford, 1986), p. 265.
34. On the second revolt of the Alpujarras, see John Lynch, *Spain under the Habsburgs*, vol. 1, *Empire and Absolutism, 1516–1598* (Oxford, 1965), pp. 211–18; Fernand Braudel, *The Mediterranean and the Mediterranean World in the Age of Philip II*, vol. 2 (London, 1976), p. 793.
35. Braudel, *The Mediterranean*, vol. 2, p. 793.
36. Lynch, *Spain under the Habsburgs*, vol. 2, *Spain and America, 1598–1700* (Oxford, 1969), pp. 44–5.
37. Kamen, *Inquisition and Society*, pp. 108–9.
38. James Casey, *Early Modern Spain: A Social History* (London, 1999), p. 226.
39. Antonio Domínguez Ortiz and Bernard Vincent, *Historia de los Moriscos* (Madrid, 1979), p. 167.
40. John. A. Jones, '*Fervor sin fanatismo*: Pedro de Valencia's Treatise on the *Moriscos*', in *Faith and Fanaticism in Early Modern Spain*, ed. Lesley K. Twomey (Aldershot, 1997), pp. 159–74.
41. Domínguez Ortiz and Vincent, *Historia de los Moriscos*, pp. 176–9.
42. Luis Cabrera de Córdoba, *Relaciones de las cosas sucedidas en la Corte de España desde 1599 hasta 1614* (Madrid, 1857), p. 464.

43. Kamen, *Inquisition and Society*, p. 112.
44. Domínguez Ortiz and Vincent, *Historia de los Moriscos*, appendix 8.
45. Miguel de Cervantes, *El Ingenioso Hidalgo Don Quijote de La Mancha*, part 2, chap. 54.
46. Braudel, *The Mediterranean*, vol. 2, p. 796.
47. J. H. Elliott, *Imperial Spain, 1469–1716* (London, 1972), p. 308.
48. Cited by Braudel, *The Mediterranean*, vol. 2, p. 797, n. 204.

Notes to Chapter 2: Traditionalism and Innovation in the Spanish Church

1. Kamen, *Inquisition and Society*, p. 64.
2. Marcel Bataillon, *Erasmo y España: estudios sobre la historia espiritual del siglo xvi* (Mexico, 1966), pp. 248–83.
3. Lu Ann Homza, *Religious Authority in the Spanish Renaissance* (Baltimore and London, 2000), chap. 2.
4. Bataillon, *Erasmo y España*, pp. 438–70; *Diccionario de Historia Eclesiástica de España*, ed. Quintín Aldea Vaquero et al. (hereafter cited as *DHEE*), vol. 4 (Madrid, 1975), pp. 2737–42.
5. Jodi Bilinkoff, *The Ávila of Saint Teresa* (Ithaca, NY, 1989), pp. 80–7.
6. Ramón Arce, *Juan de Ávila y la Reforma de la Iglesia en España* (Madrid, 1970), pp. 80–7.
7. *DHEE*, vol. 2 (Madrid, 1972), pp. 1231–4 ('Jesuitas').
8. Alastair Hamilton, *Heresy and Mysticism in Sixteenth-Century Spain* (Cambridge, 1992), p. 97.
9. Teresa de Ávila, *Libro de la Vida* (Madrid, 1986), 7:17.
10. Cited by E. Allison Peers, *A Handbook to the Life and Times of Saint Teresa and Saint John of the Cross* (London, 1954), p. 123.
11. Ibid., pp. 237–40.
12. Carlos Eire, *From Madrid to Purgatory: The Art and Craft of Dying in Sixteenth-Century Spain* (Cambridge, 1995), p. 505.
13. Letter of Charles V to Juana of Austria of 3 May 1558, printed in Manuel Fernández Álvarez, *Corpus Documental de Carlos V*, vol. 4 (Salamanca, 1979), pp. 424–5. Charles repeated the same advice to his son in the codicil to his will, dated 9 September 1558. See Prudencio de Sandoval, *Historia de la vida y hechos del Emperador Carlos V*, vol. 3 (Madrid, 1956), pp. 552–61.
14. H. C. Lea, *A History of the Inquisition of Spain*, vol. 3 (London, 1922), pp. 426–36; José Luis González Novalín, *El Inquisidor General Fernando de Valdés (1483–1568)*, vol. 1 (Oviedo, 1968), pp. 290–323; M. J. Rodríguez-Salgado, *The Changing Face of Empire: Charles V, Philip II and Habsburg Authority, 1551–1559* (Cambridge, 1988), pp. 215–19.
15. José Martínez Millán, 'Grupos de poder en la corte durante el reinado de Felipe II: la facción ebolista', in *Instituciones y Elites de Poder en la Monarquía Hispánica durante el siglo xvi*, ed. J. Martínez Millán (Madrid, 1992), pp. 137–72.
16. Letter of Valdés to Paul IV of 9 September 1558, printed in Lea, *A History of the Inquisition of Spain*, vol. 3, p. 556.

17. The 1559 Index is reprinted in *Tres índices expurgatorias de la inquisición española en el siglo xvi* (Madrid, 1952).
18. Ignacio Tellecheá Idígoras, *Fray Bartolomé Carranza y el Cardenal Pole: Un navarro en la restauración católica de Inglaterra (1554–1558)* (Pamplona, 1977).
19. Hamilton, *Heresy and Mysticism*, p. 108.
20. Kamen, *Inquisition and Society*, p. 159.
21. John Lynch, 'Philip II and the Papacy', *Transactions of the Royal Historical Society*, 2 (1961), p. 31.
22. Kamen, *Inquisition and Society*, p. 157.
23. H. C. Lea, *A History of the Inquisition of Spain*, vol. 4 (London, 1922), p. 1542.
24. Lynch, *Spain under the Habsburgs*, vol. 1, p. 251.
25. Bernard Rekers, *Benito Arias Montano (1527–98)* (London and Leiden, 1972), appendix 1, no. 40, pp. 140–1.

Notes to Chapter 3: The Reform of the Ecclesiastical Estate

1. José Sánchez Herrero, *Concilios Provinciales y Sínodos Toledanos de los siglos xiv y xv* (La Laguna, Spain, 1976); Antonio García y García (ed.), *Synodicon Hispanum*, vols 1–7 (Madrid, 1987–97); Fidel Fita, 'Concilios españoles inéditos', *Boletín de la Real Academia de la Historia*, 22 (1893), pp. 209–57; Christian Hermann, 'L'Eglise selon les Cortes de Castille, 1476–1598', *Hispania Sacra*, 27 (1974), pp. 201–35.
2. For the proceedings of the Toledan Council of 1473, see Sánchez Herrero, *Concilios Provinciales*, and for those of Seville of 1478, see Fita, 'Concilios españoles inéditos'.
3. H. J. Schroeder, *Canons and Decrees of the Council of Trent* (Illinois, 1978); Jean Delumeau, *Catholicism between Luther and Voltaire* (London, 1977); Francis Clark, *The Catholic Reformation* (Oxford, 1972).
4. *Pío IV y Felipe Segundo: Primeros diez meses de la Embajada de Don Luis de Requesens en Roma, 1563–64* (Madrid, 1891), pp. 445–7.
5. *Nueva Recopilación de las leyes de España*, vol. 1 (facs. edn, Madrid, 1965), 17, law (*ley*) iv; Lynch, *Spain under the Habsburgs*, vol. 1, p. 245.
6. See Antonio Gallego y Burín and Alfonso Gámir Sandoval, *Los Moriscos del Reino de Granada según el sínodo de Guadix de 1554* (Granada, 1968).
7. *Colección de Documentos Inéditos para la Historia de España*, vol. 9 (Madrid, 1846), p. 266.
8. Ibid., pp. 404–5.
9. Sara T. Nalle, *God in La Mancha: Religious Reform and the People of Cuenca, 1500–1650* (Baltimore, 1992), pp. 45–50 and 74–80.
10. Extracts taken from Delumeau, *Catholicism between Luther and Voltaire*, pp. 16–17.
11. J. H. Elliott, *Europe Divided, 1559–1598* (London, 1968), p. 149.
12. See Joseph Bergin, 'The Counter-Reformation Church and its Bishops', *Past and Present*, 165 (1999), pp. 30–73, for an illuminating comparative

study of the episcopates of Catholic Europe in the post-Tridentine period.

13. *Archivo Histórico Nacional* (hereafter cited as *AHN*), Consejos Suprimidos, Legajos 15192–15198; Christian Hermann, *L'Eglise d'Espagne sous le patronage royal (1476–1834)* (Madrid, 1988), pp. 155–6; B. Escandell Bonet, 'Las rentas episcopales del siglo xvi', *Anuario de Historia Económica y Social*, 3 (1970), pp. 57–90.
14. See Ignacio Fernández Terricabras, 'Por una geografía del Patronazgo Real: teólogos y juristas en las presentaciones episcopales de Felipe II', in Enrique Martínez Ruiz and Vicente Suárez Grimón (eds), *Iglesia y Sociedad en el Antiguo Régimen: III reunión científica de la Asociación Española de Historia Moderna* (Las Palmas, 1994), pp. 601–9.
15. Joseph Bergin, *The Making of the French Epsicopate, 1589–1661* (New Haven and London, 1996), chap. 8, esp. pp. 309–22.
16. Helen E. Rawlings, 'The Secularisation of Castilian Episcopal Office under the Habsburgs, *c.*1516–1700', *Journal of Ecclesiastical History*, 38 (1987), pp. 53–79.
17. José Ignacio Tellechea Idígioras, *El Obispo ideal en el siglo de la Reforma* (Rome, 1963).
18. Rawlings, 'Castilian Episcopal Office', p. 68.
19. Gil González Dávila, *Teatro de las Grandezas de la Villa de Madrid* (Madrid, 1623; facs. edn, Madrid, 1986), p. 370.
20. On Quiroga see Lynch, *Spain under the Habsburgs*, vol. 1, pp. 246–8; M. Boyd, *Cardinal Quiroga, Inquisitor General of Spain* (Dubuque, Iowa, 1954); Salazar de Mendoza, *Crónica del Cardenal de España, D. Pedro González de Mendoza* (Toledo, 1625), pp. 287–325.
21. Cited by James Casey in *Early Modern Spain*, p. 233.
22. The calculations have been drawn from Tomás González, *Censo de la población de las provincias y partidos de la Corona de Castilla en el siglo xvi* (Madrid, 1829).
23. Josué Fonseca Montes, *El Clero de Cantabria en la Edad Media* (Cantabria, 1996), chap. 3.
24. Henry Kamen, *The Phoenix and the Flame: Catalonia and the Counter-Reformation* (New Haven and London, 1993), p. 343.
25. Nalle, *God in La Mancha*, chap. 3 and appendix 3 on the educational level of the priesthood in Cuenca.
26. *AHN*, Universidades, Libro 1233-F (Colegiales de San Ildefonso), *AHN*, Inquisición de Toledo, Legajos, 264–485.
27. Bruce Taylor, *Structures of Reform: The Mercedarian Order in the Spanish Golden Age* (Leiden, 2000), pp. 420–1; Kamen, *The Phoenix and the Flame*, p. 72.
28. Taylor, *Structures of Reform*, pp. 130–3, 139–40, 143–7.
29. Allison Peers, *A Handbook to the Life and Times of Saint Teresa and Saint John of the Cross*, pp. 71–95.
30. For a detailed insight into Mercedarian reform, of which the following paragraph is a brief summary, see Taylor, *Structures of Reform*, *passim*.
31. Ibid., p. 391.

Notes to Chapter 4: The Church and the People

1. *Synodicon Hispanum*, vol. 3, Astorga 1553 (Madrid, 1984), p. 76.
2. Cited by Agustín Redondo, 'La religion populaire espagnole au xvi siècle: un terrain d'affrontement', *Culturas Populares*, 4 (Madrid, 1986), p. 337.
3. Jean-Pierre Dedieu, '"Christianisation" en Nouvelle Castille: catéchisme, messe et confirmation dans l'archevêché de Tolède, 1540–1650', *Mélanges de la Casa de Velázquez*, 15 (1977), pp. 261–94; English translation '"Christianization" in New Castile: Cathechism, Communion, Mass and Confirmation in the Archbishopric of Toledo, 1540–1650', in *Culture and Control in Counter-Reformation Spain*, ed. A. J. Cruz and M. E. Perry (Minneapolis, 1991), pp. 1–24.
4. Nalle, *God in La Mancha*, pp. 123–4.
5. Antonio Domínguez Ortiz, *Las Clases Privilegiadas en el Antiguo Régimen: El Estamento Eclesiástico* (Madrid, 1979), p. 252.
6. Kamen, *The Phoenix and the Flame*, p. 106.
7. Nicholas Griffiths, 'Popular Religious Scepticism and Idiosyncrasy in Post-Tridentine Cuenca', in *Faith and Fanaticism in Early Modern Spain*, ed. Twomey, pp. 95–126.
8. Jaime Contreras, *El Santo Oficio de la Inquisición en Galicia, 1560–1700* (Madrid, 1982), pp. 467 and 512–13.
9. Jean-Pierre Dedieu, 'Les quatres temps de l'Inquisition', in *L'Inquisition Espagnole*, ed. B. Bennassar et al. (Paris, 1979), pp. 15–41, esp. 29–31.
10. *Synodicon Hispanum*, vol. 1, Mondoñedo 1541 (Madrid, 1981), p. 73.
11. William A. Christian Jr, *Local Religion in Sixteenth-Century Spain* (Princeton, 1981), p. 167.
12. J. Tejada y Ramiro, *Colección de Cánones de todos los Concilios de la Iglesia de España*, vol. 5 (Madrid, 1855), *Concilio Provincial de Toledo* (1565–6), Sesión III, De Reforma, p. 247.
13. Nalle, *God in La Mancha*, p. 131.
14. Kamen, *The Phoenix and the Flame*, p. 119.
15. Dedieu, '"Christianization" in New Castile', p. 19.
16. Stephen Haliczer, *Sexuality in the Confessional* (Oxford, 1996), pp. 15–16 and 21.
17. Both cases are taken from *AHN*, Inquisición de Toledo (Causas de fe), legajo 32, expediente 6, and legajo 70, expediente 11.
18. Richard L. Kagan, 'The Toledo of El Greco', in *El Greco of Toledo*, ed. J. Brown et al. (Boston, 1982), pp. 57–8.
19. Jean-Pierre Dedieu, 'Le modèle sexuel: la défense du mariage chrétien', in *L'Inquisition Espagnole*, ed. Bennassar et al., pp. 313–38.
20. Contreras, *El Santo Oficio de la Inquisición en Galicia*, pp. 628–9.
21. Eire, *From Madrid to Purgatory*, pp. 178, 186.
22. Fernando Martínez Gil, *Muerte y Sociedad en la España de los Austrias* (Madrid, 1993), pp. 547–8.
23. Isabel Testón Núñez, *Estructuras mentales y vida cotidiana en la sociedad extremeña durante el siglo xvii* (Resumen de Tesis, Universidad de Extremadura, Cáceres, 1982), p. 33.

24. F. Javier Campos y Fernández de Sevilla, *La Mentalidad en Castilla la Nueva en el siglo xvi* (Religión, Economía y Sociedad según 'Las Relaciones Topográficas' de Felipe II) (Madrid, 1986), p. 72.
25. Ibid., p. 73.
26. Ibid., p. 75.
27. Ibid., p. 88.
28. Tejada y Ramiro, *Colección de Cánones*, vol. 5, De Reforma, p. 245.
29. Nalle, *God in La Mancha*, pp. 174–7.
30. Christian Jr, *Local Religion*, pp. 182–3.
31. Ibid., p. 136.
32. José Antonio Mateos Royo, 'All the Town is a Stage: Civic and Religious Festivities in Spain during the Golden Age', *Urban History*, 26/2 (1999), pp. 165–89.
33. Cited by Christian Jr, *Local Religion*, p. 172.
34. On religious drama, see Bruce W. Wardropper, *Introducción al teatro religioso del siglo de oro* (Madrid, 1967); Margaret Wilson, *Spanish Drama of the Golden Age* (Oxford, 1969).
35. Christian Jr, *Local Religion*, p. 151.
36. Maureen Flynn, *Sacred Charity: Confraternities and Social Welfare in Spain, 1400–1700* (London, 1986), p. 32.
37. On Toledan confraternities, see Lynda Martz, *Poverty and Welfare in Habsburg Spain* (Cambridge, 1983), pp. 163–8, and Carmelo Viñas y Mey and Ramón Paz (eds), *Relaciones de los Pueblos de España: Reino de Toledo*, 3 vols (Madrid, 1950–63), vol. 3, chap. 54, pp. 554–67.
38. Viñas y Mey and Paz (eds), *Relaciones de los Pueblos de España: Reino de Toledo*, vol. 3, p. 566.
39. Flynn, *Sacred Charity*, p. 118.
40. Viñas y Mey and Paz (eds), *Relaciones de los Pueblos de España: Reino de Toledo*, vol. 3, p. 560.
41. *Constituciones Sinodales* (Toledo, 1583), fol. 49*v*.
42. Eire, *From Madrid to Purgatory*, pp. 134–41.
43. Martínez Gil, *Muerte y Sociedad*, p. 528.
44. Flynn, *Sacred Charity*, pp. 137–8.

Notes to Chapter 5: The Church in the New World

1. Papal bull, *Inter caetera divinae* (1483), printed in W. E. Sheils, *King and Church: The Rise and Fall of the Patronato Real* (Chicago, 1961), pp. 78–81.
2. Papal bull, *Universalis ecclesiae regimini* (1508) printed in Shiels, *King and Church*, pp. 110–12. For detail on the Patronato Real de las Indias, see *DHEE*, vol. 3 (Madrid, 1973), pp. 1948–9; J. H. Parry, *The Spanish Seaborne Empire* (London, 1966), pp. 153–7; C. R. Boxer, *The Church Militant and Iberian Expansionism, 1440–1770* (Baltimore, 1978), pp. 77–9.
3. Lewis Hanke, *The Spanish Struggle for Justice in the Conquest of America* (Boston, Mass., 1965), p. 17.
4. Parry, *The Spanish Seaborne Empire*, p. 142.

5. On Las Casas, see *DHEE*, vol. 1 (Madrid, 1972), pp. 374–6, and Henry Raup Wagner and Helen Rand Parish, *The Life and Writings of Bartolomé de Las Casas* (Mexico, 1967).
6. A. R. Pagden, Introduction to Bartolomé de Las Casas, *A Short Account of the Destruction of the Indies*, trans. Nigel Griffin (Harmondsworth, 1992), p. xvii.
7. Las Casas, *A Short Account*, preface, p. 13.
8. On Sepúlveda, see *DHEE*, vol. 4, pp. 2433–7.
9. Parry, *The Spanish Seaborne Empire*, p. 147.
10. Christopher Columbus, *Journal of the First Voyage*, trans. B. W. Ife (Warminster, 1990), p. 3.
11. Boxer, *The Church Militant*, p. 113.
12. On the background to the evangelisation process, see Charles Gibson, *Spain in America* (London, 1966), pp. 72–3; Parry, *The Spanish Seaborne Empire*, pp. 161–5; Pedro Borges Morán, 'La Iglesia y la Evangelización', in *Historia General de España y América*, vol. 2 (Madrid, 1982), pp. 651–7.
13. Elliott, 'The Discovery of America and the Discovery of Man', in *Spain and its World*, p. 51.
14. Fernando Cervantes, 'The Idea of the Devil and the Problem of the Indian: The Case of Mexico in the Sixteenth Century' (Institute of Latin American Studies, University of London, 1991), p. 6.
15. Ibid., p. 27.
16. Fernando Cervantes, *The Devil in the New World: The Impact of Diabolism in New Spain* (New Haven and London, 1994), pp. 26–7, and *idem*, 'The Idea of the Devil', pp. 20–5.
17. Boxer, *The Church Militant*, p. 106.
18. Kenneth Mills, 'The Limits of Religious Coercion in Mid-Colonial Peru', *Past and Present*, 145 (1994), pp. 84–121.
19. Sabine MacCormack, '"The Heart has its Reasons": Predicaments of Missionary Christianity in Early Colonial Peru', *Hispanic American Historical Review*, 65/3 (1985), pp. 443–66, quotation at p. 458.
20. Boxer, *The Church Militant*, pp. 14–22, quotation at p. 18.
21. Enrique Dussel, *Episcopado Hispanoamericano* (Mexico, 1966), pp. 77, 146.

Notes to Chapter 6: Crisis and Resilience in the Early Seventeenth-Century Spanish Church

1. John Lynch, *The Hispanic World in Crisis and Change, 1598–1700* (London, 1992), pp. 1–16; Jaime Vicens Vives (ed.), *Historia Social y Económica de España y América*, vol. 3 (Barcelona, 1985), pp. 3–50, 205–22; Elliott, *Imperial Spain*, pp. 285–300; Lovett, *Early Habsburg Spain*, pp. 245–56; Patrick Williams, 'El Reinado de Felipe III', in *Historia General de España y América: La Crisis de la Hegemonía Española. Siglo xvii*, vol. 8 (Madrid, 1986), pp. 419–43.

2. J. H. Elliott, 'Self-Perception and Decline in Early Seventeenth-Century Spain', in *Spain and its World*, pp. 241–61.
3. Sancho de Moncada, *Restauración política de España*, ed. J. Vilar (Madrid, 1974), discurso 2, capítulo 2.
4. Jerónimo de Ceballos, *Discurso sobre el remedio de la Monarquía Española* (Toledo, 1620), no folio.
5. Ángel Manrique, *Socorro del clero al estado* (Salamanca, 1624; ed. Madrid, 1814), fol. 31.
6. Pedro Fernández de Navarrete, *Conservación de Monarquías y discursos políticos*, ed. Michael D. Gordon (Madrid, 1982), discurso 44, pp. 315–53.
7. A. González Palencia (ed.), *Archivo Histórico Español*, vol. 5, *La Junta de Reformación, 1618–1625* (Valladolid, 1932), especially documents 4 and 42 on the excessive growth and declining standards of the clergy.
8. *Censo de la Corona de Castilla, 1591*, facs. edn (Instituto Nacional de Estadística, Madrid, 1984); *Censo de Castilla de 1591: Estudio Analítico* (Madrid, 1986), ed. E. García España and Annié Molinié-Bertrand.
9. Felipe Ruiz Martín, 'La población española al comienzo de los tiempos modernos', *Cuadernos de Historia*, 1 (1967), pp. 189–202, and *idem*, 'Demografía Eclesiástica', in *DHEE*, vol. 2, pp. 682–733; Annié Molinié-Bertrand, 'Le clergé dans le royaume de Castille à la fin du xvie siècle', *Revue d'Histoire Economique et Sociale*, 51 (1978), pp. 5–53.
10. Felipe Ruiz Martín, 'Demografía Eclesiástica'; Domínguez Ortiz, *Las Clases Privilegiadas del Antiguo Régimen*, vol. 2 (Madrid, 1973), p. 274.
11. Elliott, *Imperial Spain*, p. 312.
12. Kamen, *The Phoenix and the Flame*, pp. 162–3.
13. Domínguez Ortiz, *Las Clases Privilegiadas*, vol. 2, p. 206.
14. Ibid., p. 275.
15. González Dávila, *Teatro de las Grandezas de la Villa de Madrid*, pp. 234–99; José Antonio Álvarez y Baena, *Compendio Histórico de las Grandezas de la Coronada Villa de Madrid* (Madrid, 1786), pp. 98–177; León Pinelo (ed.), *Anales de Madrid (447–1659)* (ed. Madrid, 1971), pp. 83–317; María F. Carbajo Isla, *La Población de la Villa de Madrid* (Madrid, 1987), chap. 6; Alfredo Alvar Ezquerra, *El Nacimiento de una Capital Europea: Madrid entre 1516 y 1606* (Madrid, 1989), chap. 1.
16. *Actas de las Cortes de Castilla*, 60 vols (Madrid, 1877–1974), vol. 26 (Cortes of Madrid, 1607), pp. 280–1.
17. *Actas*, vol. 54 (Cortes of Madrid, 1633), p. 242.
18. Juan Reglá, 'La época de los dos últimos Austrias', in *Historia Social y Económica*, ed. J. Vicens Vives, vol. 3, p. 252.
19. Ángel García Sanz, 'Castile 1580–1650: Economic Crisis and the Policy of Reform', in *The Castilian Crisis of the Seventeenth Century*, ed. I. A. A. Thompson and B. Yun (Cambridge, 1995), pp. 13–31.
20. Ángel García Sanz, 'El sector agrario durante el siglo xvii: depresión y reajustes', in *Historia de España Menéndez y Pidal*, vol. 23 (Madrid, 1989), pp. 172–4.
21. Adriano Gutiérrez Alonso, *La Cuidad de Valladolid en el siglo xvii: estudio sobre la decadencia de Castilla* (Valladolid, 1989), p. 215.

22. Lynch, *Spain under the Habsburgs*, vol. 2, pp. 35–6; Antonio Domínguez Ortiz, *Política y Hacienda de Felipe IV* (Madrid, 1983), chap. 4, pp. 227–36.
23. González Palencia (ed.), *La Junta de Reformación, 1618–1625*, document 48.
24. *AHN*, Consejos Suprimidos, Legajo 15214, 17 February 1615 (Bishop of Zamora to the Cámara de Castilla).
25. Domínguez Ortiz, *Política y Hacienda*, pp. 234–5.
26. Antonio Domínguez Ortiz, *Alteraciones Andaluzas* (Madrid, 1973), pp. 191–3.
27. *Avisos de Don Jerónimo de Barrionuevo (1654–1658)*, vol. 221 (Biblioteca de Autores Españoles, Madrid, 1968), entry for 29 November 1654.
28. *Avisos de Barrionuevo*, vol. 221, entry for 27 September 1656, and vol. 222, entry for 11 October 1656; Domínguez Ortiz, *Las Clases Privilegiadas*, vol. 2, p. 367.
29. Agustín Salucio, *Discurso sobre los estatutos de limpieza de sangre* (Madrid, 1600; facs. edn, Madrid, 1979).
30. Ibid., fols. 6*v*–7.
31. Ibid., fol. 26*v*.
32. I. S. Revah, 'La controverse sur les statuts de pureté de sang', *Bulletin Hispanique*, 73 (1971), p. 302.
33. Domínguez Ortiz, *Los Conversos de Origen Judío*, pp. 229 (Memorial from Cortes to Philip III, 1600).
34. González Palencia (ed.), *La Junta de Reformación, 1618–1625*, document 42, pp. 444–9.
35. J. H. Elliott, *The Count-Duke Olivares: The Statesman in an Age of Decline* (New Haven and London, 1986), p. 11.
36. Lea, *A History of the Inquisition of Spain*, vol. 2, p. 310.
37. Kamen, 'A Crisis of Conscience in Golden Age Spain: the Inquisition against Limpieza de Sangre', in *idem*, *Crisis and Change in Early Modern Spain* (Aldershot, 1993), p. 16.
38. Ibid., p. 18.
39. Ibid., p. 21.
40. Cited by Domínguez Ortiz, *Las Clases Privilegiadas*, vol. 2, p. 360.

Notes to Conclusion

1. Jean-Pierre Dedieu, 'Le modèle religieux', in *L'Inquisition Espagnole*, ed. Bennassar et al., pp. 282–4.
2. Kagan, 'The Toledo of El Greco', in *El Greco of Toledo*, p. 58.
3. *Constituciones sinodales del arzobispado de Toledo* (Toledo, 1601), fol. 93.

Select Bibliography

This bibliography is comprised of modern studies that have informed the writing of the text.

Alvar Ezquerra, Alfredo, *El Nacimiento de una Capital Europea: Madrid entre 1516 y 1606* (Madrid, 1989).
Arce, Rafael, *Juan de Ávila y la Reforma de la Iglesia en España* (Madrid, 1970).

Bataillon, Marcel, *Erasmo y España: estudios sobre la historia espiritual del siglo xvi* (Mexico D.F., 1966).
Benítez Sánchez-Blanco, Rafael and Císcar Pallaré, Eugenio, 'La Iglesia ante la conversión y expulsión de los Moriscos', in *Historia de la Iglesia Española*, ed. R. García-Villoslada, vol. 4 (Madrid, 1979), pp. 255–71.
Bennassar, Bartolomé, et al., *L'Inquisition Espagnole, xve–xixe siècles* (Paris, 1979).
Bergin, Joseph, 'Between Estate and Profession: the Catholic Parish Clergy of Early Modern Western Europe', in *Social Orders and Social Classes in Europe since 1500: Studies in Social Stratification*, ed. M. L. Bush (London, 1992), pp. 66–85.
——, *The Making of the French Episcopate, 1589–1661* (New Haven and London, 1996).
——, 'The Counter-Reformation Church and its Bishops', *Past and Present*, 165 (1999), pp. 30–73.
Bilinkoff, Jodi, *The Ávila of Saint Teresa: Religious Reform in a Sixteenth-Century City* (Ithaca, NY, and London, 1989).
Bossy, John, *Christianity in the West, 1400–1700* (Oxford, 1987).
——, 'The Counter-Reformation and the People of Catholic Europe', *Past and Present*, 47 (1970), pp. 51–70.
Boyd, Maurice, *Cardinal Quiroga, Inquisitor General of Spain* (Dubuque, Iowa, 1954).
Boxer, C. R., *The Church Militant and Iberian Expansionism, 1440–1770* (Baltimore and London, 1978).

Braudel, Fernand, *The Mediterranean and the Mediterranean World in the Age of Philip II*, 2 vols (London, 1976).
Burke, Peter, *Popular Culture in Early Modern Europe* (London, 1978).

Cameron, Euan, *The European Reformation* (Oxford, 1991).
Campos, F. Javier y Fernández de Sevilla, *La Mentalidad en Castilla la Nueva en el siglo xvi* (Religión, Economía y Sociedad según 'las Relaciones Topográficas' de Felipe II) (Madrid, 1986).
Candau Chacón, María Luisa, *La Carrera Eclesiástica en el siglo xviii: modelos, cauces y formas de promoción en la Seville rural* (Seville, 1993).
Cantera Burgos, Francisco, 'Fernando del Pulgar and the *Conversos*', in *Spain in the Fifteenth Century, 1369–1516*, ed. J. R. L. Highfield (London, 1972), pp. 296–353.
Carbajo Isla, María F., *La población de la villa de Madrid desde finales del siglo xvi hasta mediados del siglo xix* (Madrid, 1987).
Cardaillac, Louis, *Moriscos y Cristianos: un enfrentamiento polémico (1492–1640)* (Madrid, 1979).
Caro Baroja, Julio, *El Carnaval: análisis histórico-cultural* (Madrid, 1965).
——, *Las formas complejas de la vida religiosa (religión, sociedad y carácter en la España de los siglos xvi y xvii)*, 2 vols (Barcelona, 1995).
Casey, James, *Early Modern Spain: A Social History* (Routledge, 1999).
Censo de la Corona de Castilla de 1591 (Madrid, 1984).
Cervantes, Fernando, *The Devil in the New World: The Impact of Diabolism in New Spain* (New Haven and London, 1994).
——, 'The Idea of the Devil and the Problem of the Indian: the Case of Mexico in the Sixteenth Century' (Institute of Latin American Studies, University of London, 1991).
Chacón-Jiménez, Francisco, 'El Problema de la Convivencia. Granadinos, Mudéjares y Cristianos Viejos en el Reino de Murcia, 1609–1614', *Mélanges de la Casa de Velázquez*, 18/1 (1982), pp. 103–33.
Christian Jr, William A., *Local Religion in Sixteenth-Century Spain* (Princeton, 1981).
Clark, Francis, *The Catholic Reformation* (Oxford, 1972).
Cobos Ruiz de Adana, José, *El clero en el siglo xvii (estudio de una visita secreta a la ciudad de Córdoba)* (Córdoba, 1976).
Contreras, Jaime, *El Santo Oficio de la Inquisición de Galicia, 1560–1700: poder, sociedad y cultura* (Madrid, 1982).
——, 'The Impact of Protestantism in Spain, 1520–1600', in *Inquisition and Society in Early Modern Europe*, ed. Stephen Halizcer (London, 1987), pp. 47–63.
Contreras, Jaime and Henningsen, Gustav, 'Forty-four Thousand Cases of the Spanish Inquisition (1540–1700): Analysis of a Historical Data Bank', in *The Inquisition in Early Modern Europe: Studies in Sources and Methods*, ed. Gustav Henningsen and John Tedeschi (Dekalb, Illinois, 1986), pp. 100–29.

Dedieu, Jean-Pierre, *L'Administration de la foi: l'Inquisition de Tolède (xvie–xviiie siècles)* (Madrid, 1989).
——, 'Christianisation en Nouvelle Castille: catéchisme, messe et confirmation dans l'archevêché de Tolède, 1540–1650', *Mélanges de la Casa de*

Velázquez, 15 (1977), pp. 261–94; English translation in *Culture and Control in Counter-Reformation Spain*, ed. A. J. Cruz and M. E. Perry (Minneapolis, 1991), pp. 1–24.

——, 'The Inquisition and Popular Culture in New Castile', in *Inquisition and Society in Early Modern Europe*, ed. S. Haliczer (London, 1987), pp. 129–46.

——, 'The Archives of the Holy Office of Toledo as a Source for Historical Anthropology', in *The Inquisition in Early Modern Europe: Studies in Sources and Methods*, ed. Gustav Henningsen and John Tedeschi (Dekalb, Illinois, 1986), pp. 158–89.

——,'Les quatres temps de l'Inquisition', in *L'Inquisition Espagnole*, ed. B. Bennassar et al. (Paris, 1979), pp. 15–41.

——,'Le modèle sexuel: la défense du mariage chrétien', in *L'Inquisition Espagnole*, ed. B. Bennassar et al. (Paris, 1979), pp. 313–38.

——, 'Le modèle religieux: le refus de la réforme et le contrôle de la pensée', in *L'Inquisition Espagnole*, ed. B. Bennassar et al. (Paris, 1979), pp. 269–311.

Delumeau, Jean, *Catholicism between Luther and Voltaire* (London, 1977).

Diccionario de Historia Eclesiástica de España (*DHEE*), ed. Q. Aldea, T. Marín, J. Vives, 4 vols and Suplemento I (Madrid, 1972–5 and 1987).

Domínguez Ortiz, Antonio, *Las Clases Privilegiadas del Antiguo Régimen: El Estamento Eclesiástico* (Madrid, 1979).

——, *La Sociedad Española del siglo xvii*, 2 vols (Granada, 1992).

——, *Los Conversos de Origen Judío después de la expulsión* (Madrid, 1957).

——, *Política y Hacienda de Felipe IV* (Madrid, 1983).

——, *Alteraciones Andaluzas* (Madrid, 1973).

—— and Bernard, Vincent, *Historia de los Moriscos: vida y tragedia de una minoría* (Madrid, 1978).

Edwards, John, 'Religious Faith and Doubt in Late Medieval Soria', *Past and Present*, 120 (1988), pp. 3–25.

——, 'Religious Belief and Social Conformity: the *Converso* Problem in Late Medieval Córdoba', *Transactions of the Royal Historical Society*, 31 (1987), pp. 115–28.

——, *Religion and Society in Spain, c.1492* (Aldershot, 1996).

Eire, Carlos M. N., *From Madrid to Purgatory: The Art and Craft of Dying in Sixteenth-Century Spain* (Cambridge, 1995).

Elliott, J. H., *Imperial Spain, 1469–1716* (Harmondsworth, 1983).

——, *Europe Divided, 1559–1598* (London, 1968).

——, *Spain and its World, 1500–1700* (New Haven and London, 1989).

——, *The Count-Duke of Olivares: The Statesman in an Age of Decline* (New Haven and London, 1986).

——, 'The Spanish Conquest and Settlement of America', in *Cambridge History of Latin America*, vol. 1 (Cambridge, 1984), pp. 149–206.

——, 'Spain and America in the Sixteenth and Seventeenth Centuries', in *Cambridge History of Latin America*, vol. 1 (Cambridge, 1984), pp. 287–339.

Escandell Bonet, B., 'Las rentas episcopales en el siglo xvi', *Anuario de Historia Económica y Social*, 3 (1970), pp. 57–90.

Evennett, H. Outram, *The Spirit of the Counter-Reformation* (Cambridge, 1968).

Fernández Terricabras, Ignacio, 'Por una geografía del Patronazgo Real: teólogos y juristas en las presentaciones episcopales de Felipe II', in *Iglesia y Sociedad en el Antiguo Régimen: III reunión científica de la Asociación Española de Historia Moderna*, ed. Enrique Martínez Ruiz and Vicente Suárez Grimón (Las Palmas, 1994), pp. 601–9.

Flynn, Maureen, *Sacred Charity: Confraternities and Social Welfare in Spain, 1400–1700* (Ithaca, NY, 1989).

Fonseca Montes, Josué, *El Clero de Cantabria en La Edad Moderna* (Cantabria, 1996).

Gallego y Burín, Antonio and Gámir Sandoval, Alfonso, *Los Moriscos del Reino de Granada según el sínodo de Guadix de 1554* (Granada, 1968).

García-Arenal, Mercedes, *Inquisición y moriscos: los procesos del tribunal de Cuenca* (Madrid, 1978).

García-Cárcel, Ricardo, *Herejía y sociedad en el siglo xvi: la Inquisición en Valencia, 1530–1609* (Barcelona, 1980).

García España, Eduardo and Molinié-Bertrand, Annié (eds), *Censo de Castilla de 1591: Estudio Analítico* (Madrid, 1986).

García y García, Antonio (ed.), *Synodicon Hispanum*, vols 1–7 (Madrid, 1981–97).

García-Oro, José, *Cisneros y la reforma del clero español en tiempos de los Reyes Católicos* (Madrid, 1971).

García Sanz, Ángel, 'Castile 1580–1650: Economic Crisis and the Policy of Reform', in *The Castilian Crisis of the Seventeenth Century*, ed. I. A. A. Thompson and B. Yun (Cambridge, 1995), pp. 13–31.

——, 'El sector agrario durante el siglo xvii: depresión y reajustes', in *Historia de España Ramón Menéndez Pidal*, vol. 23 (Madrid, 1989), pp. 160–235.

García-Villoslada, Ricardo (ed.), *Historia de la Iglesia en España*: vol. 3 (2 parts), *La Iglesia en España en los siglos xv y xvi* (Madrid, 1980); vol. 4, *La Iglesia en la España de los siglos xvii y xviii* (Madrid, 1979).

Gibson, Charles, *Spain in America* (New York and London, 1966).

González Novalín, José Luis, *El Inquisidor General Fernando de Valdés (1483–1568)*, 2 vols (Oviedo, 1968–71).

González Palencia, A. (ed.), *Archivo Histórico Español*, vol. 5, *La Junta de Reformación, 1618–1625* (Valladolid, 1932).

Gracia Boix, Rafael, *Autos de fe y causas de la Inquisición de Córdoba* (Córdoba, 1983).

Griffiths, Nicholas, 'Popular Religious Scepticism and Idiosyncrasy in Post-Tridentine Cuenca', in *Faith and Fanaticism in Early Modern Spain*, ed. Lesley K. Twomey (Aldershot, 1997), pp. 95–126.

Gutiérrez Alonso, Adriano, *La Ciudad de Valladolid en el siglo xvii: estudio sobre la decadencia de Castilla* (Valladolid, 1989).

Gutiérrez, C., *Españoles en Trento* (Valladolid, 1951).

Haliczer, Stephen, *Sexuality in the Confessional* (Oxford, 1996).

—— (ed.), *Inquisition and Society in Early Modern Europe* (London, 1987).

Hamilton, Alastair, *Heresy and Mysticism in Sixteenth-Century Spain* (Cambridge, 1992).

Hanke, Lewis, *The Spanish Struggle for Justice in the Conquest of America* (Boston, Mass., 1965).

Harvey, L. P., *Islamic Spain, 1250 to 1500* (Chicago and London, 1990).
Henningsen, Gustav, *The Witches' Advocate: Basque Witchcraft and the Spanish Inquisition (1609–1614)* (Reno, 1980).
Hermann, Christian, *L'Eglise d'Espagne sous le patronage royal (1476–1834)* (Madrid, 1988).
——, 'L'Eglise selon les Cortes de Castille, 1476–1598', *Hispania Sacra*, 27 (1974), pp. 201–35.
Highfield, Roger, 'Christians, Jews and Moslems in the Same Society: the Fall of *Convivencia* in Medieval Spain', in *Studies in Church History*, ed. D. Baker, vol. 15 (Oxford, 1978), pp. 121–46.
Hillgarth, J. N., *The Spanish Kingdoms, 1250–1516*, 2 vols (Oxford, 1976–8).
Homza, Lu Ann, *Religious Authority in the Spanish Renaissance* (Baltimore and London, 2000).

Jones, John A., '*Fervor* sin *fantatismo*: Pedro de Valencia's Treatise on the *Moriscos*', in *Faith and Fanaticism in Early Modern Spain*, ed. Lesley K. Twomey (Aldershot, 1997), pp. 159–74.

Kagan, Richard L., 'The Toledo of El Greco', in *El Greco of Toledo*, ed. Johnathan Brown et al. (Boston, Mass., 1982), pp. 57–8.
Kamen, Henry, *Inquisition and Society in Spain in the Sixteenth and Seventeenth Centuries* (London, 1985).
——, *The Spanish Inquisition: An Historical Revision* (London, 1997).
——, *The Phoenix and the Flame: Catalonia and the Counter-Reformation* (New Haven and London, 1993).
——, 'A Crisis of Conscience in Golden Age Spain: the Inquisition against *Limpieza de Sangre*', in *idem*, *Crisis and Change in Early Modern Spain* (Aldershot, 1993), article VII.
——, 'The Expulsion: Purpose and Consequences', in *Spain and the Jews: The Sephardic Experience, 1492 and After*, ed. Elie Kedourie (London, 1992), pp. 74–91.

Ladero Quesada, Miguel Ángel, *Mudéjares de Castilla* (Valladolid, 1969).
Lapeyre, Henri, *Geografía de la España Morisca* (Valencia, 1986).
Lea, Henry Charles, *A History of the Inquisition in Spain*, 4 vols (New York and London, 1922).
León Tello, Pilar, *Judíos de Toledo*, 2 vols (Madrid, 1979).
Liss, Peggy K., *Isabel the Queen: Life and Times* (New York and Oxford, 1992).
Llamas Martínez, Enrique, *Santa Teresa de Jesús y la Inquisición Española* (Madrid, 1972).
Longhurst, John E., *Erasmus and the Spanish Inquisition: The Case of Juan de Valdés* (Albuquerque, 1950).
Lorenzo Pinar, Francisco Javier, *Actitudes religiosas ante la muerte en Zaragoza en el siglo xvi: un estudio de mentalidades* (Zamora, 1989).
Lovett, Albert W., *Early Habsburg Spain, 1517–1598* (Oxford, 1986).
Lynch, John, *Spain under the Habsburgs*, vol. 1, *Empire and Absolutism, 1516–1598* (Oxford, 1965).

——, *Spain under the Habsburgs*, vol. 2, *Spain and America, 1598–1700* (Oxford, 1969).
——, 'Philip II and the Papacy', *Transactions of the Royal Historical Society*, 5th series, 11 (1961), pp. 23–42.

MacCormack, Sabine, '"The Heart has its Reasons": Predicaments of Missionary Christianity in Early Colonial Peru', *Hispanic American Historical Review*, 65/3 (1985), pp. 443–66.
MacKay, Angus, 'Popular Movements and Pogroms in Fifteenth-Century Castile', *Past and Present*, 55 (1972), pp. 33–67.
Márquez, Antonio, *Literatura e Inquisición en España (1478–1834)* (Madrid, 1980).
Martínez Gil, Fernando, *Muerte y Sociedad en la España de los Austrias* (Madrid, 1993).
Martz, Lynda, *Poverty and Welfare in Habsburg Spain: The Example of Toledo* (Cambridge, 1983).
Mateos Royo, José Antonio, 'All the Town is a Stage: Civic and Religious Festivities in Spain during the Golden Age', *Urban History*, 26/2 (1999), pp. 165–89.
Mills, Kenneth, 'The Limits of Religious Coercion in Mid-Colonial Peru', *Past and Present*, 145 (1994), pp. 84–121.
Miscelánea conmemorativa del Concilio de Trento (1563–1963): estudios y documentos (Madrid, 1965).
Molinié-Bertrand, Annié, 'Le clergé dans le royaume de Castille à la fin du xvie siècle', *Revue d'Histoire Economique et Sociale*, 51 (1978), pp. 5–53.
——, *Au Siècle d'Or: L'Espagne et ses hommes: la population du royaume de Castille au xvie siècle* (Paris, 1985).
Monter, William, *Frontiers of Heresy: The Spanish Inquisition from the Basque Lands to Sicily* (Cambridge, 1990).
Muchembled, Robert, *Popular Culture and Elite Culture in France* (London, 1985).

Nalle, Sara T., *God in La Mancha: Religious Reform and the People of Cuenca, 1500–1650* (Baltimore and London, 1992).
——, 'Inquisitors, Priests and the People during the Catholic Reformation in Spain', *Sixteenth Century Journal*, 18 (1987), pp. 557–87.
——, 'Popular Religion in Cuenca on the Eve of the Catholic Reformation', in *Inquisition and Society in Early Modern Europe*, ed. Stephen Haliczer (London, 1987), pp. 67–87.

O'Reilly, Terence, 'Melchor Cano and the Attack on the Spirituality of Saint Ignatius Loyola', in *From Ignatius Loyola to John of the Cross* (Aldershot, 1995), article IV.

Parry, J. H., *The Spanish Seaborne Empire* (London, 1966).
Pérez Villanueva, Joaquín (ed.), *La Inquisición Española: nueva visión, nuevos horizontes* (Madrid, 1980).

Rawlings, Helen E., 'The Secularisation of Castilian Episcopal Office under the Habsburgs, *c.*1516–1700', *Journal of Ecclesiastical History*, 38 (1987), pp. 53–79.

Redondo, Agustín, 'La religion populaire espagnole au xvi siècle: un terrain d'affrontement', in *Culturas Populares*, 4 (Madrid, 1986), pp. 329–69.

——, 'Luther et l'Espagne de 1520 à 1536', *Mélanges de la Casa de Velázquez*, 1 (1965), pp. 109–65.

Rekers, Bernard, *Benito Arias Montano (1527–98)* (London, 1972).

Revah, I. S., 'La controverse sur les statuts de pureté de sang', *Bulletin Hispanique*, 73 (1971), pp. 263–306.

Rodríguez-Salgado, M. J., *The Changing Face of Empire: Charles V, Philip II and Habsburg Authority, 1551–1559* (Cambridge, 1988).

Ruiz Martín, Felipe, 'La población española al comienzo de los tiempos modernos', *Cuadernos de Historia*, 1 (1967), pp. 189–202.

——, 'Demografía Eclesiástica', in *Diccionario de Historia Eclesiástica de España* (*DHEE*), ed. Q. Aldea et al., vol. 2 (Madrid: Insitituo Enrique Flórez, 1972), pp. 682–733.

Salomon, Noel, *La vida rural castellana en tiempos de Felipe II* (Barcelona, 1973).

Sánchez Herrero, José, *Concilios Provinciales y Sínodos Toledanos de los siglos xiv y xv* (La Laguna, 1976).

——, 'Vida y costumbres de los componentes del cabildo catedral de Palencia a finales del siglo xv', *Historia, Instituciones, Documentos*, 3 (1973), pp. 485–532.

Schroeder, H. J., *Canons and Decrees of the Council of Trent* (Rockford, Illinois, 1978).

Shiels, W. E., *King and Church: The Rise and Fall of the Patronato Real* (Chicago, 1961).

Sicroff, Albert A., *Los estatutos de limpieza de sangre: controversias entre los siglos xv y xvii* (Madrid, 1985).

Taylor, Bruce, *Structures of Reform: The Mercedarian Order in the Spanish Golden Age* (Brill, 2000).

Tellechea Idígoras, José Ignacio, *El Arzobispo Carranza y su tiempo*, 2 vols (Madrid, 1968).

——, *Fray Bartolomé Carranza y el cardenal Pole: un navarro en la restauración católica de Inglaterra (1554–1558)* (Pamplona, 1977).

——, *El Obispo ideal en el siglo de la Reforma* (Rome, 1963).

Testón Núñez, Isabel, *Estructuras mentales y vida cotidiana en la sociedad extremeña durante el siglo xvii* (Cáceres, 1982).

Thomas, Keith, *Religion and the Decline of Magic* (Harmondsworth, 1978).

Thompson, I. A. A., *War and Government in Habsburg Spain, 1560–1620* (London, 1976).

——, 'El Reinado de Felipe IV', in *Historia General de España y América: La Crisis de la Hegemonía Española. Siglo xvii*, vol. 8 (Madrid, 1986), pp. 443–519.

Vicens Vices, Jaime (ed.), *Historia Social y Económica de España y América*, vols 2 and 3 (Barcelona, 1985–8).

——, 'The Decline of Spain in the Seventeenth Century', in *The Economic Decline of Empires*, ed. C. M. Cipolla (London, 1970).

Viñas y Mey, Carmelo and Paz, Ramón (eds), *Relaciones de los Pueblos de España ordenadas por Felipe II: Reino de Toledo*, 3 vols (Madrid, 1950–63).

Wagner, Henry Raup and Parish, Helen Rand, *The Life and Writings of Bartolomé de Las Casas* (Albuquerque, 1967).

Williams, Patrick, 'El Reinado de Felipe III', in *Historia General de España y América: La Crisis de la Hegemonía Española. Siglo xvii*, vol. 8 (Madrid, 1986), pp. 419–43.

Wolff, Philippe, 'The 1391 Pogrom in Spain: Social Crisis or Not?', *Past and Present*, 50 (1971), pp. 4–18.

Woodward, Geoffrey, *Spain in the Reigns of Isabella and Ferdinand, 1474–1516* (London, 1997).

Wright, A. D., *Catholicism and Spanish Society under the Reign of Philip II, 1555–1598 and Philip III, 1598–1621* (Lampeter, 1991).

Index

A Brief Account of the Destruction of the Indies (1542), 104
Acosta, José de, SJ (1540–1600), Jesuit historian and missionary, 111–12
Alcalá de Henares, university of
  centre for Polyglot Bible project, 29, 31
  centre of humanist scholarship, 29
Alcántara, Pedro de Fray, OSF (1499–1562), founder of Discalced Franciscans, 36
Alpujarras revolt, I (1499–1502), 15–16; Alpujarras revolt, II (1568–70), 19–20
Alumbrados, 28, 29, 30, 31, 33, 34, 36, 40, 41, 44, 46
Amerindians
  conversion of, 107–10
  religious backsliding of, 110–13
  see also Idolatry campaigns in New World
Ampudia, Pascual de (*d.*1512), Abp Burgos (1496–1512), 53
Anticlericalism, 120–3
Arbitristas, 120–3, 124–7, 142
Arias Montano, Benito (1527–98), biblical scholar, 48–9, 158 (Profile)
Autos de fe of Protestant heretics (1559–60), 41–2 + Table 2.1
Ávila, Juan de (*c.*1499–1596), religious reformer, 32–3, 43, 153 (Profile)
Ávila, Teresa de, *see* Jesús, Teresa de

Bernáldez, Andrés (*d. c.*1513), chronicler and priest, 7–8, 12
Biblical scholarship, attacked by Inquisition, 47–9; *see also* León, Fray Luis de; Arias Montano, Benito
Bishops in the New World
  appointment of, powers of, 114–16
  see also Patronato de las Indias
Bishops in Spain
  education, 64–5
  ideal bishop, the, 66
  income in early seventeenth century, 132–3 (Table 6.4)
  income in late sixteenth century, 62–3 (Table 3.1)
  policy of appointment of under Ferdinand and Isabella and Charles V, 52–3
  policy of appointment of under Philip II, 63–7 + Table 3.2
  principles underlying post-Tridentine reform of, 58–9
  promotional/diocesan structure, 59–61 + Map 1

Bishops in Spain – *continued*
residence, 66–7
social origins, 64
state service, 66–7
see also Patronato agreements
Borja, Francisco de, SJ (1510–72), General of Society of Jesus, 43, 155–6 (Profile)
Brotherhoods
and the Council of Trent, 97–8
in Toledo, 96–7
increase in number of, 96
work of, 95–6

Cámara de Castilla, 66
Cano, Melchor, OSD (1509?–1560), scholar and censor of Inquisition, 34–5, 45–6, 106, 154–5 (Profile)
Carmelites
foundation of Discalced branch, 36
limitations of post-Tridentine reform, 74–6
see also Jesús, Teresa de
Carranza y Miranda, Bartolomé de, OSD (1503–76), Abp Toledo (1557–76), 154 (Profile)
adversaries, 45–6
charged with heresy by Inquisition, 39, 43, 44–7
conflict: crown *v.* papacy, 46–7
treatise on episcopal office, 66
trial verdict, 47
Carrillo de Acuña, Alfonso (1412–82), Abp Toledo (1466–82), 52
Castilian census (1591), 124, 125, 127
Castilian Cortes
and the *limpieza de sangre* debate, 140–1
criticism of growth of religious orders, 129–30
Cazalla, Agustín (*c.*1510–1559), Valladolid heretic, 40–1
Ceballos, Jerónimo de, *arbitrista*, 122, 127
Christianisation programme, 79–81
catechism training, 79–80
ten commandments, 80–1
prayers, 80–1 + Table 4.1
see also Sacraments, observation of; Inquisition and minor heresy
Church councils
see Council of Trent, implementation of via provincial church councils
Clergy/Clerical estate
see Ecclesiastical estate
Cofradías
see Brotherhoods
Columbus, Christopher (1451–1506), 100, 107
Commentaries on the Christian Catechism (1558), 43, 46
Conventual rule
eradication of and replacement by observant rule, 55, 73, 74, 108
Converso
and innovation in religious life, 28, 29, 33, 35, 36, 48
anti-*converso* tensions, 6
creation of, 1–2
culture of, 3–4
persecution of by Inquisition, 7–10
suspicion of, 4–5
see also New Christians; Jews
Convivencia
notion of, 1–2
reflections on breakdown of, 26
survival of, 3–4, 15, 18
Corpus Christi, 94–5
Council of Aranda (1473), 51
Council of Seville (1478), 51
Council of State
and *limpieza de sangre* debate, 141
Council of Trent (1545–63) and ecclesiastical reform
decrees of, 54–5
implementation of via diocesan synods, 57–8
implementation of via provincial church councils, 56, 58, 67, 84, 86, 92, 98

implementation of via seminaries, 71–2 + Table 3.4
outcomes and limitations of, 76–7
policy of Philip II, 55–6
see also Bishops in Spain; Priesthood in Spain; Religious orders in post-Tridentine Spain
Council of Trent (1545–63) and the reform of popular religious culture and discipline, 79, 82, 84, 85, 86, 87, 92, 94, 97, 98–9
Covarrubias, Diego de (1512–77), Bp Segovia (1564–77), President Council Castile (1572–77), 66
Crisis in seventeenth-century Castile, 119–20
Cruzada tax, 46, 135
Cult of saints/relics, 92–3
of Virgin Mary, 93

Décima eclesiástica, 137; *see also* Ecclesiastical estate in seventeenth-century Spain, taxation of
Demographic crisis, 119, 124–5, 133
Discalced Carmelites, *see* Carmelites

Ecclesiastical estate in New World
clash of authority between secular and regular branches, 114–16
Ecclesiastical estate in post-Tridentine Spain
see Council of Trent and ecclesiastical reform
Ecclesiastical estate in pre-Tridentine Spain
condition of/criticism of, 50–1
reform of/limitations of under Ferdinand and Isabella, 51–2; under Charles V, 53
Ecclesiastical estate in seventeenth-century Spain
criticisms of, 120–3
growth in size of regular branch, 75 (Table 3.5), 127–30 + Table 6.2
growth in size of secular branch, 126–7
income/wealth of, 130–5 + Table 6.4
opposition to taxation of, 136–8
regular clergy in Madrid, 128–9 + Table 6.3
size of in relation to lay society, 124–6 + Table 6.1
taxation of, 135–8 + Tables 6.6, 6.7
Egidio, Dr Juan (*d.* 1560), Sevillian heretic, 39–40
Enchiridion Militis Christiani (1503), 28, 29, 30
Encomienda, *encomendero*, 103, 104–5
Episcopate
see Bishops in Spain; Bishops in the New World
Erasmus/Erasmianism
attacked by Inquisition, 30–2
discussed at Congregation of Valladolid (1527), 30
support for in religious and intellectual circles, 28–30
Evangelisation of New World debate, 101–7
Excusado tax, 135, 136 (Table 6.6), 138

Fernández de Navarrete, Pedro, *arbitrista*, 122–3, 127, 141
Fonseca, Alonso de (*c.*1476–1534), Abp Toledo (1523–34), 29, 31
Fresneda, Fray Bernardo, OSF (1509–77), Bp Cuenca (1562–71), 46, 58

Ginés de Sepúlveda, Juan (1490–1573), writer of treatise on justification of conquest, 105–6
González de Ávila, Gil (*c.*1578–1658), historian and priest, 126
González de Mendoza, Pedro (1428–95), Abp Seville (1474–82), Abp Toledo (1482–95), 7, 52–3, 148 (Profile)

Granada, Fray Luis de, OSD (1504–88), writer of devotional literature, 43, 66
Greco, El (Domenikos Theotocopoulus) (*c.*1541–1614), painter of *The Burial of the Count of Orgaz* (1586–88), 67, 144
Guerrero, Pedro (1501–76), Abp Granada (1546–76), 19, 33, 153–4 (Profile)
Guevara, Niño de, Inquisitor General (1599–1602), 22, 140, 141

Hernández, Francisca de, *alumbrada*, 30–1, 40
Holy brotherhoods, *see* Brotherhoods
Humanist tradition
  in New World, 108, 111, 117
  in Spanish Church, 28–30

Idolatry campaigns in New World, 112–13
Illuminists, *see Alumbrados*
Inquisition, the Spanish
  and attack on religious innovation/Catholic reformers, 30–2, 32–7
  and minor heresy, 82–4 + Table 4.2
  establishment and function, 6–7
  Index of prohibited texts (1559), 42–4
  Index of prohibited texts (1583–4), 44
  methods, 10
  reaction to, 8–9
  regional activity, 9–10
  victims, 7–8

Jesús, Teresa de, OCarm (1515–82), founder of Discalced Carmelites, 35–7, 75, 157 (Profile)
Jews in Spain
  anti-semitic tensions, 4–7
  conversion of, 3
  expulsion of, 11–13
  segregation of, 11
  tolerance of, 2
  see also Converso
Jiménez de Cisneros, Francisco, OSF (1436–1517), Abp Toledo (1495–1517), 15, 29, 53, 108, 149 (Profile)
Junta de Reformación (1619), 123; (1623–8), 141, 142

Laínez, Diego de, SJ (1512–65), General of Society of Jesus (1558–64), 35
Las Casas, Bartolomé de, OSD (1474–1566), defender of Indian rights, 104–7, 149–50 (Profile)
León, Fray Luis de, OSA (1527–91), biblical scholar and poet, 37, 47–8, 157–8 (Profile)
Limpieza de sangre (purity of blood) movement
  creation of laws/statutes, 4–6 + Table 1.1
  intervention of Cortes, 140–1
  intervention of Council of Inquisition, 140–2
  intervention of Council of State, 141
  seventeenth-century debate, 139–42
Local religion, *see* Popular religion
Local saints
  feast days of, 91 (Table 4.5), 93–4
  veneration of, 90–1 + Table 4.4
  vows to, 91–2 + Table 4.5
Loyola, Ignatius, SJ (1491–1556), founder of Jesuits, 33–5, 43, 151–2 (Profile)
Lutheranism in Spain
  definition of Lutheran, 37
  discovery of influences in Seville (1558), 39–40 + Table 2.1
  discovery of influences in Valladolid (1558), 40–1 + Table 2.1
  objectives of anti-Lutheran campaign, 41–2
  role of Valdés in detection and punishment of, 38–9

Manrique, Ángel Fray, OCist (1577–1649), *arbitrista*, Bp Badajoz (1646–9), 122, 125
Manrique de Lara, Alonso (*d.*1538), Inquisitor General (1523–38), Abp Seville (1523–38), 29, 30, 32, 39
Mariana, Juan de, SJ (1536–1624), historian, 44, 48, 49, 159–60 (Profile)
Martínez de Siliceo, Juan (1486–1557), Abp Toledo (1546–57), 5–6, 45, 151 (Profile)
Mendicant mission in New World
  early stages, 107–10
  later stages, 114–16
Mercedarian order, post-Tridentine reform of, 74, 75 (Table 3.5), 76
Millones tax, 119, 137, 138 + Table 6.7
Moncada, Sancho de, *arbitrista*, 121, 125, 127
Montesinos, Antonio de, OSD (*d.*1540), defender of Indian rights, 102–3
Moors in Spain, tolerance of, 13–15
Morisco
  after-effects of expulsion of, 24–5
  creation of, 1–2, 15–16
  expulsion of (1609–11), 22–4 + Table 1.2
  failure of integration of, 20
  intolerance of in Granada, 18–20
  intolerance of in Valencia, 20–2
  protection from inquisitorial investigation, 18
  survival of Islamic culture, 16–17
  see also Alpujarras revolts I and II

New Christians
  and religious innovation, 28, 29, 33, 36, 40
  and the Inquisition, 9, 10
  relationship with Old Christians, 139–42
  stigma attached to, 2
  see also Converso; *Limpieza de sangre* movement; *Morisco*

Observant rule, *see* Conventual rule
Old Christian values, 4, 7, 9, 139–42, 143, 144
  see also Limpieza de sangre movement
Osuna, Francisco de, OSF (*c.*1492–*c.*1540), writer of devotional literature, 35, 44

Papacy, and the Spanish Church
  Sixtus IV (1471–84), 7, 8, 52; Innocent VIII (1484–92), 52; Alexander VI (1492–1503), 52, 100; Julius II (1503–13), 100; Adrian VI (1522–3), 53; Pius IV (1559–65), 46, 55; Pius V (1566–72), 46–7, 74; Gregory XIII (1572–85), 47, 75; Clement VIII (1592–1605), 21; Paul V (1605–21), 23; Alexander VII (1655–67), 138
Patronato agreements on ecclesiastical appointments, 52–3
Patronato de las Indias, 100–1, 113
  see also Bishops in the New World
Pensions on ecclesiastical incomes, *see* Ecclesiastical estate in seventeenth-century Spain, taxation of
Pérez de Ayala, Martín (1503–66), Bp Guadix (1548–60), Bp Segovia (1560–4), 57
Plague (1596–1602), 119, 124; (1647–52), 124, 133
Polyglot Bible projects, *see* Alcalá de Henares, University of; Arias Montano, Benito
Ponce de la Fuente, Dr Constantino (*c.*1502–60), Sevillian heretic, 39–40, 43
Popular religion
  definition of, 78–9
  practice of, 89–99
  see also Council of Trent and the reform of popular religious culture and discipline

Priesthood in Spain
  appointments to, 71
  educational level of, 72–3
  parochial structure, 68 (Map 2), 69–71 + Table 3.3
  post-Tridentine reform of, 67, 69
  role of, 67
  seminaries for training of, 71–2 + Table 3.4
Priesthood in the New World
  failure to generate native roots, 113–14
Protestant Church, *see* Reformed Church
Protestantism in Spain, *see* Lutheranism in Spain
Provincial church councils, *see* Council of Trent, implementation of via provincial church councils
Pulgar, Hernando del (1430?–1491), *converso* chronicler at court of Ferdinand and Isabella, 3, 8, 11
Purity of blood, see *Limpieza de sangre* movement

Quiroga, Gaspar de (1512–94), Abp Toledo (1577–94), 20, 33, 36, 44, 48, 49, 66–7, 72, 146, 156–7 (Profile)

Reconquest, the, and the shaping of Spain's religious identity, 1–2
Reformed Church, the
  the establishment of and reaction of the Inquisition to, 27, 31
  the spread of its influences to Spain, 37–8
Religious orders in post-Tridentine Spain
  growth in size of, 75 (Table 3.5), 127–30 + Table 6.2
  limitations of reform, 74–6
  objectives of reform, 73–4
  see also Carmelites; Mercedarian order, post-Tridentine reform of; Society of Jesus
Ribera, Juan de (1532–1611), Abp Valencia (1568–1611), 21–3, 158–9 (Profile)
Rojas y Sandoval, Cristóbal (1502–80), Bp Cordoba (1562–71), 57

Sacraments, observation of, 84–9
  baptism, 85–6
  bigamy, 83 (Table 4.2), 86–7
  confession, 85
  extreme unction, 87
  marriage, 86–7
  mass, 84–5
  masses for the dead, 88–9 + Table 4.3
Salamanca, University of, *see* Biblical scholarship
Salucio, Fray Agustín, OSD (1523–1601), writer of treatise on purity of blood, 139–41
Seminaries, *see* Council of Trent and ecclesiastical reform
Sesso, Carlos de (*d*.1559), Valladolid Protestant, 40, 46
Society of Jesus
  in Spain, 33–5, 67, 74, 75 (Table 3.5)
  in the New World, 112, 113
Spiritual Exercises, 34, 35
Statutes of purity of blood, *see* *Limpieza de sangre* movement
Subsidio tax, 135, 136 (Table 6.6), 138
Synods, *see* Council of Trent and ecclesiastical reform

Talavera, Fray Hernando de, OSJ (1428–1507), Abp Granada (1493–1507), 8, 15, 17, 53, 108, 148–9 (Profile)
Tapia, Fray Pedro de, OSD (1582–1657), Bp Cordoba (1649–52), Abp Seville (1652–7), 138
Taxation of ecclesiastical estate, *see* *Cruzada* tax; Ecclesiastical estate in seventeenth-century Spain, taxation of; *Excusado* tax; *Subsidio* tax

Tithe, 130, 131, 133, 134 (Table 6.5), 137 (Table 6.7)
Torquemada, Fray Tomás de, OSD (1420–98), first Inquisitor General of Spain (1483), 6, 7, 9
Trent, *see* Council of Trent

Universities, *see* Alcalá de Henares, University of; Biblical scholarship, attacked by Inquisition

Valdés, Fernando de (1483–1568), Inquisitor General (1547–65), Abp Seville (1546–68), 38–9, 42, 43, 44, 45, 47, 150–1 (Profile)
Vergara, Juan de (1492–1557), humanist scholar, 31–2, 152 (Profile)
Vitoria, Francisco de, OSD (1480?–1546), defender of Spain's legal title to Indies, 103
Votive feast days, *see* Local saints

Yepes, Juan de (John of the Cross), OCarm (1542–91), founder of male branch of Discalced Carmelites, 75

Zumárraga, Juan de, OSF (1468–1548), Abp Mexic (1527–48), 108, 110, 111